31143011352524
364.1536 Cacho, L
Cacho, Lydia,
Infamy :

Main

INFAMY

INFAMY

HOW ONE WOMAN BROUGHT AN INTERNATIONAL
SEX TRAFFICKING RING TO JUSTICE

LYDIA CACHO

Translation by Cecilia Ross

SOFT SKULL PRESS
AN IMPRINT OF COUNTERPOINT

Copyright © 2016 by Lydia Cacho

All rights reserved under International and Pan-American Copyright Conventions. No part of this book may be used or reproduced in any manner whatsoever without written permission from the publisher, except in the case of brief quotations embodied in critical articles and reviews.

Library of Congress Cataloging-in-Publication Data

Names: Cacho, Lydia, 1963–author.
Title: Infamy : how one woman brought an international sex trafficking ring to justice / Lydia Cacho.
Other titles: Memorias de una infamia. English
Description: Berkeley, CA : Soft Skull Press, [2016] | Includes bibliographical references and index.
Identifiers: LCCN 2016008775 | ISBN 9781593766436 (alk. paper)
Subjects: LCSH: Cacho, Lydia, 1963– | Child prostitution—Mexico—Cancâun. | Child pornography—Mexico—Cancún. | Women journalists—Mexico.
Classification: LCC HV6570.4.M6 C33613 2016 | DDC 364.15/36—dc23
LC record available at http://lccn.loc.gov/2016008775

Cover design by Kelly Winton
Interior design by Domini Dragoone

SOFT SKULL PRESS
An Imprint of Counterpoint
2560 Ninth Street, Suite 318
Berkeley, CA 94710
www.softskull.com

Printed in the United States of America
Distributed by Publishers Group West

10 9 8 7 6 5 4 3 2 1

To my father, for his love and solidarity.
To my fellow journalists, today and always.

To hold back this looming darkness,
let us add our voices to the word,
let us make pacts of love,
truces of doubt,
let us not want for roses,
or poems,
or songs.

We must be intolerant of silence,
so that
Not one woman more
will be despoiled of April,
the wind,
and the rain.

"Not One Woman More" (a fragment), Guisela López

CONTENTS

INFAMY

INTRODUCTION

One night in 1999, I was preparing to leave the offices of the magazine where I worked as editor in chief in Cancun, Mexico. My boss had gone home a short while earlier, and my secretary was waiting for me at my car. I had just activated the building's alarm and closed the door when, on turning around, I suddenly found myself face to face with a man I thought I recognized. He pressed a gun to my forehead, and exhaling a bitter stench of tobacco as he spoke, he said that if I stuck my nose into his private life again, I'd be dead. Then he turned on his heel and walked away. My blood had turned to ice. I got in the car, trying to decide how best to respond, what the most appropriate course of action would be. There was no good answer. Threatening someone with death—even at gunpoint—is not a crime in Mexico. The man with the gun didn't want to kill me, he just wanted to let me know that he could. He was the owner of a brothel that masqueraded as a tropical dance club. He had a sort of bunker there where he was holding a group of young Cuban women against their will. I had published an article about it in a Cancun newspaper a few months earlier, prompting the Mexican authorities to close the club and the Cuban authorities—who were colluding in the temporary "migration" of exploited dancers—to cut their ties to this well-known local businessman and lawyer.

This individual considered his business-cum-criminal life a private matter, as do thousands of those who exploit women and young girls and boys all over the world. On several occasions since that night, I have faced armed men seeking to silence me with threats, violence, attempts on my life, even jail. So far none have managed to silence me. I have investigated all manner of mafias throughout my career as a journalist, writer, and defender of human rights. The deaths of esteemed colleagues have marked the passing years, and their bravery is a daily inspiration to me. I have been kidnapped, jailed, and persecuted for many years. My life is in danger today, as are the lives of the majority of those colleagues of mine who rebel against impunity and violence. My story is relevant because I am one of thousands of activists and journalists who refuse to stand silently by in the face of such atrocities as child pornography, human trafficking, the sale of weapons to hired teenage assassins, or the murder of journalists working to ensure that their societies understand the circumstances that are changing or even destroying them.

The story you hold in your hands is the biography of a complex life where love and esteem are ever-present, as are hate, extreme violence, and even death. In this book, you will find an accurate, in-depth analysis of the *mafiosos* who orchestrate the sale and purchase of young girls and have confessed their crimes as producers of child pornography as well as their ties to powerful politicians in Mexico, the United States, and the rest of the world. You will hear the words of those who tried to kill me for having given voice to the girls and boys who managed to escape their networks of abuse. You will learn who these small Latin American children bought and sold in Mexico are. But you will also discover the bravery of these young survivors, you will discover shared human compassion and the will to change an entire country, and you will discover how tragedy can become an instrument of social transformation.

One afternoon, I was watching the first *Matrix* film with a group of teenagers in the shelter I founded in Cancun for the protection of women and children. I like to use this movie when working with young people in order to discuss how we all have to make decisions and accept consequences. In the film, intelligent machines have come to enslave humans in order to exploit their vast stores of vital energy. Because it would be far too cumbersome to keep the entire human population as slaves if its individuals were aware of their situation, the machines create the Matrix, a prefabricated virtual reality within which people live, deluded as to their true condition. For the enslaved humans, the matrix they live in is an unshakable reality where happiness depends on following the rules. The character Morpheus manages to awaken the protagonist, Neo, from this virtual reality. In his confusion, Neo attempts to mount a resistance within the preexisting context, but Morpheus reminds him that he was raised in an intangible prison he can neither see, nor smell, nor touch. *This* prison is in the mind, and that is the genius of the Matrix. Neo's task, his challenge, is to learn to understand freedom from within a different paradigm than the one he has been exposed to since he was a boy; he must transform reality and his way of looking at the world in order to free himself and others.

Reality is erected upon human experience, upon our conception of the world, and this conception is fluid: it is constantly changing and transforming. Once we understand that the cultural matrix we were brought up in is a prison backed by patriarchal powers, a prison that generates abuse, violence, and slavery, we have two choices: Those of us who seek a pattern of social interaction not based on the abuse of others, who desire freedom without violence, can unite; or we can submit to those who tell us that there is no freedom without violence. I chose the first path, and I have accepted the consequences.

In reality, the "Lydia Cacho cause," as writer Roberto Saviano has dubbed it, represents the efforts and sacrifice of a large number of individuals working to build a world free from violence. But because this cause befell me, my loved ones have also suffered threats, and they worry along with me. The violence unleashed in the wake of my book *The Demons of Eden: The Powers Protecting Child Pornography*, which exposed networks of power in the political and business worlds, has most definitely extended to the brave journalists whose selflessness prevented the triumph of campaigns on the part of these same networks to distort or bury my findings. The bravery of the upright government workers, congresswomen and men, lawyers, and judges who put their jobs on the line in order to defend their ethical convictions and stand in support of justice for the victims of child abuse is likewise commendable. I wrote the first half of this text at a time of anxiety and desperation, when I was locked in a judicial battle against state governor Mario Marín and Kamel Nacif, two men who were protecting the head of a child pornography and money laundering ring that was in turn backed by powerful lawyers, politicians, and businessmen with connections that can be traced all the way up to the presidency of Felipe Calderón. Now, years later, I am taking up these memoirs again, ahead of my appearance at the Inter-American Court of Human Rights, with clear evidence about how and where these people are living, these people who created such a horrific trail of abuse, corruption, and death, these people who are so vilely in debt to society. Many are the lessons I have learned.

Before she died, my mother made me promise that I would never open the door to spite or anger, that no matter how much suffering I faced, I would remember that my task—in journalism, in activism, and in my family life—is to build. And peace, she explained to me, can only be built when we are moved and inspired by the desire for a free and happy life for ourselves and the whole of humanity.

"They want fear to control you, my daughter," she told me, "but *you* must use hope and dignity to control *it*; you must not allow your spirit to be colonized by anger or hatred, because these things will blind you." My mother could never have imagined how powerful the mafias her daughter would find herself confronting would be, but her lessons have helped me to remain strong, even if I have to spend the rest of my life fleeing my enemies, these powerful mafias that buy, sell, and abuse young girls and women.

I have learned during my many years of persecution that freedom, as Octavio Paz wrote, is not simply the ability to do whatever one likes; rather it is being able to make a decision—yes or no—and to accept the consequences of that decision. I am, therefore, and despite the circumstances, a free woman—a free woman in an oppressive Mexico, where the rule of law is not a reality but merely a pipe dream.

For my mother, for myself, and for all women. This is what I say to myself every morning when I wake up. With this book I have placed in your hands, I am crossing over into new territory, possessed of the most powerful tools at my disposal: truth, freedom of speech, and proof.

Lydia Cacho
February 2016

1

WHO IS LYDIA CACHO, ANYWAY?

One year and eighteen days after I was first remanded to prison and then released on bond pending trial (and, in an ironic twist, given around-the-clock police protection as a result of the threats I had received from Succar Kuri and others), my lawyer, Xavier Olea, phoned to wish me a happy 2007 and ring in the good news: A Mexico City judge had just acquitted me on all charges of defamation. The call came as I was traveling home from Holbox Island, in Quintana Roo, where I had spent New Year's Eve in the company of friends and my romantic partner. Jorge drove, while I sat in the passenger seat listening to Xavier's gravelly but upbeat voice. I began to cry and was having trouble speaking. I just kept repeating, "Thank you, thank you," over and over again. Concerned, Jorge asked me what had happened.

At a loss for more words, all I could say was, "I'm free again, I've got my freedom and credibility back." And with that, I pressed my body against his, and he hugged me tight with his right arm, his left hand still firmly on the steering wheel.

"You never lost your credibility," he told me.

I replied simply, "What kind of credibility can a journalist have if they've been sentenced for defamation?"

I cried long and hard, as though I had a river flowing through my soul. But these were no longer tears of fear or disappointment, they were salt-tinged drops overflowing with newly won freedom and certitude, for the authorities had stripped me not only of my freedom but of my credibility as well, and now that I had them back, I could move forward.

On the ride home, I watched the jungle landscape slip past along the highway, the same jungle that had stared back at me, endless and dark, as I sat in a speeding car one year earlier, penned in by State Judicial Police agents and terrified. As though bearing my freedom aloft in a ritual act of homecoming, we returned home in silence, seeking out each other's hands to hold from time to time, accompanied by the quiet joy of the music of Queen. I recalled the words of Eduardo Galeano: "Music holds the soul together." *It sure does*, I thought.

As soon as we arrived at my home in Cancun, I picked up the phone and called my family and close friends; each one echoed the other's thoughts, declaring that when we do right, the truth always prevails. I don't know whether that's entirely true, but I did feel the need to celebrate this first small victory of mine in the overwhelmingly large battle for justice. Shaking off the case against me was like rising out of a deep well and feeling my lungs fill with a sudden rush of air. Day and night, throughout it all, I would remember that I was just an ordinary citizen struggling against an ever-changing and shifting monster that uses governmental and criminal muscle to crush anyone and anything that gets in its way. I wanted to return to my tribe, to my family. To my origins, to all that had prepared me to resist and rebel against abuses of power.

A STRONG, UNITED, LOVING TRIBE

It was 1969. I was a girl of six, and my grandfather would plonk me down at his side, pour himself a glass of port, and tell me stories about how I'd gotten to be the way I was—forever asking and questioning, bold and fearless, never conformist, wild and affectionate. He was always telling me that ours was a family with a great many stories to tell, a great many questions to ask. In that irrefutable, sage tone of his, he would unravel the mystery of my eternal question—*Why did I feel like this, all mixed up and restless, while the other girls didn't?* His answer was always the same: because I was a child of many cultures, because I had the blood of Portuguese sailors, Moorish conquerors, and strong, valiant Gallic women flowing in my veins. And there was my father's family, too—on that side, I held within me the counsels of the conquered indigenous peoples of Mexico, and those of lone Mexican soldiers. That's why I rebelled against authoritarianism and the forced imposition of ideas, my grandfather said (and he repeated it before he died), because it had fallen to me to do something with all that knowledge and pain passed down from my ancestors.

"This is what life after death is," he said years later, referring back to those childhood conversations. "You carry your dead on your shoulders in your own life, you carry their wisdom and their stories." One might easily think that my grandfather's words were nothing more than the sentimental folly of a sweet old fool. But considering I have survived torture, a police kidnapping, and a brief but terrifying imprisonment, considering I have received death threats from organized criminal groups and experienced a number of attempts on my life, more than one might also say that my Grandpa Zeca knew what fate was holding in store for me.

My grandfather was a Portuguese man born into a line of peasants and sailors, of dark complexion and strong build, and tough as an ox; he had kind, sparkling eyes and large hands that were always ready to embrace, share, work the land, or write stories. No one ever had to teach him anything about poverty and injustice because he had experienced them firsthand. He was born in April 1909. One year later, on October 5, 1910, the First Portuguese Republic was created, and soon after came World War I. In January 1919 there was a brief civil war in the country, which lasted just one month and ended in Oporto, my grandfather's land. He told me that monarchy aside, there wasn't much difference between Portugal's history and the history of Mexico. Between 1910 and 1926 alone, Portugal went through forty-six different governments; the people had no choice but to adjust rapidly to living with poverty and the ignominy of tyrants and corrupt politicians.

My grandfather married a French woman who was born in Lyon in April 1915, an intelligent woman with a prodigious memory, alabaster skin, and a pair of immaculate green eyes. She was the daughter of a woman who—according to those in the town where she lived—had the gift of clairvoyance; she could sense danger and see what lay in people's futures. Having a social conscience was not an intellectual luxury for my grandparents; it was simply a way to survive in a Europe caught between wars and social upheavals. In 1931, he was twenty-two and she was sixteen; they had friends and family in France, Spain, and Portugal, and they quickly learned the importance of solidarity and political awareness.

My grandmother had a sweet smile, and she was an extraordinary student of history, one of those people who have an absolutely clear understanding of the fact that life is too short for regrets and that it is human pride that prevents us from recognizing that social uprisings are merely the tiny steps that clear the way for those who will come after us. Marie Rose, her shining, green eyes fixed on mine, would drill into me the notion that we must not allow life to dwindle away in the agonizing prison-labyrinth of fear of the enemy: "We are not building the present, we're building the future. That's why fear is actually a tool for our minds; it keeps us alert so that we can think and blaze a way forward."

She was a master of simple pleasures, an extraordinary cook, a woman capable of glimpsing fate and contemplating the universe from the shores of her soul's inner peace. The only time I ever knew her to be scared was when she was diagnosed with a brain tumor at age eighty. She passed away surrounded by my mother, my two sisters, and myself. And out in the vegetable patch the two had planted, my grandfather, lost in heaving sobs, felt his soul crumble with the pain of bearing witness to the death of his partner in love and life.

My grandfather was an explosive man and to know his wrath was to discover what even the most loving of men is truly capable of. She was the mistress of his inextinguishable, tender strength. Both liked to say that rebellion against all forms of slavery ran in our blood. They must have been on to something because they themselves rebelled, choosing to cross an entire ocean and settle in Veracruz. And they brought my mother, Paulette, along with them, so that she, too, could meet her manifest destiny.

Paulette was born in Lyon, France, in 1935, and it was at the age of six that she set sail for Mexico with her mother. While my grandfather was working to free himself from all the political entanglements back in France, my grandmother was being greeted on the opposite shore by friends who had fled during the war. Meanwhile, Portugal was under the rule of dictator Salazar, "God's Anointed One," and his highly feared political police force, the PIDE. Detractors of the regime were tortured and jailed at the Peniche and Caixas prisons and the Garrafal concentration camp. All around him, my grandfather's different support networks were struggling to survive in a world dominated by Franco, Mussolini, and Hitler.

My grandmother told me how from 1936 to 1939, her friends fought for a new state against Franco in the Spanish Civil War, and how from 1939 to 1945, the madness of the Great War taught them the value of food and friendship as well as a love of life and an appreciation for social and inner peace.

My mother grew up in Mexico, in a home where life was celebrated—and death and injustice remembered—in frequent gatherings held with other wartime refugees. You could just as soon find them listening to a Chabela Vargas record as enjoying some *fados* sung by Amalia Rodríguez, who used to visit my grandparents' house along with her guitarist. My mother felt Mexican, and she learned to be at ease in each of her two very different worlds.

When she was a teenager, she spent some time studying in France and Portugal, where she fell in love for the first time but nevertheless returned to Mexico. During a soirée she attended with her best friend Lucero at the home of a military engineer, she was introduced to a handsome man, tall and trim, with a deep voice, long eyelashes, and brows arched like two crows in flight. Shortly afterward, they found themselves pledging their eternal love before a priest in the Santa Rosa de Lima church in Mexico City.

I inherited my father's strength of will as well as his eyes, his gaze. My longing for freedom was a gift passed down from my grandmother and grandfather, and my understanding of the real world was given to me by my mother; my two sisters and three brothers taught me that love is limitless just as long as we know how to forgive one another, as long as we learn to love each other for our similarities and explore our differences without starting a war over them. From my father's father, a soldier who was known as somewhat of a lone wolf, I learned how heartrending it can be to watch a good man bend to the rules of machismo and live by the dogma of the patriarchy before finally self-destructing, old and alone.

My siblings and I grew up in an atmosphere where there were both difficult times and fun and games. We were raised by a serious, hardworking father and a cheerful mother—a psychologist and classical ballet dancer who liked to read us old Russian tales and was an avid soccer fan (a Club América fan, to be exact)—in a middle-class apartment in the Mixcoac colony of Mexico City. From a young age, I learned my address by heart, in case my tendency to get wrapped up observing people and listening to their stories—favorites among my many distractions—ended up leading me far from home. "My name is Lydia Cacho Ribeiro, I live at Donatello 25, apartment 104," I would recite for my mother, who made me memorize our telephone number as well.

Before I was born my parents had two boys and a girl, and after me came a sweet, loving boy followed by the youngest of all, Myriam, who grew up to become a psychologist and shaman, an invaluable figure in my adult life, an ally in my battles for peace and equality.

In a painful series of deaths, I lost my grandmother, then my grandfather, and then on February 24, 2004, my mother bid me good-bye as I held her in my arms at the end of a extended battle with hepatic cancer.

My family is—just as my mother orchestrated it to be—a strong, united, and loving tribe. Together, we partake in various causes of peace and their exciting and joyful or bitter and disappointing outcomes. At the most trying of times, my sisters and my brothers are always there to chart a course through shared tears, to declare, "Enough with this outrage!" and to relax in one another's company at a table bowed under the weight of dish upon dish of our grandmother's best recipes.

"Just what are you made of," Germán Dehesa asked me once in an interview, "that allows you to face such ignominy with a smile and keep your faith alive?"

"I was raised to never give up" was my reply.

And that is true. I was born in 1963 into an unconventional home. My mother held a degree in psychology, but her real vocation lay elsewhere than in private practice; she had no interest in becoming a master of the Freudian couch. She preferred to be out on the streets, working in Mexico City's communities. She told me that when her friends asked her why she didn't use her knowledge to earn some serious money, she would smile and insist—in that passionate voice she inherited from her father—that Mexico was plagued by inequality, that she had to do her part to promote equality, and that "you don't build that from inside an office, you do it in the trenches, on the streets."

My mother would take my siblings and me to what in those days were called "the lost cities" of Mexico's capital. People live there among heaps of trash, in houses pieced together with cardboard, surviving in some cases on little more than a single tortilla a day. My mother, her brothers, and a group of young people were working to try to help the women and men living in these places to develop a sense of community, to demand schools, and to improve their way of life.

I can't imagine that my mother could have had any idea just what effect seeing those little girls and boys in the slums on the outskirts of town would have on my soul, right down to its innermost depths. While she and her colleagues gave talks, I would attempt to play with my peers, only to discover with alarm how girls my age were physically unable to hold a pencil in order to make the simplest of drawings, how boys the same age as my brothers didn't even have enough energy to kick around the ball we'd brought them as a present. They would just squat there on the loose dirt, their noses crusted over with dry snot, their tangled, matted hair grown into nests for tiny, jumping insects. When I discovered they ate a single meal of black beans and tortillas a day—and sometimes only tortillas—I despaired.

At that young age, somewhere between seven and ten, a child has no idea what to do with the strange feeling brewing inside her that some omnipresent force is lying to us and controlling our reality. A child's understanding of the cruelty of poverty and corruption is entirely devoid of any ideological implications; that's precisely why the emotions evoked by it are so intense, even leading to feelings of anxiety. We are educated in the idea that we are all equal, but the real-life differences between us appear insurmountable, and the answers adults give us are never enough to counter what our innocent eyes see out there in the world, all that we come to question. We begin to perceive some flicker of the truth, but then our schoolteachers spend a lifetime training us to doubt the wisdom of our intuition, to second-guess that part of our conscience that is so well attuned to feelings of human compassion and prompts us to ask ourselves *why* this or that person has to live a life mired in poverty, violence, and ignorance, while we wonder what it is that makes us so different.

At some point in their own childhood, these teachers were told that this is the way the world works; with a single blow, the intuitive child within them, the feeling girl or boy who refused steadfastly to believe the prevailing discourse of violence as a instrument of control, was destroyed. Some became victims of racism, physical abuse, machoism, or sexism, while others took it upon themselves to execute, enforce, and perpetrate the "one true Mexican reality." I later learned *patriarchy* was the name of that socio-political system I grew up to reject and confront.

But millions of us grew to understand that cultural values are simply constructs of the human mind and that anything built can be transformed. Then some of us, although not all of us, chose to act accordingly. To contemplate giving one's life to defend an ideal is not, in this context, a reaction to some vacuous notion of self-sacrificing heroism. Rather it is the product of ideological conviction and—surprising though it may seem—a deep love of life and a desire to live happily, with dignity.

In my own case, thankfully, neither my mother nor my teachers tried to snuff out my budding intuition. On the contrary, they did their best to feed it, to set me on the path of philosophy, debate, and reading. I discovered the concept of otherness, as well as my own right to live a life of dignity, free from violence. In a Mexico where nothing good comes to women who dare speak a word of protest, I learned to rebel. And life, with its gradual accumulation of hardships, taught me to cloak my defects and cultivate my virtues in the best way I could. My mother kept quoting Carl G. Jung, reminding us that contradiction between subjective assumptions and external facts is what gives rise to problems. Most of my teen friends wanted to cling to their innocent childhoods; I on the other hand could not wait to become an adult woman to be able to do things about what I saw as a chaotic society in which I felt like an outcast, a rebellious angry girl.

I have never been faint of heart. Like my nephew Santiago, I was born with the fearlessness of a Portuguese sailor setting out to sea in search of new life. "*E se mais mundo houbera, lá chegara*," as my grandfather used to say—meaning the world might be bigger and vaster than you think, and one must search for the hidden secrets of humankind. As a girl, I had no trouble lifting up wriggling spiders by their legs; I would write on any scrap of paper I could get my hands on, and scribble all over the walls. At the age of five, seated atop my tricycle, with a magic cape knotted around my neck, I launched myself off the roof of our building's garbage shed to prove that I could fly. A fractured tailbone and two weeks spent under virtual house arrest enlightened me to the fact that Aladdin and his flying carpet were, alas, just a fairy tale. I would awake at night and ask my sister if the starry sky, the ceiling of the Universe, could fall down and cover our heads while we slept. And once, after a nun explained to me that God is everywhere and sees everything, I asked my mother how I might send a letter to the Supreme Being in order to request that He cover His eyes when I went to the bathroom, because I didn't like the idea of Him seeing me in such a state.

My mother's friends warned her that she shouldn't be bringing us up that way—socially maladjusted, rebellious, and confronted from a very young age with the truth of suffering in society—not to mention answering all our questions on any topic—including sexuality and abuses of power—as though we were adults. Her response was that being a mother doesn't make you anyone's keeper but rather a guide, someone responsible for human beings that must one day leave the nest and go out into the world. "Daughters and sons are given to you for a short time; they don't belong to you, they're human beings, individuals taking shape in order to consciously become the best possible version of who they are. I much prefer to raise a tribe of maladjusted women and men than a gaggle of mediocre specimens," she'd explain to us. Her passion was Portuguese, like her father's, and her convictions as unshakable as cathedral walls.

My mother trusted us. That's why when I was a child and would ask her why there were so many poor people, so many boys living in dumps and girls using shawls to carry around babies born out of violence, she would reply, "It's unfair, I know! And because you and your brothers and sisters can see the suffering and understand it, because you have the privilege of getting an education and three meals a day, it is your duty to prepare yourselves to help change the future of your country."

Sometimes we'd just stop asking, because to conceive of your self as part of a national tragedy is a notion that no adolescent girl can truly contemplate without resistance. I would much rather go to the Casa del Lago cultural center in the Chapultepec forest, where I took free painting lessons and could dream up sweet, idyllic water-color universes and then build tents out on the patio of the house where my friends and I would mount expeditions to Egypt in search of the lost treasures of the pharaoh Hatshepsut.

Years later, my mother invited me to join her on some work-shops with groups of teenagers; I rebelled against such uncertainty. I loved my school—Colegio Madrid—and its liberal atmosphere, where students could debate ideas without having to conform to the patriarchal designs of submissive, artificially beautiful women. But I hated mathematics and any other subject that seemed useless to me. I didn't care whether I passed or failed these courses; I preferred literature. I wanted nothing more than to write about everything going on around me and to play basketball. Several of my closest friends are from that period of my life.

My mother urged me to study arts at the Casa de la Cultura Mixcoac, one of the first cultural centers in Mexico City. It was all we could afford, so I spent a few afternoons a week in literature, poetry, or painting workshops, or in history courses taught by Dr. Ballester, founder of the city's Hellenic Cultural Center. It is to him that I owe my knowledge of the rebelliousness of Aspasia of Mileto and my desire to travel to Greece and follow in the footsteps of Pericles.

Years later, when I turned sixteen, my mother founded an organization for the development of women, and my sisters and I completed a program that would allow us to lead workshops there. Then
one day I moved to Paris, to relearn the language of my ancestors.
I cleaned houses to make a living, until at the age of twenty-three,
after several years of studying, traveling, and working, I decided that
I needed to go and live by the sea, to get in touch with the sailor
residing deep within my soul, the one my grandpa Zeca had talked
so much about. And rising up before me was an image of Cancun as
an unspoiled paradise, a terra incognita, an appleless Eden.

AN EDEN WITHOUT DEMONS

I had first seen the Cancun and Cozumel coast on a trip years
earlier, when I learned to scuba dive at the age of seventeen, and
I immediately fell in love with the sea and the jungle; the clear
water caves and the wilderness reminded me that life on the earth
is good, regardless of the cruelty people embody. I promised myself
that one day I would burn my ships in order to settle in the tropics.
It turns out I had no ships to burn, other than an English boyfriend
who didn't share my sense of adventure. But I nevertheless gathered up my few belongings—mostly books and music records—and
set out for a new life of inwardness to find my own voice, in search
the honest rhythm of the revolutionary feelings that I had been
nesting for a while.

I wanted to write by the sea, to set sail, to know and understand the world as well as my own place in it. I hoped to find
inner peace as I paddled around under the waves. I had just gotten
my official certification as a scuba diver from some friends of my
brother Oscar's. This handful of marine biologists had helped me
venture into the silent, submarine world where we learned to love
the planet from within its very own reservoirs of life-giving liquid.
I had found Paradise, some said—peace to understand life and all
its miracles, said I.

Cancun had come into existence just twelve years before. It was an eminently masculine society, made up of construction workers and engineers, which led to the creation of a superficial and somewhat prostituted community of capitalists, moneymakers, and money launderers that clashed with the eco-scientists, musicians, hippies, and writers in search of their own kind of paradise.

At its inception, the city was meant to be a beacon for investment and capital, and its planning was entirely lacking in cultural or educational foresight. Women came later and had to adapt themselves to a strange world that had neither hospitals nor schools but did have plenty of cantinas and brothels. The state's capital city, Chetumal, itself had a long history as a corrupt border town founded by contraband smugglers and marauders. Chetumal was originally a prison town for guerrillas and Zapatista revolutionary leaders. They mixed and matched smugglers, contractors, petty thieves, and revolutionary prisoners to create a political culture of corruption and extortion. These same groups later gave rise to the city's political class. All of which—despite the fact that businessmen from all over would then descend upon the region and alter its landscape, some with good intentions and others with money to be laundered or an unsavory past to escape from—goes a long way toward explaining why Cancun is the way it is today.

A few months after arriving, I began to write stories—short cultural pieces for the local newspaper, *Novedades*. After a while I met a woman who would become a dear friend of mine. Lía was married to a hotel manager, and she and her friends were hungry for culture, social integration, and good schools for their young daughters and sons. We organized the first of the several conferences my mother would give in Cancun on sexuality, relationship dynamics, and women's rights.

Shortly afterward, I met Salvador, who had been a successful dentist in Mexico City before he, too, decided to burn his ships and follow his childhood dream to become a sailor. At his side, I learned to sail, and eventually the two of us graduated as sailing captains in

Florida to chart our own routes and courses. We made a pact to sail around the world together. I became an expert sailor, and on board a friend's boat, I learned how to harpoon fish so that we would have something to eat whenever we went out on the high seas. We made several trips around the islands of the Caribbean with another couple on a thirty-eight-foot Irwin sailboat. During one of those voyages, on which I was always the official cook, an intense storm that left my body frozen in fear taught me to always breathe deeply, come what may; on another, we found ourselves having to flee together in our friend Pepe's boat from modern-day pirates and drug traffickers off the coast of Belize. But the rest of our trips were calm affairs, full of love and fun. I would always pack two suitcases: one small one with my bikinis and a few articles of lightweight clothing, and one large one filled with books and notebooks, everything I needed to read, write, and draw.

On the first long voyage we took, from Miami to Guatemala's Rio Dulce and from there on to the Cayman Islands, we spent nearly four whole hours snorkeling one afternoon. As we floated in the cool, calm Caribbean waters, I was unaware of any physical pain. What wonders of marine life were before me, entire families of turtles and dolphins, sharks minding no one but themselves! But by the time we got back to the boat, my legs had grown numb, to such an extent that I was unable to stretch my muscles even slightly in order to relieve the cramping pains.

I remembered this day fifteen years later, on the night of December 16, 2005, when during my "police kidnapping," the State Judicial Police agents who were torturing me asked if I could swim, and one of them told me they were planning on throwing me into the sea once we got to Champotón, in Campeche. My legs felt numb then, too, paralyzed with adrenaline and weariness—the pain felt familiar and it reminded me of that sailing trip with Salvador.

While the agents joked about throwing me out to sea, a wave of conflicting emotions washed over me. *Yes, I can, I can swim,* I thought. *Just like that day we were out on the sailboat; I swam for four hours.* But now I was sick, just getting over a case of infectious bronchitis, and I had a fever I couldn't shake. And in the battle raging in my mind between hopefulness at my chances for survival and the fear that was keeping my mind alert, I first pictured myself feeling strong, having plenty of stamina, swimming, watching as terra firma drifted farther and farther off and the waves carried me away from the police agents, safe and sound, seeking out the help of a night fisherman. But then I felt my cramped, useless legs and felt myself sinking, helplessly spent, into the sea.

FIRST CAUSES

Salvador and I were married for thirteen years. Throughout that time, I wrote stories dealing with women living in southeastern Mexico's Maya region. In 1988 my mother introduced me to a friend of hers, Esperanza Brito de Martí, an extraordinary, wise, and loving elder woman. I had coffee with her one day, and I told her that I had taken a few journalism courses and attended several literature workshops, and that although I was essentially self-taught, I hoped to become a real journalist. Esperanza laughed at me—she had an acid sense of humor I would later come to understand and enjoy—then she asked me to write her an essay explaining why it was impossible to be a good self-taught journalist. And so with Esperanza running the magazine *FEM*, I began writing for it. *FEM* was the Mexican equivalent of *Ms.*, the American feminist magazine cofounded by Gloria Steinem.

Alaíde Foppa and several friends of hers founded *FEM* in the 1970s. This was at the same time that women in my mother's generation were coming into their own and out of the closet as feminists. My mother was in touch with the European feminist philosophers such as Simone de Beauvoir and Luce Irigaray, whilst most Mexican feminists had adopted the American women's movement discourse more linked to the civil rights movement and the anti-war upheaval.

Alaíde Foppa, Rosario Castellanos, Tina Modotti, Marcela Lagarde were the Latin American women bringing together feminist philosophy and political rebellion for women and girls in my country. I listened to them on the radio, I read their poetry and their essays again and again. They made my generation believe we could become their living utopia of empowered women, agents of change, owners of our destiny.

I was first turned on to *FEM* when I was in high school, and when I read the things these women were writing, I realized that they were expressing exactly what I had been thinking and feeling all along—I knew there had to be another tribe out there beyond my own family, one I could belong to, one in which I would have the freedom to make my own choices, to think for myself, to reimagine and re-create the world. Back then I never imagined that I would one day have the privilege of seeing my words find a home among those of my teachers, that I would be brought under the welcoming wing of women like Esperanza and Alaíde, or Marcela Lagarde, the friends and pupils of Simone de Beauvoir, readers of Susan Sontag and Gloria Steinem.

In 1989 I met journalist Sara Lovera, the teacher of an entire generation of provincial female journalists and the founder of *La Doble Jornada*, the first feminist supplement to be published in the major national newspaper *La Jornada*. Controversial, passionate, at times intolerant and gruff, Sara was first my teacher and later my friend, as well. I attended workshops and certificate programs in investigative journalism, feature writing, and reporting. I felt right at home as I came into contact with numerous journalists who were also working as women's rights activists. I began publishing pieces in the national media before working up the courage to start my own editorial column in Cancun's *La Crónica*, a paper run by Fernando Martí, Esperanza's son. Back then I went to Mexico City to buy books—the entire collection of Ryszard Kapuscinsky, everything written by Eduardo Galeano, Truman Capote, Joan Didion, Tom

Wolfe, and the German journalist who later became a friend and an advisor when I began investigating mafias: Gunter Wallraf.

Ever since that first column in *La Crónica*, I have never gone a day, not even a single bleary Monday, without writing. And when *La Crónica* eventually disappeared (as a result of a hostile outburst by then-governor Mario Villanueva Madrid, whose ties to the Cartel of Sinaloa landed him a spot in the Altiplano detention center and later an extradition to the US where he is still paying for money laundering for organized crime). I found myself writing for several different papers over the years—*Novedades, Por esto!*, and *La Voz del Caribe*.

I went on to write articles for *La Doble Jornada* and diverse feminist magazines, I published a book of poems, and I spent a good deal of time out and about, camera in hand, interviewing people, trying to understand what life was like for them in this made-up paradise in the Southeast corner of Mexico.

In 2003 Sara Lovera and Lucía Lagunes of Mexico, Mirta Rodríguez Calderón of Cuba, Rosalinda Hernández and Laura Asturias of Guatemala, and I cofounded the Mexico, Central America, and Caribbean Journalists' Network. This international network gradually shifted its focus to an analysis of the world from a gender perspective. At the time of its creation, I was a correspondent for the news agency CIMAC, and I happily joined this new family of women and men who shared—and continue to share—the dream of practicing a form of journalism that is ethical, professional, and non-sexist. At the beginning we were twelve; by 2016 the network has more than six hundred members all over the Spanish-speaking world.

I learned to combine my journalism and activist work with a private life that gave me spiritual balance. Throughout this period, Salvador and I would often spend time on a small boat, simply sailing around, reading, talking and making love. This allowed me the chance to lose myself in works of literature, to write in my diaries, and to start down the path of Buddhist literature. I meditated morning and night and learned how to deal with my emotions in a way that complemented what I had learned from my psychologist mother, who had taught me to question everything, to understand and analyze myself, and to accept my emotions in order to transform them. My forays into Buddhism and a daily yoga practice taught me new ways of structuring my inner peace in a constant search of balance with my obsessive behavior to do many things at the same time, to write and disclose, to investigate and to find explanations for what seemed inconceivable, such as systematic femicide or pervasive child abuse perpetrated by family members. I began to branch out, and while I continued to be involved in writing political analysis, I began to publish a newspaper column on Saturdays and eventually became the editor of a local magazine.

I did a report on HIV/AIDS, interviewing a group of young, gay, HIV-positive individuals who asked me to tell the true story of the institutional abuses suffered by people with the virus. I agreed to their request, and after journeying into the belly of the beast and coming into contact with fear, sickness, and discrimination in hospitals and morgues, my dear friend Lía and I helped them create a nonprofit organization. We secured an abandoned building and with the help of my husband, Salvador, transformed it into the region's first hospice for HIV/AIDS patients. The time I spent in this world of paradoxes, pain, discrimination, and death forever changed my life.

Lía and I became versed in first aid treatments, and several of the young men whose tenderness and courage had secured them a spot in our hearts later ended up dying in our arms, abandoned by their own families, who feared the modern-day pest. Then one fine afternoon, as a young man named Carlos left my trembling, tear-filled eyes to contemplate the overpowering presence of death, I knew that he would be the last person I would allow to pass away in my arms. I decided to set out in search of life again, to explore the world of HIV prevention, to write about it—to try to find the light amid the darkness. The mood of psychic despair, depression, and abandonment of that young generation of gay men could not be soothed by poetry or friendship. I recall so many days and nights reading out loud the most beautiful poems by Emily Dickinson, Garcia Lorca, Neruda, and Walt Whitman, hoping their souls—and mine—would find solace in the fine words of others, as mine had failed me a while ago. I had no explanation for a decade of official denial of HIV/AIDS, for the cruelty and abandonment of the ill. I was never afraid of contracting the virus, but I was secretly afraid of finding comfort in death.

I signed up for a United Nations program and went to New York on a United Nations Development Fund for Women (UNIFEM) project. There I met two women who changed my life: Stephanie Urdang, a South African journalist in charge of the Gender HIV/AIDS program, and Madhu Bala-Nat, a Hindu expert in charge of the UN Joint Nations Program on HIV/AIDS (UNAIDS) link to UNIFEM. To this day I cherish their friendship and am in awe of their knowledge and ability to navigate in the awful bureaucracy at the UN in order to make the best out of the worst.

After my trip to New York I flew to Senegal, Africa, and as I stood there in an orphanage, surrounded by hundreds of parentless girls and boys all suffering from AIDS, my feet suddenly felt the entire weight of life bearing down on them, all the consequences of death and silence. It was then that I decided to explore the tragedy of this pandemic. To this day, I have never shaken the weight of the apocalyptic vision of hundreds of children's eyes boring into mine, perhaps trying to find in my expression a lost mother's face, in my gestures a dead father's arms. I can still feel myself surrounded by the singular scent on the skin of those small human beings who held their arms out to me, yearning for a little human warmth from someone who would not spurn them; "A kiss, a kiss" they would beg when we visited them in their hospice, its corrugated metal roof burning under the sub-Saharan African sun. A reporter is never supposed to get personal, the great teachers of journalism wrote in their books; theory meant nothing to me during that month in Africa, so I hugged them for hours, I played with raggedy dolls, I told them stories in French, and they taught me a few words in Wolof. We sang together and among them I became a child. Back at the hotel at night I cried and wrote long love letters to my husband.

I wrote reports and articles, I appeared on television and radio shows, and I traveled to several countries as well as throughout my own, listening to the stories of thousands of women who found themselves languishing under the yolk of the human immunodeficiency virus. Never have I felt so moved and simultaneously so useless as when I stood before the United Nations General Assembly Hall and explained the situation of women and girls with HIV/AIDS in Mexico. I returned several times to that historic building in New York, where the dignity of nations and the misery of their inhabitants are the subjects of debate and negotiation. And I felt emptier than ever. All the speaking and writing—what good does it do anyone, apart from feeding my own ego when I get to see my name in print? And so I turned my eyes once more to Mexico, to the jungle near Cancun.

SEEKING REFUGE FROM VIOLENCE

I spent countless hours with my mother, hatching plans for the creation of a horizontally integrated women's organization, one that would allow us to grow, become strong, and help other women without falling victim ourselves to either the political system or the macho, patriarchal order. Our women's organization quickly began to bear fruit, several men joined forces with us, as well, and our dream became a reality.

A group of friends, women who believed that a different world was possible, founded a nonprofit called Estas Mujeres [These

Women], where we held workshops on civil rights and equality. Our feminist group was a success; Bettina, Celina, Miren, Mariarosa, Priscila, Guillermina, and I were "the only crazy women in town" talking about gender equality and the possibility of women taking a stand against violence in Cancun. María Rosa Ochoa, a cultural columnist and theater actress, suggested that we produce a radio show that we later called *Estas Mujeres*. That project lasted several years and was a great success. On the show, we called upon women to defend their rights. These women spoke invariably about the violence they suffered as being an obstacle that limited their ability to work, to be free, and to be happy. They spoke about their father's sexual abuse, their husband's rape, their boss's sexual harassment; they talked about all sorts of discrimination, be it of race or gender. Unbeknownst to us, we opened the Pandora's box of our corner of paradise—we mentioned the unmentionable, and for that we had to pay our dues.

I was working as an editor at the magazine *Cancuníssimo*. My associate, Vicente Álvarez, and I came up with a plan to create a magazine that would serve as a forum where women could discuss their issues. To test out the idea, I began by writing a supplement in a local newspaper called *Esta voz es es mía* [This Voice Is Mine], and when we saw the overwhelming reaction of readers, we threw ourselves headlong into the creation of the new magazine, which we called *Esta boca es mía* [This Mouth Is Mine]. Shortly thereafter, we produced a television show of the same name, which enjoyed wide regional acclaim. We were breaking down paradigms—feminist programming on Televisa? *Yes.* A complete success. Until, that is, the holder of the broadcasting license canceled the show five years later because he "considered it obscene" for us to be speaking openly about such topics as female condoms and the G-spot. It was all right to portray women as victims of violence, especially indigenous women, but censorship fell upon us in the year 2003 for speaking about empowerment and female sexual freedom.

Abused women would show up at the radio or television station asking for help. We would refer them to the Federal Public Ministry, but their requests for assistance would be turned down. The authorities said there was nothing that could be done for these women, because the law established that spousal battery was not a crime if the resulting injuries cleared up in less than fifteen days. And so the women would return to the radio station and tell of their troubles at the Attorney General's Office.[1] We brought this group of women together into a formal organization and decided to advocate for a change in the laws that would allow violence against women to be prosecuted as a crime. It took more than ten years to achieve the integral law we now have, but we managed to locate some congressmen willing to bring the law up for debate. By mid-2007, the Ley General de Acceso a las Mujeres a una Vida Libre de Violencia [General Law on the Right of Women to a Life Free from Violence] was passed in the state of Quintana Roo as well as the rest of Mexico.

With institutional support lacking, and in the wake of a wave of publicity we had managed to garner for the topic in the press and on television, victims of domestic abuse started to come to us. Then one afternoon, discussions with these women brought us to a decision—we would open a formal space for the protection of domestic abuse victims. My experience with the HIV hospice acted as a foundation for the creation of this second nonprofit organization.

A single dramatic experience would then change my perception of gender violence forever. I was returning from an investigative trip in the state of Guanajuato, in central Mexico, and paused in my journey to take a break at a truck stop. A slim but muscular blond man followed me into the women's restroom. When I came out of the stall to wash my hands, he sprang at me, immobilizing me. He then attacked me, raped me, and left me for dead. When

---

1. Translator's Note: The Mexican Attorney General heads both the Office of the General Prosecutor and the Federal Public Ministry.

I eventually dared to move again, I telephoned my mother. I was taken to a hospital in an ambulance to Mexico City; I had a few broken bones, a dislocated arm and hip, and several fractured ribs. Naturally, I only learned all of this at the hospital; I was completely unable to explain to the doctor how I had managed, given my injuries, to stand up and walk out of the restroom under my own strength. Quite simply, I had experienced the power of adrenaline and the will to survive.

Once I was discharged from the hospital, I went through my entire recovery process in the company of my family, and I had one of the most powerful epiphanies of my life. I suddenly understood the great importance of these networks of unconditional support, like the one I was so lucky to have in my family and closest friends.

The experience was a wrenching one. Among other lessons, I realized that I had behaved quite cavalierly when I had previously had the nerve to ask victims of violence to bare their souls to me in interviews. When the unforeseeable circumstances of life then forced me into their position, I felt that I should avail myself of that same nerve, and steel myself. It was one of the great lessons in humility of my existence. I came across a United Nations statistic stating that every eighteen seconds, a woman or girl is raped in Mexico. Why was I any different? Perhaps because I'm a journalist of some notoriety in my own city? No, I'm just another Mexican woman trying to survive in her homeland. And neither I nor any other person deserves to be a victim of violence.

Time passed, and with my arm still in a sling and a few broken bones that hadn't quite yet healed, I returned to Cancun. In the meantime, my marriage of thirteen years was about to come to an end, for reasons of diverging interests. We had each grown in opposite directions, and so three months after my return we decided to separate. I left our home and moved into a small apartment that I had been using for several years as a studio. Little by little, I reconstructed my life on my own. I was happy; I felt I could do whatever I wanted without having to worry about anyone or anything. I found new sources of strength, and I began confronting my fears and transforming my pain into positive projects and actions.

One morning I went to meet with my colleagues and friends in our favorite coffee shop. My friend Ruben, who used to be the editor-in-chief of *Por esto!*, told me that his sources had confirmed governor Mario Villanueva was responsible for the attack back in Guanajuato. It was his way of taking revenge for our journalistic work. We were never able to prove that he gave the order for me to be raped in that bathroom, but years later when he was sentenced in the US for his ties to organized crime, a man that used to be a part of his security detail corroborated the information.

We finally opened the women's aid center and high-security shelter. Right when we had located a suitable building and were preparing to outfit it accordingly, the friends with whom I had planned everything pulled out of the project. They said it was too much for them—they had families of their own, and victim assistance wasn't their area of expertise. Some of them were afraid of the potential retaliation from the powerful husbands of the women who began seeking our assistance. At that point, I turned to my mother.

"This project is indispensible," she told me, "and women will come" whose destiny it is to be a part of this mission. She was right; the project gained an unimaginable strength and local community power.

Slowly but surely, those extraordinary people did come, and they built a strong, solid, professional space in which women and their children could rebuild their lives and regain their right to dream and live with dignity, free from violence.

The first to join the mission were Fernando Espinosa, director of the Fundación Oasis, and Guillermo Portella, a Spanish hotel owner who was inspired by our project and secured the donations we required to open the aid center and shelter. Our victim assistance model requires two separate facilities: a public day center providing free legal and social work services as well as psychological and personal security assistance, and a high-security shelter on the outskirts of the city where domestic abuse victims whose lives were in danger could take refuge with their children for periods ranging from three to six months while we worked with them in a safe space, helping them to resolve their situation and draw up a plan to rebuild their lives.

Next, I contacted Claudia, a psychologist and feminist; Edith, a social worker; Magdalena, head nurse; and Irma, our sweet, energetic administrator. We found a small house in which to set up and inaugurate the women's crisis center, which we organized following an American shelter model. When we began to realize that many of the victims coming to us for assistance and protection were married to or involved in relationships with members of the police force or syndicates such as the taxi drivers' union (which is known to be running protection rackets), I began to use my investigative reporting skills to find out just who we were up against. We then worked quickly, in conjunction with victims and other social networks, to develop a security and investigation model that would take this important information into account.

Some of the women we saw had fallen victim to the actions of men of great power—to drug lords or individuals tied to organized crime and the trafficking of women and children—and others to construction workers, middle-class men, peasants, or bricklayers, or to chauvinist businessmen and politicians.

At a national conference on human rights, I met Alicia Leal and her Alternativas Pacíficas de Monterrey [Monterrey Peaceful Alternatives] team from Nuevo León. They were the first to open a high-security shelter for domestic violence victims in Mexico. She invited me to join a small group of people working to create a network of women's shelters across the country. We signed right up. I used the skills I developed in creating the journalists' network to embark on this new endeavor.

Necessity forced me to take over the running of our Comprehensive Women's Care Center (CIAM), namely because nobody wanted the director's job. I set about reading books on criminology and victimology, and I signed up for training courses at the Texas-based National Training Center for Domestic and Sexual Violence, run by Debby Tucker, my dear friend and amazing teacher. I attended the courses while still managing a magazine; my journalist's salary went to cover part of the admission costs. Little by little, various journalist and businessmen friends began sponsoring our staff members, underwriting their salaries. But the Mexican IRS[2] would not approve our nonprofit's tax-deductible status until we were able to demonstrate that we had been working continually in victims' assistance for a minimum of two years. We were trying to achieve what was already a reality in other countries—we wanted Congress to assign public resources to cover part of our operating costs. After all, victim protection is a responsibility of the state, and nonprofit organizations such as ours merely share in the collective duty to work for the betterment of citizens' lives. Our goal was to see public policy against violence become institutionally enshrined.

To that end, I began to study the history of shelters for battered women in other countries. We learned of a sizable number of instances in which women had been killed by their partners, sometimes at the very doors of the shelters in which they were seeking refuge, their aggressors having figured out their whereabouts. And such incidents occurred across the United States and Spain, as well as in Mexico and the United Kingdom. We decided to develop an investigation strategy that might help put us a step ahead of the perpetrators of these types of assault, while I used my journalistic work to denounce acts of corruption on the part of both aggressors and judicial authorities. I spoke with the CIAM team and we came to a unanimous decision: If we were going to work to build peace, we would inevitably have to confront the most brutal forms of violence,

---

2.   Translator's Note: Mexico's federal tax collection agency.

and to do so, we would need to have peaceful, intelligent, innovative, and—most important—professional strategies at our disposal.

I learned to appreciate my youth and my obsessive stamina as I kept three jobs at the same time. My only salary came from my job as a freelance journalist and magazine editor, so at night I would write articles and essays that I'd sell to magazines throughout the world. Ever since we opened the shelter I decided I would never have a salary as a human rights advocate. We were working toward getting public money invested in our organization, so I found it unethical to receive public money as an activist while continuing to investigate and write about gender issues, fighting the powers that be. Many friends questioned what they called an extreme decision. In time I knew I did the right thing. My enemies—drug lords, human traffickers, and corrupt politicians—were looking for something fishy in the organization's books, yet they never found it. In a country like Mexico where almost everyone has a small corruption crime under the pillow, I had to make sure mine was free of anything other than a small sandman ghost. My obsession with accountability and transparency was applicable not only to the public officials I was investigating, it applied first and foremost to myself. My father taught me that peace of mind comes from being coherent in one's actions and words, and if I was determined to promote and defend the right to have rights, I really needed the biggest protection of them all: honesty and knowledge.

When I turned thirty-seven, everything I had learned about journalism and human rights advocacy came together—the pieces of the puzzle finally all fit, everything made sense. I was up for the task, or at least I believed myself to be.

We set up a variety of international networks, some aimed at training, some at protection, others at information gathering—networks of like-minded, mutually supportive organizations working together to keep one another out of harm's way. One afternoon, my good friend journalist Ricardo Rocha, who had come to Cancun to tour the CIAM shelter, said these words to me: "A good reporter should investigate every story as though it's the last one they will ever cover in their life." Taking this advice to heart, we investigated every story of violence that the women we were protecting brought to us. Our team was now juggling seventy cases a month involving women whose lives were in danger, most of them due to human trafficking, forced prostitution, and domestic violence; meanwhile, society at large lived in a state of willful ignorance regarding the true magnitude of the problem. Over the years, we have seen dozens and dozens of criminals, pedophiles, rapists, and potential perpetrators of femicide pay for their crimes. And even more importantly, we have witnessed how hundreds of survivors of these acts of violence were able to reconstruct their worlds without the fear of losing their lives for daring to stand up and declare: "Enough is enough!"

Among the various security strategies implemented at the shelter, we had digital video cameras installed to record the perimeter of the center twenty-four hours a day, in order to capture evidence of any attacks or threats that might come to be made, as well as recording the faces of the aggressors themselves. Following the first occasion on which death threats were received at the shelter—threats that were made by an arms dealer from Torreon who also acted as an informer for the Nuevo Leon attorney general—we purchased a specialized telephone device to record such threats to be able to hand them over to the authorities as evidence when required. We reported those first threats to the national Attorney General's Office (PGR, Procuradía General de la República) and the Assistant Attorney General's Office for Special Investigations on Organized Crime (SEIDO, the Mexican equivalent of the DEA), just as we would do years later, at the end of 2003, when Jean Succar Kuri threatened me over the phone.

I visited shelters similar to ours in New York, Texas and Spain, and over time we drew up a victims' assistance model that was specifically adapted to the reality of our location, which, because of the high level of corruption and the utter lack of institutional justice in the Mexican system, was a radically different one than that of other countries. We knew what was being done in Torreon, in Aguascalientes, and in Mexico City, places where shelters for victims of abuse had been opened but were struggling because armed husbands or pimps would simply show up at the shelters and threaten the teams' lives. Alicia Leal in Monterrey, the extraordinary lawyer Luz Castro in Chihuahua, and Ester Chávez and her Casa Amiga team in Juarez were all experiencing the same attacks. Each of them was working to protect women in her respective city, but all of them were essentially defenseless—abandoned by the state, mistrustful of corrupt local police, and threatened by a variety of aggressors. The women and men who make up these organizations are, nevertheless, transforming the nation, and all of them consider that their work is well worth the risk.

At this point, we were living our lives caught between the beacons of hope and a yearning for freedom from violence on the one hand, and the dark shadows of injustice and abuse of power on the other. Jesús, the kindhearted therapist in whom I've been depositing my innermost worries this past year, once gave me the following advice: "You must learn to carry a lantern in one hand, to light your path; to carry a knife in the other, to defend yourself; and to not be blinded by the light." I came to the understanding that being a pacifist and working to eradicate violence does not mean bowing to the wills of others but rather learning to defend yourself while still holding true to your principles.

One morning a powerful local drug dealer who used to rape his children and batter his wife came to the crisis center. He had a shotgun and was accompanied by two other gunmen armed as if they were going to war. "Potenciano" (his alias) yelled at us from the outside, "Bring my wife or bring Lydia Cacho. I will kill you both for defying me." We immediately called the police, they arrived, and once they saw the military weapons the gang members were bearing, they quietly bowed out. On the phone, I desperately asked the chief of police why his men had left. He answered calmly, with what sounded like shame on his voice: "Listen, Señora, give the guy his wife and children back, or they will kill you all."

I was in my office, accompanied by our team's psychologist, our lawyer, and our social worker. We stared at each other as I hung up after calling the police chief something along the lines of "a useless coward." I then proceeded to spend an hour talking to the gunman through the video-porter system, telling him we did not have his family. He said he was going to kill me and then shot at the crisis center. Finally after several calls we were able to get the Federal Police to arrive; two patrols came, they talked to the men, and just like that the gunmen got into their cars and left. We had everything on tape. The next day I gathered the entire team from the shelter and the crisis center and introduced them to a judo instructor. For days he taught us all—from the nurses and social workers to the driver and the psychologists—how to take a gun away from an attacker. We practiced and practiced until we got a hold of it. We then created a risk analysis protocol and a safety instruction manual to rescue victims who find themselves in situations of extreme danger. We trained for months. Many people came to help us; a friend of mine who used to belong to a SWAT team reviewed our protocols and instructed me for two hours every night for four months, until I knew how to handle everything from kidnappings to death treats, from group crisis to how to attend to gunshot wounds. Everyone on the team knew the rules: We were to always travel in pairs, and we all had satellite radios that back then were only used by criminals or specialized police forces. We understood this was war: the trenches were the streets, the homes of millions of families, the shelter's door. We saved money to have the main doors armored, including bulletproof glass. We were pacifists but we refused to be victimized by losing sight of the dangers involved in defending the rights and freedoms of others. As a journalist I knew every fact has to be backed by evidence, so we had cameras installed everywhere, with 24-hour recordings sent to a remote hard disk.

The Succar case would put to the test the principles I had stood fast by my entire life. When the mafia demons eventually came, we had already spent years building up our networks and gaining experience; we had matured enough to face the heart of darkness.

2

BRAVE GIRLS, IMPLACABLE TORMENTORS

In October 2003, Emma, a young girl with nut-brown hair and an innocent face, approached a former teacher of hers, Margaret, and asked her to help her report a man named Jean Succar Kuri for child pornography and rape. Margaret put her in touch with Verónica Acacio, a lawyer and the president of the nonprofit child-protection organization Protégeme [Protect Me], who agreed to represent her along with a number of other underage girls, and assist them with their case. On October 27, Quintana Roo state attorney general Celia Pérez Gordillo gave her authorization to the assistant attorney general to obtain video recordings of a conversation between Emma and Succar Kuri, with the aim of gathering evidence for the case. In the conversations taped at a local restaurant in Cancun, Succar admits to having raped girls as young as five. At this point, the Quintana Roo daily *Por esto!* had already been offering full, detailed coverage of the case blaming the girl victims who had somehow "sexually provoked the businessmen," and a few days later all the papers in the state had picked up the story, now blaming the mothers of the victims for not being present. On October 29, business magnate Kamel Nacif and his lawyers orchestrated Succar Kuri's escape, after receiving a warning that the latter was to be arrested the following day. I had begun documenting the case and investigating Succar Kuri. I invited Verónica, the lawyer, to my TV program to discuss child abuse and the unethical behavior of the authorities and the press that insisted on re-victimizing the victims and letting the abusers out of sight.

The very next day, October 30, Succar's wife, Gloria Pita, telephoned Emma and her mother and warned them to retract the accusations against her husband, or else. Two phone calls were recorded—with the consent of the assistant attorney general—in which Gloria can be heard admitting clearly and specifically to having explicit knowledge regarding her husband's acts of child rape and to being in possession of pornographic videos of Succar Kuri with several young girls. Among these, Gloria warned, were videos of Emma participating in sexual acts with her husband and other girls. The pornographer's wife told the young girl she would make the videos public if she went ahead with the criminal case.

On November 2, Emma reported Jean Succar Kuri again, this time to the PGR, for child pornography and for having raped her repeatedly since she was thirteen years old, as well as her younger sister and her cousin, eight and nine years old respectively, and several other girls of six. In her testimony, she stated that Succar brought girls over from the United States in order to offer them to Kamel Nacif Borge, Miguel Ángel Yunes Linares, and Alejandro Góngora Vera; she also stated that Succar claimed to be under the political protection of renowned politician Senator Emilio Gamboa Patrón and that thanks to this association, he was untouchable. In the days after she filed her report, Emma sought out Óscar Cadena, who had risen to fame years earlier with his Televisa program *Ciudadano infraganti*, a poor imitation of *60 Minutes*. Emma asked Óscar to interview her on his local TV show, because she feared her life was in danger as a result of having reported her rapist. Cadena agreed, and the interview was broadcast on local TV only to become a scandal that again placed the blame on the victim.

On November 4, a second underage girl gave her testimony to the police. She told how, beginning when she was six years old, Succar Kuri raped and filmed her. Another victim, still a girl at the time, gave her statement and testified that she met Succar Kuri when she was in kindergarten, at a neighbor's home, and that he had begun abusing her when she was just five. Three more minors who had never even met Emma gave statements attesting to similar facts a few days later. I kept following the case while, at the same time, investigating two other cases of sex trafficking from Argentina and Venezuela to Cancun and Florida. Nightclubs were filled with young women from Colombia, Argentina, Venezuela, and the US; they publicized themselves in local newspapers, and male journalists and immigration officials would visit these pole dancing joints and brothels for free—after all, the owners wanted to have the press and authorities on their side. Ever since Colombian kingpin Pablo Escobar built his mansion in Tulum, on a piece of land offered to him by the governor of Quintana Roo, I had quietly followed the trails of drug traffickers in the Caribbean who bring young women and girls through the Belize and Guatemala borders. My source at the DEA in Cancun kept telling me to stay away from that issue. Human trafficking for sexual exploitation was not yet recognized by Mexican authorities at the beginning of 2003. The governors made sure the Caribbean destination had no bad press at all, and the fact that Colombian drug lords, Russian mafias, and Mexican cartels had settled here was supposed to be a secret. Anyone who dared to expose them was—accordingly to authorities—damaging the economy of a tourist state. Just two years earlier, in May 2001, ex-governor Mario Villanueva was arrested for his links to organized crime; even though the big news was published in *The New York Times*, many local reporters such as me and others working for *La Crónica* newspaper had been reporting on this fact for years. When I told my DEA source that I was studying the criminal phenomena of forced prostitution and international networks linked to the cartels, international mafias, and human smuggling, he warned me I might be left alone or worse yet . . . I would be persecuted.

On November 7, 2003, the Third Court issued a search warrant for the Solymar Villas, owned by Succar. Among the items found in the search was an envelope containing hundreds of pornographic photographs of girls from Mexico and other countries. Roughly 20 percent of these photos showed boys under the age of sixteen engaging in sexual relations with small girls or being abused by older men. According to the federal authorities, twenty compromising videos filmed by Succar himself were recovered in the search but later disappeared. A year later, Cancun police agents were discovered putting them up for sale at US$40,000 a pop.

The victims' situation was becoming dangerous, and it was at this point that Emma came to me. She asked me to help her, as a journalist, to tell her story, because she was at risk of being murdered. She later agreed to allow CIAM Cancun to assist her and some of the other victims.

On November 12, international police organization INTERPOL announced that it had initiated an investigation against Jean Thouma Hanna Succar Kuri for "money laundering" and that the investigation would cover at least eight resort cities across the country—cities where Succar also owned residences, clothing and jewelry shops, restaurants, and other properties. Little by little, information came to light that pointed to the trafficking of minors for the purposes of exploiting them in the sex tourism industry, putting them at the service of affluent Mexican and American men. The girls and young women, unaware of the full magnitude of the situation, told how Succar had taken them to Los Angeles and Las Vegas, where they were forced to have sex with businessmen who were friends of their exploiter. They also explained that American girls were taken to Cancun to be exploited there, although none of them knew what had become of these girls afterward. Among the scores of porno-graphic photos recovered by the federal agents, there is one showing a small girl barely four years of age, with blond hair styled in a Prince Valiant cut, bound at the wrists and naked, and before her is the nude body of an older man with a large paunch, his erect penis posi-tioned directly in front of the child's frightened face.

Not even the federal agents assigned to the operation knew how to react to the feeling of revulsion these images provoked. Not even they, the professional investigators, could detach themselves from the impulse of fear such acts of cruelty generate. Every one of them, debating at length about possible criminological hypotheses, was struggling to find the right words to describe the fugitive pedo-phile and his accomplices. A sort of fellowship, born of the anguish caused by the extreme acts of brutality the evidence was pointing at, began to be felt by all those working to carry out a proper investiga-tion and protect the victims. Fear permeated the entire atmosphere, and no one was immune to its effects, not even the most seasoned of federal agents. I saw more than one shed tears of grief and desolation at the simple thought that they might not be able to stop this net-work of pedophiles. Every one of us cried, some holding each other's gaze silently, trying to control our breathing in order to continue the search for clues, and others in the privacy of our own homes as we wracked our brains in an attempt to understand what could possibly move these men to destroy the lives of such helpless beings. There were a plethora of questions, but the answers were few and fruitless. For a long while, the only thing that kept us going, kept us strong, was the thought of those girls' bravery. If they, who had gone through all the seven circles of hell, were still capable of standing and telling their stories, then none of us had the right to give up.

THE MEETING / EMMA AND THE APARTMENT

One rainy evening in November 2003, some time after eight o'clock, I had just locked up the office to go home when my cell phone rang.

It was a woman who had seen me on television; some mutual friend had given her my number. Very evidently distressed, she told me that there was a problem with a friend of her daughter's and asked me to please come to her house because she had no idea how to deal with the situation. When I asked her if it was an emergency or if it could wait until the following day, she replied that it was a matter of life and death. I got in my Jeep, dug out a notebook and pen, and copied down her address. On the way I used my radio to call Claudia, the psychologist at the shelter, in order to let her know where I was going. If I did not call her within two hours it was important that she look for me. Safety was by then an everyday issue.

I drove to a middle-class neighborhood of government housing complexes made up of three-story buildings consisting of six or eight units each. The street was dark; it was the middle of hurricane season, and it had been raining. The rows of identical buildings made it hard to find the right address. I finally spotted it, next to a faded, crumbling wall. Before getting out of the car, I dialed the woman's cell phone number to let her know that I had arrived; then I looked carefully around, pulled a canister of pepper spray out of my purse, and readied it in my hand. In the other hand the radio was ready to call in case of an emergency. I walked along the sidewalk, surrounded on all sides by an intense, unsettling blackness, until I reached the staircase leading up to the woman's apartment. When I saw that she was waiting for me in the open doorway, I tucked the pepper spray back into my bag and gave her a quick wave.

I ducked into the apartment, where the woman greeted me with a kiss on the cheek and a look of desperation on her face. She was slender, about forty, with short hair gathered up at the back. Her expression was dark and sweet but veiled with anguish. She wore a flowery cotton dress and a lightweight pink sweater (it was a cool time of year, when locals can often be seen sporting sweaters and jackets). The apartment was very small, and the first thing I noticed were two girls—first the woman's daughter, a beautiful, black-haired girl who was standing at her mother's side, and then a young blond girl with fine features and brown eyes, her face distorted with fear and sobbing. Her face looked like dirty windows on a rainy night and her eyes were bloodshot from her heavy cries; she wrung her hands anxiously and looked at me in alarm, scrutinizing me in silence. It was the woman who spoke first.

"Well . . . this is Emma. I explained to her that I know you, that you have a television program and you help abused women. She saw your show and asked me to call you, because she needs help. If you need anything, please just let me know." She offered me a glass of water, placed it hurriedly into my hands, and disappeared into the adjoining room, her arm around her daughter.

The young girl seated before me was experiencing a breakdown. She collapsed in tears and told me that she had reached her wits' end, pleading with me to please help her. The television in the kitchen was switched on to a soap opera. The two of us were sitting on a tiny sofa near the window, not two yards from the small kitchen where the TV set hung from one wall. I moved to turn it off when she began speaking, in order to focus better on what she needed to tell me, but she stopped me abruptly; she told me not to turn it off, that we needed to have it on because the nightly newscast was going to mention something about her case. Then she proceeded, speaking haltingly. She had filed a report against the man who raped her for years, she began. The sound of the television set droning almost menacingly in the background will always accompany my memory of the rest of the story this girl told me that night.

She started in, giving me a rather fractured explanation of the situation. She first told me that when she was barely thirteen years old, a friend of hers invited her to meet a very kind man she knew who would let them use the pool at his hotel, a villa resort in the tourist area of the city. Her friend explained that he was a very rich man whom everybody called "El Johnny"; he owned jewelry and clothing stores as well as the villas, and he made a habit of giving the girls gifts and buying them school supplies, books, fancy clothes, and so on. So her friend introduced them, and it turned out that the man was in fact using them sexually in exchange for giving them money. Emma was jumping all over the place in the way she told me the story, skipping back and forth between different explanations in no particular order, clearly weary of having had to tell the same story to so many different people and on so many different occasions. She was visibly frightened, and at several points in the conversation she started to cry. Her entire body was shaking and she said that she no longer trusted anyone, she felt like she was about to go crazy, and she was extremely scared. I could see all the post-traumatic stress disorder symptoms in her voice, attitude, and gestures.

I tried to provide some solid support for her and help her to distance herself mentally from the story that was causing her such distress. I took her hands in mine and asked her to breathe slowly and take a sip of water. I told her my name and said that I could only imagine what she was going through, acknowledging I was aware it must have been extremely difficult. She replied that she knew I had written something in the paper about her case, she knew that I had defended her rights. She asked me why I had done such a thing without knowing her. I explained that she was a very brave girl and that I despised the manner in which some journalists had been discussing her situation. I explained how and why I thought the judgmental news coverage was utterly inappropriate and a violation of her human rights. I impressed upon her that she was not responsible for any of it.

"What happened to you was a crime, a crime committed by an adult against a minor. The law is on your side," I said, knowing full well the weight and impact my words would carry with her. I had first heard about her case through the local media, at which point I simply did what I'm most specialized at doing and wrote an editorial analyzing the rights of sexual abuse victims. "Thousands of women survive this sort of thing and manage to be happy again," I said, looking her straight in the eyes, "but none of them has done it alone."

Right away, Emma began to calm down. A faint smile crossed her lips and a red flush returned to her cheeks. Just then, the intro music to Joaquín López Dóriga's newscast started playing. She whirled around to face the television set and sat frozen, like a gazelle poised to flee from a coming attack. As the newscaster read out the headlines for the night's top stories, we heard him announce, with that loud tone of a fascinated newscaster who is ecstatic about his scoop, that later on in the broadcast a scandalous video would be shown highlighting the confessions of a pedophile. The young girl at my side underwent another instant transformation—she began begging me to call the station and make them halt the broadcast, but I didn't understand what she was talking about.

"You're a journalist, please, call López Dóriga! Call him and tell him not to show the video." Then she started repeating over and over, "They're going to kill me, they're going to kill me! Please, stop them." And finally, in a fit of desperation, "You don't know who these people are!"

And it was true, I had no idea who the ghosts were that had caused this poor girl to work herself into such a terrified fervor, so closely resembling the dread that must grip a soul upon hearing its death knell.

The news team relayed information about Succar and showed a portion of a video in which he is seen speaking not only openly but also coolly and calmly about having raped several five-year-old girls. At that very instant, a cell phone rang. We both started at the sound. Young Emma gaped at the phone in terror for a moment. Then she answered, moved the earpiece closer to me so that I could listen in, covered the mouthpiece with her hand, and whispered urgently, "It's El Johnny's son."

A young man's voice began spitting insults down the line.

"Emma, you bitch, I'm watching the news, I saw what you did to my dad, and either you drop this whole thing, or I'm going to kill you."

He hung up, and Emma broke down again. She slumped against me, and I hugged her quietly, trying to gauge the level of danger she was in, and the level of danger those of us choosing to help her might also be in.

I asked her about Succar's son. She told me that he never went anywhere unarmed, that he was American, that he lived in California, somewhere right outside Los Angeles, and that she was convinced he could kill her, that he was capable of that and much more.

"Why is he going to kill you?" I asked. She dove headlong into her response, talking a mile a minute about Succar Kuri's powerful friends. Politicians with direct access to the president, congressmen, governors . . . Her words gathered pace, painting a picture of the man who was the very portrait of absolute power. Then she stopped suddenly, and I asked her about her mother. Her tone changed, and a look of sadness came over her face. She told me that her mother was an alcoholic and very poor. She lived with her stepfather—a mechanic—and neither one of them fully understood what had been going on, or even really knew the whole truth of the matter. She looked down at her hands, which she had busied by continually twisting and untwisting a scrap of wet tissue, and said that her mother was a very uneducated woman, that her mother was in fact angry but at the same time scared.

From one moment to the next, she began shaking again, saying that they were going to find her, that for all she knew, they might be listening in on her right now. She turned to me and said, "I need you to help me, because you're a journalist; we could use your program to tell the truth. If not, they're going to kill me. And they're going to kill my mom, and my little sister, and me, and my cousins, because we did it, we reported them." She went on, repeating the same sentences over and over, each time a little quieter, as though they lost some of their intensity with every repetition.

Meanwhile, López Dóriga's program continued, still on the same topic.

I asked Emma, "Is that you in front of him?"

She nodded, her eyes welling up again as she saw her blurred face on screen.

"Make it stop, make it stop, please, talk to someone," she sobbed, and she pressed the telephone into my hand. "Make it stop, tell them to stop it right now," she wept.

"I don't have the power to halt a Televisa broadcast, I have no power over it at all," I insisted, but she continued to plead with me, so I got out my own cell phone and dialed Ernestina Macdonald, Televisa's Cancun correspondent.

"Ernestina, do you know if they're going to show any more videos of Emma and Succar on the news? Please, make sure they don't show the girl's face—it's very dangerous!"

Ernestina replied very coldly, "No, the girl's face won't be shown, only the rapist's."

It was the first time I ever saw the video. When I heard some of the things said on it, my breath caught, bile heaved up into my throat, and my mouth went dry. I looked at the girl at my side; I couldn't even begin to imagine how she was feeling. Her eyes were fixed on the screen, and the two of us listened in silence. She continued wringing her hands, as though trying to cleanse them of some nonexistent filth. Then I felt a hollow sensation in the pit of my stomach, and a chill ran through my body as I stole a glance at her out of the corner of my eye, wondering at the courage it must have taken for her to sit down and film her tormentor like that.

The video was recorded at the outdoor dining patio of a downtown restaurant. The sound quality is very clear, and Succar Kuri's face can be seen as he speaks, sips at his juice, and twirls his straw around in the glass almost happily. He smiles now and again while speaking. Emma's face as she asks him her series of questions is seen blurred only a few times. But you can hear the nervousness in her voice; it is the anxiety of a victim risking exposing herself to her aggressor in order to obtain evidence against him—in this case, a tacit confession. Near the end of the filmed portion of their conversation, she gets what she's looking for:

> SUCCAR: Lesly was coming over to my place from the age of eight to twelve. Lesly took baths with me, she was with me a long time, she slept whole weeks with me, and I never did anything to her.
>
> EMMA: But you would kiss her, and touch her.
>
> SUCCAR: But I'm telling you, that's all allowed! Because that's the risk you take when you go to some lonely old fuck's house, it's all part of the risk. Her parents just said, "Oh, he takes care of my daughter, he takes care of my daughter." All that's allowed. For instance, I say to Lesly, "Bring me a girl who's four," and if she says, "She's already been fucked," and I see if she's been fucked already, then I see if I'm gonna stick my dick in her or not. You know this is my weakness, it's my kink, and I know it's a crime and it's not allowed, but it's so much easier this way, because a tiny little girl like that doesn't stand a chance, because you can convince her really easily, and then you fuck her. I've been doing it my whole life, and sometimes they try to trick me, because they want to stay with me, because I've got a reputation for being a good father . . .

I was truly at a loss for what to say. It was a lot of awful information to take in. Night had fallen, and I wanted to run, to get out of there, but I tried to concentrate. *My God*, I thought, *how many girls are there? Where are they?* But it was neither the time nor the place to bring up my own worries; it was time for this girl to be heard and for me to make sure I understood the story she was telling me, so that I could help her. I took a deep breath and asked her the questions that would draw us away from the tangled emotions brought on by her harsh, violent descriptions and lead us instead to concrete pieces of information. I had to call on the whole of my training and experience as a reporter—*Find the truth, find what lies beneath, don't get sucked in, allow yourself to be moved but don't get sucked in*, I thought, trying to steady my mind.

Emma explained to me that the recorded conversation had been submitted to the state Assistant Attorney General's Office. Assistant attorney general Miguel Ángel Pech made copies of the tape and sent them to the press, timing their distribution to coincide with his public announcement that an investigation had been launched to look into the child pornography and prostitution ring headed by the Lebanese-born businessman.

Emma and I spent two hours talking. She repeated that there were hundreds of photographs and scores of pornographic videos with her and other girls as young as five. I don't know where I continued to draw my strength from, but I copied down the stories as she relayed them to me and did my best not to imagine the pain these poor children must have suffered—the personal anguish I was experiencing was unbearable. I tried to outline some strategies she could follow to protect herself, anything to prevent her from continuing to go over the story in all its detail, because just the thought of that inevitably drove her into a state of impossible distress. I promised her that we would do whatever she wanted.

"We need to get my little sister and the other girls back—they've been locked up at the DIF[3] and they're really scared," she said.

"Why are they locked up?" I asked, surprised, as I understood public child protection services were guarding these kids.

"Because we filed our report and now they don't want them to be with their mothers. Leidy Campos, at the Attorney General's Office, says it's the mothers' fault for not taking care of them. . . . But they didn't know anything, I swear, I swear," she insisted, her eyes glistening and damp. "El Johnny filmed us the first time and

---

3. Translator's Note: Sistema Nacional para el Desarrollo Integral de la Familia, the Mexican Child protection services.

then showed us the videos to keep us quiet. Once you were in with him, you couldn't get out."

Years later, it would become clear just how many girls and boys were keeping quiet because of Succar's threats. In time I interviewed and counted two hundred children.

I asked Emma if she could spend the night there at her friend's apartment so that she would be safe until I could take her to my office the next day, when we could figure out a plan to rescue the girls and protect their families. She said she could.

I knocked on the door to the bedroom where the woman who had called me on Emma's behalf was waiting. She stood up, and I spoke to her quietly to assure her that everything was going to be fine. She embraced me and then asked in a whisper if I thought someone might really kill the girl. I replied that I couldn't be sure and we would have to investigate matters further, but that she would be safe there in her home.

"She's a good girl," I said, "but she's suffered a great deal."

I left the apartment, got into my truck, and put on some jazz music. I turned the volume up as far as it would go and lost myself in the silky voice of Sade as I focused on breathing deeply, attempting to calm myself down on the drive home.

The following day, I awoke at five in the morning, drank a large glass of orange juice, and stepped out onto the balcony. The beauty of the landscape spread out there before me stood in stark contrast to the version of Cancun paradise I had discovered the night before. I rolled out my yoga mat and exercised for more than half an hour. Afterward, before getting into the bath, I recall that I gazed down at the silver-sheened mirror of the lagoon and then up to the pristine sky and thought to myself, *We'll shed light into the darkness, fearlessly. Those girls are alive, and we're going to protect them.*

I drove to the office, all the while running over in my head the different possible strategies I could present to my CIAM team. I had to keep reminding myself to concentrate on what we could do now rather than on the horror of what had already been done. Like a mountain climber who knows that she and her companions have no choice but to rappel their way down to the bottom of a chasm, I took silent stock of my emotional tools, like someone counting and bundling up safety cords, hammers, and bolts—for if one is to avoid falling into the abyss, the hardware that supports her must be secure—and I made a mental list of strategies: what people to go to, what calls to make, what favors to ask of friends, what information to share with colleagues in the event the situation turned out to be as dangerous as I feared.

Emma came into the office at ten that morning. I had outlined some ideas with my team, and we had contacted the municipal child protection service office. When I called my friend Verónica Acacio, the lawyer and activist, and explained to her what had happened, she told me this was the same extremely delicate case she had mentioned to me a few months prior. I became uneasy and tried to recall what she had told me on that earlier occasion. We never mention specific information about cases, or victims' names, over the phone, so I decided my discussion with Verónica would have to wait. Generally speaking, CIAM and Ms. Acacio's Protégeme organization would refer cases to one another depending on the specific area of specialization of each institution, so I never imagined that Verónica was already aware that the Attorney General's Office had concrete leads pointing to organized crime in the Succar case. Later, she would be the one to remind me of two key names: Kamel Nacif and Emilio Gamboa.

On the afternoon of November 21, 2003, the nation's attorney general, Rafael Macedo de la Concha, made his first public appearance in the PGR's newly refurbished Cancun offices, and he used it to speak about the Succar case. I was sitting right in front of him. He chose his words carefully as he addressed the press, his face virtually devoid of expression:

The Federal Investigations Agency [AFI][4] and INTERPOL are working jointly to determine the whereabouts of Jean Thouma Hanna Succar Kuri, who is also the subject of an active investigation for alleged money laundering.

A murmur of incredulity rippled across the room. The journalists there had spent more than thirty days trotting out the different stories that had already come to light. They'd published photographs where the victims' faces were clearly visible, as well as portraits of their mothers. By also showing photographs of the exteriors of the victims' homes, neighbors would be sure to figure out who the mothers of all the victims were, and to judge them for having—allegedly—handed their daughters over to a pedophile.

Meanwhile, I called Mexico City to speak with the director of INTERPOL, having been introduced to him by a friend of mine who specializes in topics having to do with violence. I told him who I was and about the work we were doing at CIAM. Then I suggested to Emma that she tell him everything she knew, and she agreed. Straight away, we hopped on a plane to the capital city. I took Emma to INTERPOL's offices and waited in the adjoining room while she told director Ricardo Gutiérrez who the powerful men protecting Succar Kuri were. Then she handed over all the evidence she had, and we returned to Cancun.

After a lengthy process involving various efforts and agreements with the state DIF and the PGR, Emma and her family, as well as three additional girls and boys and their families, were admitted to CIAM Cancun and began receiving protection and specialized care. Emma received outpatient psychiatric assistance. Verónica Acacio

---

4. Translator's Note: Agencia Federal de Investigación, Mexico's main investigative police force, organized under the national Office of the Attorney General (PGR). It has since been replaced by the Ministerial Federal Police (PFM, Policia Federal Ministerial), with many of its former agents having been transferred to the preventive Federal Police force, the second of Mexico's federal-level police agencies, which operates under the Secretariat of Public Security (SSP, Secretaría de Seguridad Pública).

acted as her lawyer throughout the process, while we helped with the development of a security strategy. Emma asked me to assist her in getting in touch with different media outlets that could help her tell the truth of her story; we agreed that the public would be better able to appreciate the significance of the fact that Succar Kuri had been arrested in the United States if the story was publicized there, also. Several papers—including *The Arizona Republic, The Dallas Morning News*, and others—interviewed her and the mothers of some of the other victims. Emma's fortitude despite the occasional, momentary losses of composure to be expected in such circumstances, as well as her tenacity and bravery, made her the object of much admiration.

After the customary four months had gone by, plans were drawn up for the families to relocate and continue receiving external therapy, in accordance with our assistance protocol. If victims spend any longer than that at the shelter, what they conceived of initially as an oasis of calm can quickly become a suffocating confinement. For the good of their psycho-emotional health, they must begin to rebuild their lives. It now fell to them—in particular to the mothers and, in those cases where they were present in their children's lives, the fathers—to remain firm and not allow themselves to be co-opted by Succar Kuri. The PGR's victim assistance and human rights branch had an obligation to protect them and follow up on their cases, but they never did.

Emma asked to go to Mexico City. My friend Ricardo Rocha, a journalist who had covered the Succar Kuri case on his morning news show and in *Reporte 13*, knew the victims and had been profoundly moved by their stories. Emma was now twenty-one years old—although she has always looked much younger than she really is—and Rocha offered her a position working in news production. And so this now bright-eyed young woman moved to the capital city, with Protégeme and Verónica Acacio agreeing to pay for her schooling. She found lodging in a fantastic apartment in the Coyoacán district with a writer who was a friend of hers, an adult who could look after her. Whenever she moved around the city, she did so by car, with a chauffeur, to shield her from Succar's threats. This form of protection was extremely costly, but fortunately there were plenty of people dedicated body, soul, and pocketbook to the goal of preventing Succar from bringing his victims back into the fold. And the authorities were revealing even more names of individuals associated with his organized crime network.

The victims' families continued their external therapy, but finding themselves worn down by the PGR's endless questioning and the emotional relapses of their twelve- and thirteen-year-old children, they grew angry with the authorities. Months went by, and they were continually required to submit expert psychological and medical status reports.

One afternoon Lety, the mother of one of the girls, asked to speak with me privately. She is a sweet woman, although she has been deeply affected by her daughter's suffering. No longer able to cope, she spoke insistently.

"We've spent a year in this situation—when is it going to end? This is torture."

I relayed Ms. Acacio's estimate that Succar's extradition to Mexico could take between one and two years more. Years of pent-up anger finally broke through her calm, resigned exterior.

No, she said, she'd already been told that the trial could take another two years. It was absolutely impossible; neither she nor her daughter and son who had been abused at the hands of Succar and his powerful friends would be able to survive if they were forced to live with this open wound for so long. It was agony, she said, and she was right. Mrs. Lety decided to remake a life for herself and her children in a different state. She said that when Succar was brought over, they would come back for the trial. No one can possibly judge this woman without putting themselves in her shoes; she had all the right in the world to want to close that horrifying chapter of her life. The crawling pace at which the authorities were operating had become a boon to her children's aggressors.

Slowly, while the sluggish wheels of bureaucracy were making life hellish for the victims, Succar Kuri and Kamel Nacif's lawyers were scouring the victim assistance networks in search of the families. They made threats and offered money. Some of the families accepted, and others did not. I got involved in the investigation to such an extent that I had to fly to the US several times in order to understand the mafia links and the criminal power Kamel Nacif—Succar's partner—had over politicians. That was the first time I saw Nacif´s criminal files for tax evasion in Nevada.

A year and a half after we at CIAM first got involved in the Succar case, new girls who had been abused by these man were still turning up at our door. Their new stories brought tales of incompetence on the part of the police investigators, stories of girls who were taken to California and never came back, of underage American girls brought to Mexico to forcibly have sex with Succar's friends. The criminal connections were becoming clearer, but at the same time, my various sources and contacts revealed that thanks to the powerful influence of Kamel Nacif—who is a friend of Senator Miguel Angel Yunes Linares—and ex Minister of Interior Emilio Gamboa Patrón, the case had been indefinitely stalled at the PGR. Now Succar might go free, and the families with who we were still in touch were terrified at the possibility.

THE DEMONS ARE CAPTURED IN PRINT

In December 2004, reporter David Sosa, a friend of mine, got in touch with me because the publishing house Random House was looking for a journalist to tell the Succar Kuri story; I told him that I would help him, that publishing the ignominious acts of such pedophiles would be a good idea because it might help get the case moving to the federal courts. We met to go over the information I had: an index of the investigation that included hard data on money laundering, international sex trafficking, child pornography rings, several powerful politicians involved, and a couple of assassinated girls. Once he saw the details, and read aloud the names of the powerful men involved, Sosa told me that he was no longer interested in participating and that I would have to write it on my own. It was too dangerous, he said, not worth the risk.

I then traveled to Mexico City, and the publishers gave me 10,000 pesos for the book. Two airplane tickets later (for trips I took to interview my sources at the PGR and INTERPOL), and the money was gone. Three months had gone by when I gave the publishers the manuscript of *The Demons of Eden: The Powers Protecting Child Pornography*. I wrote it in just a few weeks, but I had been preparing the documentation for the previous two years. My husband at the time, a journalist from Guadalajara, read it before I sent it, and we discussed the risk involved. But by the time the book was ready I had already survived several death threats, an assassination attempt, and a couple of car chases with gunmen trying to scare me to stop my investigations. And deep inside me, no matter the risk, I knew it was something I had to do.

I flew to Mexico City a couple weeks before the book launch. By that time the antidrug czar Jose Luis Santiago Vasconcelos knew me quite well; he had to send his men to our shelter a couple of times when I had the first assassination attempt and again when hit men surrounded our office and asked me to get out or else they would launch grenades to get me to stop. At the shelter we were protecting young women victims from organized crime networks dedicated to human trafficking of girls and women for the tourism sex industry. We had also protected children abused by then-famous drug lords. He knew our work quite well, and he read my weekly newspaper columns and investigations.

Quickly I realized the book launch could become a tragic event. A couple days earlier, the editor-in-chief of Random House had been summoned to the office of the newly appointed Federal

Police Bureau undersecretary Miguel Angel Yunes. The children I interviewed had accused Yunes of being one of the clients of the sexual exploitation ring. I gathered enough evidence, including child pornography videos and photos, to publish his full name. One of the federal attorneys who helped me get evidence (and who ended up receiving death threats for protecting the children) shared official documents he was sure would "evaporate" from the official files once Yunes took office.

Yunes had summoned the editors, a first for Random House Mexico, and when they politely refused to censor me, he followed up by issuing an express threat.

I called Vasconcelos and explained Yunes's threat, and his response was immediate. He tried to convince me to stop the book launch until he could make sure I would not be murdered. "Your book has evidence that can make an important part of the federal government crumble. This is an international human trafficking network, Ms. Cacho." I said I was not backing off, not only because my investigation was good, honest, socially pertinent, and well documented, but because I had made a promise to all the girls and boys who trusted me with their stories. He then told me the antidrug office (SEIDO, the Mexican DEA) would be guarding me at all times, and from then on I would be officially assigned four secret service agents to be with me for the rest of my life.

The night of April 15, 2005, two days after my 42nd birthday, the famous journalists Carlos Loret de Mola, Denisse Merker, and Jorge Zepeda presented the book at the Jaime Sabines Cultural Center in Mexico City. We were surrounded by a heavily armed detachment of SEIDO consisting of 15 special agents who had been ordered by the prominent antidrug office's assistant attorney general at the time, José Luis Santiago Vasconcelos.

I looked at my editors, and they could not believe their eyes. For the first time in their life, they had to present a book while surrounded by special policemen to protect us from the Federal Police agents. A few days prior to the presentation, while the publishing house was organizing a press tour to promote the book, I was seated in the office of my editor, Ariel Rosales. At one point during our meeting, Faustino Linares, the director of Random House Mondadori at the time, stepped into the room. He was a senior editor who had recently come over from Spain to run the Mexican office, and he asked us, in his characteristically sweet, almost phlegmatic voice, "Who is this Mr. Miguel Ángel Yunes?"

Ariel and I glanced warily at each other before replying that he had been a senator, wanted to become governor of the state of Veracruz, and had been serving for the past few months as undersecretary of Federal Police.

"I see. Well, he called me; he wants me to go see him at his office today, in an hour or two hours, ideally."

We asked Faustino to take a seat; he needed to understand who this particular political figure was and the role he played in the story of my book, which he evidently had not read.

I showed him a folder containing photocopies of some of the documentary evidence obtained during my investigations, and I warned him that Yunes was going to try to stop the book launch. And that's precisely what happened. Faustino and Ariel went down to the offices of the Federal Security Police. In the meeting, Yunes alleged that his name should never have appeared in the book. They explained to him that I had done nothing more than transcribe the declarations officially submitted in the Succar Kuri case and the investigation on the historic links he had with a drug lord from the Gulf Cartel. At that point, Yunes read them letters from several public servants, letters that exonerated him, he said, from any responsibility in the case. Those same letters had already been published in *La Jornada*, when Yunes exercised his rebuttal rights after one of the daily reports alluded to the fact that his name had come up at the pedophile's trial. After personally reading the letters out loud, he attempted to persuade Faustino and Ariel that they be read at the book presentation, as well, and that the publishing house make a statement reproaching me and saying that they did not approve of my having included the name of Miguel Ángel Yunes in one of their books. Naturally, the director refused, although he did offer to have me interview Yunes and publish his side of the story in a new edition. Under no circumstances would he ever speak to me, Yunes replied. So they suggested that he could write a piece explaining his position. This text and facsimiles of the letters he had just read to them at the meeting could appear in the appendix of the new edition. They were also willing to have the editor read Yunes's text at the book presentation and give a summary of the contents of his letters. He said he would think about it but that the publishers needed to think about his initial proposal as well.

After the meeting, Yunes telephoned to press the issue and even sent over a messenger to ask whether they were going to accept his offer. They would not, but their counterproposal to him still stood, they replied. Faustino gave me a detailed account of the meeting, we discussed it, and we agreed—we would have to alert the authorities.

We looked at each other, and Faustino asked us out of the corner of his mouth, almost in a whisper, "Just what do they have on this Yunes guy?"

The book launch went off without a hitch, under the watchful eyes of Alejandro Góngora—the former head of the National Tourism Development Fund (FONATUR) and Emilio Gamboa's representative in the latter's business dealings with the Fund, as well as one of Succar Kuri's associates. He attended the presentation in the company of a lawyer. Half of the *mafiosos* I had investigated were sitting there at the book launch; amongst 200 people they quietly took notes and had a man taking pictures.

Over the course of the following months, some of the roadblocks in the Succar case began to be cleared and progress slowly started up again, all thanks to the fact that journalists had chosen to present the story in the proper light and focus on what was truly important—child pornography, sex trafficking, and the dangers of Succar being set free. And all manner and ilk of new witnesses started cropping up, too. Never imagining the impact my request would end up having, I had asked the publishers to print my personal email address on the book's back cover. Almost overnight, I began receiving hundreds of emails. At first they trickled in, just a few dozen every week or so, but I soon found myself flooded with more than one hundred per week. They came from female and male readers of all ages, some telling me how my book had prompted them to recall the abuses they themselves had suffered in childhood, others simply thanking me for telling this important story. But most importantly, I was contacted by young adults from Cancun between the ages of twenty-four and twenty-six who wished to speak with me after having read my book. I met with some of them, and what I learned was absolutely astonishing; the number of young people who knew about Succar Kuri and his obsession for young girls and boys was far larger than I had ever guessed.

Some of the individuals I spoke with had studied at the La Salle, a religious high school in Cancun, and they told me that when they read the book, they finally understood a large portion of what they had seen going on around them when they were in school. According to them, it had been common, albeit unspoken, knowledge at the school for a decade now, a well-known secret that these teenage girls and boys had zealously kept without understanding the consequences of their silence.

As the months passed, the book was no longer a hot topic in the press, but the calls and reports from readers concerned about this and other, similar cases continued unabated. I went on with my life, still working at CIAM and, with an eye to a future book, still investigating cases involving the trafficking of women and children.

Occasionally, one of the victims in the Succar case would alert us to the fact that new death threats had been made and that Succar's lawyers had been hanging around outside the schools looking for his victims (especially the youngest girls), or outside their houses looking for their mothers, and offering to pay them between US$10,000 and US$20,000 if they agreed to accompany them to their offices to sign a document retracting their accusations. We advised the victims as best we could and reported the threats to the authorities, but nothing was done. The only outcome was that a few of the mothers—two, in particular—accepted the lawyers' offers of money and were forced first to sign a statement admitting their retraction and then to bring their children in to testify. Their strongest motivating factor—and the most credible one, given the climate of impunity in Mexico—was that Succar was sure to be set free, and that if they didn't cooperate, he would order that they be killed, eliminated by any means necessary.

THE EMPIRE STRIKES BACK

One mid-May afternoon in 2004, Emma telephoned to say hello. To my horror, she then went on to explain that Succar had finally managed to locate her. My blood turned to ice in my veins. We had spent months doing everything we could to help her make a new, dignified life for herself, so that she could study and receive therapy, so that she could have a job that would allow her to see that money can be earned through honest work and that what Succar had taught her in her adolescence—that women and girls are only good for one thing: prostitution—is false. She told me that Succar had located an uncle of hers who lived in Mérida and had telephoned him personally from his Arizona prison. Her uncle had then called her and told her he thought she should listen to what Succar had to say.

I felt impotent listening to what Emma was telling me. I had been in a meeting with Alicia Leal, the director of the Alternativas Pacíficas de Monterrey shelter, when she called, and I let Alicia listen in. As the conversation went on, I found myself struggling to find the right words. Emma was now defending her rapist, alleging that things hadn't really been so bad. Alicia caught my eye and whispered, "It's the Stockholm syndrome."

I knew how difficult it is for victims of this sort of crime to break the paradoxical bonds linking them to their aggressors, but this was too much. The girls were finally free from Succar now, thanks in part to the pressure of various human rights organizations; he had been arrested on an INTERPOL warrant on February 4, 2004, in Chandler, Arizona. Nevertheless, Emma insisted that I simply didn't understand just how powerful Succar's friends were.

"They're going to kill us, Lydia. It's better that we negotiate."

I tossed out every argument I could think of; a sense of desperation took over and clouded my mind, and I ran out of things to say. Alicia, an expert in victim assistance, had a trip to Mexico City planned for the following days, and she offered to go and speak to Emma there. Emma agreed. But a few days later, my phone rang again—this time it was Alicia, and she sounded worried. She explained that Emma's concept of her relationship with Succar exhibited a mixture of fear, love, and neediness. After all, there's a reason this type of abuser likes to get his claws into these girls and boys when they're still young, during their formative, preteen years, because that way he can manipulate his victims' view of themselves and the world. They are able to link abuse and sex, love and fear, power and submission in their victims' psyches, sometimes for the rest of their lives.

Several weeks later, as the summer of 2004 neared its end, Emma disappeared from Mexico City. She canceled her cell phone account, she didn't say good-bye to a single person, and she never returned to school. We searched worriedly for her, but no one had any knowledge of her whereabouts. Meanwhile, there were other women and children who needed our help, and so life, despite everything, went on.

Ten months later, in May of 2005, I had gone home for the night and was checking my email, when a chill ran down my spine—there, right before my eyes, was an email from Emma, a scattered explanation telling me that Succar Kuri's lawyers had taken her to Los Angeles and that she was afraid that now that he was going to be set free, they were going to kill her and all the other girls and boys. A few disconnected pieces of information and a sort of veiled apology for something she said was about to happen was all Emma wrote, but something in her email seemed off. Although the tone of her words was apparently filled with anger against me for having published the book, she also, at one point, said that it was good that I had written it, because "now Succar would not touch any more little girls." She asked me not to look for her, because she was going to do what she had to do. Yet again she was in the eye of the storm, as a victim who longs for the rapist father figure's love and forgiveness. She was sacrificing herself and at the same time she was back in California with the family and the luxuries she had grown accustomed to. Prostitution needs training, intense expert training to break girls into little distorted pieces and then convince them that the only way for them to feel whole again is if they are touched by the hand of the men who own them.

A few days later, during Carlos Loret de Mola's morning newscast on Televisa, Emma appeared wearing a small crystal bead in the center of her forehead, Hindu-style, her hair permed and bleached a shade of blond identical to that of Succar's wife. On national television, she recited a prepared speech, defending Succar Kuri and alleging that my book was full of lies. I sat next to my husband, holding hands in front of the television, frozen with incredulity, an overwhelming feeling of sadness washing over me. "This is the power of traffickers," I said to Jorge, "they own girls as slaves, they break them and they break them until they take their human dignity away."

"No, no, Emma, they're going to destroy you," I heard myself speak to the television set, as though she could hear me through the screen.

Dumbfounded, I returned to the office in a state of apprehensive expectancy, but the silent suspense didn't last long. My colleagues in the press, all the people who had helped Emma and believed in her, began telephoning me, expressing their indignation; even those newspaper reporters who had always been so willing, through thick and thin, to give her voice and cause a platform felt betrayed. I must have gone over the scientific explanation of Stockholm syndrome and post-traumatic stress disorder twenty different times with the various people calling me. Once at the office, the team got together to hash out their impressions. The social worker assigned to Emma's case cried as she explained that she felt overpowered by anger and sadness. There we were, Succar Kuri's threats still hanging over us, every one of us operating under a tremendous amount of emotional strain resulting from the constant expenditure of effort required to listen to the abhorrent stories told to us by the girls Emma had brought in to us. And now this same young woman who had been given more opportunities than any of the other victims was siding with Succar.

Why is she sacrificing herself? we all asked. To protect her tormentor? For money? We stared unbelievingly, agape, at one another. Supporting and protecting victims is a calling, not just a job. Our team has always been guided by the philosophy that we work because we believe we can help to create a country free from gender violence. We are all survivors who have chosen to become teachers of peace and act as sympathetic companions who know how difficult the path of personal transformation can be. And now the question on everyone's mind and lips: *What are we going to tell the other girls?*

Several of the mothers were already up in arms. Emma had sold herself out to the same abuser who—in their eyes—had destroyed the lives of so many underage girls, and they were not about to forgive her. One of these mothers went to the Attorney General's Office and reported Emma for having forcibly taken her five-year-old daughter to Succar Kuri's Solymar villa resort complex. The pedophile's revenge was exacting its desired effect: It was sowing division, uncertainty, and fear among the survivors. The mobsters were strategically creating mayhem; with the victims broken down in emotional despair, it would be more difficult to keep them going until the court trial of the pedophile ring leader and his accomplices.

I found myself thinking back to that line in her email where Emma apologized to me for something she said was about to happen and thinking that this television appearance must have been what she was referring to. It would be several months before it came to light that behind Emma's co-optation lay not only Succar Kuri but also none other than Kamel Nacif, his associate and accomplice, who had put up US$300,000 for Succar Kuri's defense and the buying of some witnesses.

Around this same time, while Succar's arrest was making international headlines, a young Salvadoran girl who had been sexually exploited by Succar Kuri and Kamel Nacif also disappeared. No one knew whether she was still alive or if she had been murdered. Wenceslao Cisneros, one of several lawyers over the years to have represented Succar Kuri for a time before eventually stepping down, talked to me and claimed that his former client told him that the girl would never be seen again—he had her killed. According to recorded telephone conversations, Kamel Nacif paid Succar Kuri US$2,000 to bring the girl to the Solymar Villas in Cancun so that he could "fornicate" with her.

I had been planning to spend my September 2005 vacation traveling, a much-needed trip to relax after all the pressure, the long hours, and the threats accrued over the course of this exhausting Succar Kuri case. Jorge and I had promised each other that we would discuss the case no further. I had done everything that was in my power; now it fell to the authorities to do their part. After all, the girls were still getting their therapy, a few had chosen to go home with their mothers, and the case would not be allowed to move forward—assuming it ever would—until Succar was extradited. CIAM had continued to take on dozens of similar cases; they were almost all resolved successfully, and the team had gotten the chance to share in the joy of families who were now able to go back to their lives without the shadow of violence looming over them, the joy of women who were now able to rebuild their dignity and their lives.

But my vacation was canceled one day when I was returning home from Oaxaca, where I had been filming a report on the poverty affecting women migrating from the Sierra region there. I had a fever when I boarded the plane home, and by the time we landed, I was in need of hospitalization. I spent two weeks in the hospital with acute renal complications (I had undergone surgery and lost one of my kidneys when I was eighteen years old), which led to a case of infectious pneumonia that kept me in critical condition for several more days. In the company of family, friends, and Jorge, I began to recover, somewhat weakened but on the path to health.

I was finally able to resume traveling in November of that year. I went to Spain with the Artists Against Violence Network campaign, and while I was there, the singer Cristina del Valle and I planned a concert to take place in Mexico City's Zócalo Square in January of 2006. The concert would be part of a campaign against femicide and gender violence. It would be election season in Mexico, so part of the plan was to meet with the different presidential candidates in order to get them to commit to working against femicide and gender violence. By November, all of the candidates save one—PRI[5] candidate Roberto Madrazo—had signed on. Despite this show of support, Andrés Manuel López Obrador would end up canceling at the last minute with no explanation. Madrazo would refuse to meet with us, leaving the campaign's representatives to appear before the press accompanied by Felipe Calderón—in his first electoral act—and Patricia Mercado. Both candidates would give impassioned speeches

5. Translator's Note: Partido Revolucionario Institucional, the Institutional Revolutionary Party is one of Mexico's three main political parties. It is a centrist-to-left-leaning party considered by many to be a state party, having held power continuously for seventy-one years, until 2000. Mexico's current president, Enrique Peña Nieto, is a member of the PRI.

in which they expressed their determination to combat gender violence, human trafficking, and the culture of impunity.

But all that was still to come. After planning the concert in Spain, I flew to Sri Lanka at the invitation of Amnesty International to attend the Global Summit of Women Human Rights Defenders. On December 15, I returned to Cancun, eager to put the unfortunate year behind me and with no other desire than to calmly look forward to the holiday break. But Governor Mario Marín was about to make his entrance into my life, and it would upend far more than just that Christmas.

3

KIDNAPPED BY
THE STATE

It was Friday, December 16, and it was raining. The Cancun streets were slick with water, and the air was cool. It was 11:45 in the morning on my first day back at work after returning from my trip to Spain and Sri Lanka. I'd left the diner where I had met some colleagues for breakfast, I'd switched on the music, and I was driving unhurriedly to the CIAM offices. I called to let them know I'd be there in fifteen minutes; my bodyguard would be waiting for me at the corner of the building. Following the threats I had been receiving from Succar Kuri, his accomplices, and other aggressors since 2003, both the National Human Rights Commission (CNDH) and the Chamber of Deputies had requested that the PGR provide me with protection. Vasconcelos from SEIDO had already assigned three federal agents to act as my bodyguards, and they had been working with me since the book launch in Mexico City.

I did not notice anyone following me; I'm in the habit of checking my rearview mirror often. It had been raining since early that morning and the streets were flooded. As my light gray Ford approached the streets surrounding the Supermanzana 63 district of dive bars, brothels, and liquor stores, the rain gave way—as it often does in the Caribbean—to a bright, glittering morning. A rainbow arced across the sky as I pulled up at a stoplight. I sat musing for a moment on how privileged I am to live in the tropics, where the pure, fresh air and the humidity were doing such wonders to soothe the symptoms of my bronchitis. I was just a few days away from completing the course of antibiotics I had been prescribed.

I turned onto 12th Street. When I'd parked my truck and turned off the engine, a small car drove past, and then I got out of my vehicle. Suddenly, a silvery blue car with Puebla State plates stopped in the middle of the street, blocking the way, and three dark-skinned individuals jumped out, one of them wearing a white T-shirt and a shoulder holster that clearly had a gun in it. Another held a pink folder in his hand and was walking very quickly toward me. I looked to my left—behind me on the street was a white Jeep Liberty. I scanned it for plates—this one was from Puebla, too. At both corners, cars where closing the street. At that moment, I was convinced they were contract killers, although I didn't know who might have hired them. Then I glanced down the street toward the intersection—a red car was blocking it, and a man standing outside the CIAM offices was gesturing to another close by. I thought they were about to shoot me, and my heart froze.

The man with the folder shouted as he approached me, "Lydia Cacho, easy now, don't try anything, you're under arrest."

There were two men coming at me head on, and another slipped around the side of my car. Terrified, and hardly realizing what I was doing, I pushed the car alarm button on my key ring and tried to climb back in, but by that time one of the men had already reached me, and he quietly pulled out a gun and hissed, "Don't try anything, and don't call your bodyguard, or we're sure to have some fireworks on our hands."

They know I have bodyguards, I thought.

"On what charges? Who's charging me?" I managed to ask once or twice, trying to maintain my composure.

But the only response I got from them was, "We're taking you to the Puebla jail."

Meanwhile, two of the men were speaking hurriedly, one repeating, "Don't resist, or we're gonna have some fireworks on our hands," and the other threatening me, "Yeah, and journalists sometimes get killed by stray bullets."

Like a slap to the face, the echo of his words knocked the air straight out of me, and I felt instantly nauseated. And they were all almost as nervous as I was. The man with the pink folder kept shoving it in my face, opening it to show me—but all of the pages inside were blank. I didn't have enough time to understand what was going on. The second agent pulled out his badge wallet but wouldn't let me look at it to see his name. It was as though they were putting on a show for someone else's benefit. It was pure madness.

A series of confused questions flashed through my mind: *Puebla? Why Puebla?*, I thought. *Are we defending some woman from Puebla?* If we were, I wouldn't know about it—the CIAM team had been working continually, but I'd been out of the country for the past fifteen days.

My car alarm continued to blare, and I knew that my colleagues were probably watching everything over the closed-circuit security system we'd had installed around the exterior of the building; we'd been prepping for emergencies for years.

I told the police agents several times, "My federal bodyguards have to come with me."

The State Judicial Police agent standing next to me grabbed my forearm, holding his gun in his other hand, and repeated once again, anxiously, that I shouldn't give the order to my bodyguards, because if I did, we would end up in a shoot-out. I found myself telling them in a whisper, "Okay, okay calm down, I am not ordering anything."

From his post at the corner, agent Toledo, one of the three bodyguards on my security detail, witnessed everything that was happening. Later he would tell the Office of the Special Federal Prosecutor for Crimes Against Journalists that when he saw what was going on, he thought the agents had come over from the State Judicial Police to help me with my work: "I called the head of the bodyguard detail and told him, 'I think Ms. Cacho is going to do one of her rescues.'" (He was referring to the fact that when women call the center and their lives are in danger, we go out to their places of residence in order to rescue them and their children. My bodyguards had accompanied me on a few of these rescue operations. We disarm the aggressors and call the police, who generally refuse to set foot in anyone's home for fear of being sued by the aggressors for breaking and entering.) Later the female bodyguard told authorities that Toledo told their boss some men were taking me, and the boss asked, "Are they policemen?" He said they *looked like* policemen. So the boss apparently told them to let them take me.

While this was going on, the police agent with the folder repeated several times that I had better cooperate; I told him that I would, I asked him to please remain calm, and I assured him that I would put up no resistance. Just then, "Cronos," CIAM's head of security, stepped out into the street. They all saw him, and the armed agent standing at my side became extremely agitated and practically screamed at me, "Tell your bodyguard to stay put—tell him not to shoot or there's gonna be fireworks!"

He was now jamming his gun into my left side. I lowered my voice and said as calmly as possible, "Please, he's a colleague of mine, we don't use weapons here, he's not armed, I swear."

"Cronos" approached us slowly, his head lowered and his palms facing front to show that he wasn't carrying any weapons, and he spoke slowly and deliberately, his voice carrying a hint of apprehension I'd never heard from him before.

"Everything is fine, we don't use weapons; I just want to know what's going on."

The police agent holding the pink folder—later I would learn that this man was Comandante Montaño—went through the same ridiculous charade all over again, showing him the blank pages, opening and closing the folder quickly, and said, "She's under arrest for defamation, we have an arrest warrant, we're taking her to the Puebla jail."

I heard the word *defamation*, but it still didn't make any sense.

Our head of security replied, "Very well, gentlemen; allow me to accompany her."

Though my captors made no response, he stuck by my side. I glanced out of the corner of my eye and saw two more men sitting inside the Jeep Liberty behind us. We were ordered to remain calm and told that nothing bad would happen. As we approached the agents' vehicle, Montaño opened the back door and out stumbled a woman, no older than thirty, with dyed blond hair. She held a video camera in her hand and was attempting to hide it under her light-colored clothing. She ducked her head, as though trying to shield her face, and hurried over to the Liberty while taping everything.

We got in the car. Then one of the men began speaking over the radio to some of the others, and we peeled out quickly. When we reached the corner, the man in the passenger seat turned to Montaño and said, "Follow the others!"

The red car that had been stopped at the corner, a Jetta, pulled out now, too, and I was able to pick out the heads of four men inside. I slipped my hand inside my purse, which I was clutching against my stomach, and slowly pulled out my cell phone.

Montaño said, "If you behave, we won't have to handcuff you." His nervousness was due, I suppose, to the thought that my body-guard might try to rescue me from them.

"Cronos" discreetly took out his own cell phone, dialed the office, and said out loud, "We're going to the state attorney general's office."

I started typing out a text message to my husband; I was afraid that if I made an actual call, they would take my phone away from me, but I managed to write, *I'm in custody, they're taking me to Puebla.*

To my relief, I saw that the agent seated next to me hadn't noticed a thing, because he and the others were too busy making sure nobody was following us. So I dialed Jorge, who lives in Mexico City, and, holding the phone in my lap without bringing it to my ear, I said out loud, "You have me in custody and you're taking me to Puebla. What are the charges against me?"

This time, the agent saw my telephone. He was holding his gun in his hand, and he ordered me to hang up—I'd have the right to make phone calls once we reached the state attorney general's office. I handed the phone to my colleague; I thought that if we did as we were told, they might not end up beating us. I looked over at "Cronos," wondering, *What if this is an abduction and they disappear us both?*

A jumble of anger and fear came over me. I thought that "Cronos" had made a mistake, because as head of security for all of CIAM, he ought to have stayed with the team; after all, he'd already gotten a good look at the individuals who were carrying me off. I didn't say anything, because I knew that everything had been recorded—the center's security team has a hard drive to store the twenty-four-hour-a-day footage from the cameras surrounding the building. And sure enough, the recordings from that day, which we later submitted to the authorities, confirmed my description of the arrest.

"Cronos" and I rode along in silence while the State Judicial Police agents spoke among themselves and made phone calls, the man in the passenger seat occasionally giving instructions. Behind us was the white Liberty, and when we had nearly reached the state attorney general's office, a green Suburban caught up with us as well. We were driving at top speed. As we approached the building where the Office of the Attorney General for the state of Quintana Roo is housed—not fifteen minutes after I had first gotten into the car—I saw that the agents had spoken the truth and we really were going to the Attorney General's local Cancun offices, so I lowered my guard. It was not until that moment that I discovered I had practically stopped breathing altogether; the tension had petrified my lungs, I was inhaling barely enough to keep from passing out, and I felt at once lightheaded and jittery. I took in a large gulp of air and was instantly seized with a loud fit of coughing that interrupted the agents as they exchanged instructions. I turned urgently to "Cronos" and said, "Don't let them take me out of here until you see my lawyer."

The last thing I had a chance to hear him say was his quintessential, "Yes, Ms. Cacho, don't you worry."

We sped into the building. I never thought the sight of the main entrance to the Cancun state attorney general's building could produce such a wonderful feeling of relief in me. The light green, semicircular walls suddenly made me feel safe. *They're not hit men! This is legal, and I'm going to come out of it*, I thought.

Meanwhile, CIAM's lawyer and one of my administrative colleagues had left the center as soon as they saw on the cameras that we had driven away. They'd received that first call from "Cronos" and were heading over to the state attorney general's offices. Araceli Andrade, the center's head lawyer, began making calls, intending to secure an injunction. Almost immediately, the cell phone of our other colleague, who was driving, rang—it was our social work coordinator from back at the center.

"Be careful, you're being followed," she warned them. The feed from the security cameras had shown that just seconds after the two women ran out to their car and drove off, a Suburban that was parked near the individual I had seen standing outside the office went after them.

We were hustled into the state attorney general's building; then the men turned to "Cronos" and said, "Here we are, now we're going to take her to see her lawyers."

The two of us exchanged glances one last time. No words were spoken, but it seemed to me that my anguish was mirrored in his face.

They rushed me down toward the holding area. A couple of people who were waiting at the entrance to the building recognized me, but I wasn't able to see their faces, and then the agents shoved me toward the hallway, pulling me and pushing me.

"That's Lydia Cacho, the woman from TV . . ." I heard a woman say as she held a baby in her arms.

One of the agents alerted the others: "They've seen her . . . quick, get the papers, you son of a bitch."

They closed ranks around me so that no one else could see me. The green walls of the state attorney general's building, the dark hallway, and the table that stood at the entrance to the holding area were all empty. Like a child torn from her mother's arms, I craned around to look behind me, hoping to see someone who might know where these agents were leading me, their hands gripping, their fingers digging into me like claws.

We went into one of the holding cells, and Comandante Montaño ordered me to take a seat. The whole thing was almost schizophrenic—as a number of local police agents streamed into the small room, which was furnished with chairs and a single old desk, Montaño changed his tone of voice; he was behaving so kindly now that it made me even more nervous.

"Please, I have the right to speak with my lawyer . . . I'm sick, I have bronchitis, I have the right to see a doctor," I repeated several times, obviously distressed but doing my best to adopt an attitude of equanimity, or so I hoped.

"Agent Montaño," a man spoke into the Comandante's ear. Two more agents walked into the room, and they appeared to recognize me; they were from Cancun.

Montaño held my gaze and said, "Yes, yes . . . settle down"—his tone became almost paternalistic—"we're going to let you see your lawyer, and you can bring your medicine and everything. Just remain calm so we don't have to handcuff you and we don't set off any fireworks. You wouldn't want to get shot by a bullet, now, would you? I'm told you're a real feisty one." He and the other men laughed and then turned their attention to the paperwork before them.

Seated in a black, vinyl chair in a room surrounded by a mix of Puebla and local Cancun police agents, I attempted to gather my thoughts. A lot of people were speaking at once, and documents were changing hands constantly and quickly. Suddenly, a local police agent who recognized me approached my chair. He was a young man, he caught my eye, and without saying a word, he spilled some papers onto the floor next to where I was sitting.

As he slowly gathered them back up, he leaned in toward me and whispered, "Ma'am, don't let them take you in the car . . . they're going to off you . . . the attorney general hasn't signed off on this, ask them to let you see him."

His words hit me like a sharp sword thrust deep into my soul, destroying the little sense of calm I had felt.

Just then, four more State Judicial Police agents stepped into the room. The atmosphere was stuffy; when I tried to breathe, I was met by a thick odor of tobacco mixed with sweat. The young man who had come over to warn me had now scurried away. I tried to recapitulate—*Would they really dare kill me?* I felt a shiver run through me, and I scanned the eyes of the other policemen, searching for some reassuring glance, someone to get me out of there. Suddenly, a tall, heavyset man I had never seen before pushed through the conflux of agents and told me quickly that he was a friend of Benjamín de la Peña, a lawyer and friend of mine from Cancun.

"Do you need anything?" he asked.

I was dizzy, I didn't know how to respond, and before I could, I heard a woman's voice loudly demanding to be let in. Seconds later, I saw the small figure of Ana Patricia Morales, a member of CIAM's board of trustees and the vice president of the Quintana Roo Hotel Association, elbowing her way over to me. I stood up and instantly heard Montaño's voice ordering me, "Sit down!"

I didn't comply immediately; I embraced Ana Patricia for a few brief moments and whispered to her, "Don't let them take me— they're going to kill me."

"Sit down!" the Comandante barked angrily. This time, I obeyed. I looked over at Montaño, who was holding up a pair of handcuffs and gesturing with them from where he stood behind Ana Patricia. With her iron determination and self-confidence, she told me not to worry, that defamation was a minor crime that did not warrant imprisonment.

"I'm going to speak with the attorney general and see what all this fuss is about." As she left the room, I could hear her voice trail off as she told the agents to hold tight since I had the right to request that my lawyer review the petition for my arrest.

"Yes, yes, of course," Montaño replied, with that syrupy tone of his I would come to know so well.

"Moreover, Ms. Cacho is ill, she was just released from the hospital, we have the hospital records to prove it; if you take her anywhere, she mustn't travel by highway, because her health is delicate," I heard the voice of my friend insist, now speaking from the hallway outside the holding cell.

Weeks later, Ana Patricia would tell me that as soon as she left the room, she telephoned my friend Lía to ask her to get a copy of my hospital record. Lía called my doctor, who immediately sent over a copy of my records to show that I had indeed been hospitalized two months earlier for acute bronchial pneumonia. The records attested to a ten-day period spent in the hospital, and the insurance bill was included in the file. But unfortunately it was too late.

When Ana Patricia left, Montaño and two other agents laughed mockingly. One of them said, right to my face, "Nosy fucking bitches, now you're scared, aren't you?"

One of the local agents grabbed my arm with no warning, lifted me from the chair, and he and three additional men led me rapidly out of the room.

"Where are we going?" I asked.

They were restraining me as we walked, and the thinnest of them responded in a flat, callous tone, "Shut your mouth."

They jostled me along quickly until we reached the consulting room of the state attorney general's in-house doctor, and they sat me down in front of her. One of the men stood behind me, while the other three waited outside the glass door. The young doctor was surprised to see me. She gave me a quick examination, and while I was in the middle of answering some of her questions, I was seized by another fit of heavy coughing. In her report the doctor wrote that I showed signs of infectious bronchitis. She handed the document over to the Cancun agent and told me that I should take my medicine and be careful not to catch cold.

Montaño looked me in the eye, and in that fraction of a second I understood then that my removal from the safety of these offices was inevitable. As he and the other agents escorted me back down the hall, I spotted my coworkers, CIAM's lawyer, and my bodyguard standing some eight yards away, and without thinking, I shouted with all my might to Óscar Cienfuegos, the head of my federally mandated security detail, "You guys follow me, call Vasconcelos at SEIDO, they're going to kill me!"

"Okay, Okay!" he shouted back. That was the last time I saw his face.

I was rushed back to the office in the holding area. A local agent picked up my purse, which someone had taken from me and placed on the table. "Give this to one of your people, because if they"—meaning the Puebla agents—"take it, who knows what might happen to your belongings," he said.

I nodded. He took my purse and cell phone and handed them to someone standing outside. I heard an agent tell them not to worry, that they were going to wait for my medical report to arrive. Meanwhile, Ana Patricia was insisting that she be allowed to speak with state attorney general Bello Melchor Rodríguez. She wanted to make sure that all the paperwork was in order, that a cooperation accord was in fact in place between the Puebla and Quintana Roo authorities. Ms. Morales is a member of the Security Consulting Council for the Office of the State Attorney General, and months later she told me that that day was the first time the state attorney general had ever refused to meet with her. We later learned that he was speaking with the governor, who was part of the plot for my illegal arrest.

While all this was going on, a call came into the line at the holding area. One of the men picked up the phone and said, "It's the boss."

Montaño walked over to me and bent down so that his face was level with mine. I couldn't tell if his voice was kind or sarcastic, because I was paralyzed with fear as I listened to him say, "Behave now, and we won't have to cuff you. We're good people, don't make us angry, we're just doing our job."

I stared back at him and nodded, and then, speaking just as quietly as he, I replied, "Okay."

Moments later, two agents stepped up to me, one on each side; they yanked me up by the arms, and I heard one of them say, "Easy now, lady . . . we're going to take you to see your lawyer and get your medicine."

They exchanged a brief look and led me out of the room. Then one of the men behind me grabbed hold of my hands, positioning my two fists at my back, while the other two agents immobilized my forearms. Quickly, an agent positioned himself in front of me, and they practically ran me out of the building's back door. A second later, I felt a sharp yank at the back of my head. Someone was pulling my hair with rage; I buckled in pain and allowed myself to be pulled along. A few moments later, the man dragging me by the hair hurled me into the back of a car. I fell with my hands behind me. The whole thing was extremely fast and unexpected. I was slow to react; I slumped on the seat, half fallen onto the floor. I heard the two front doors slam shut.

"Get down, get down!" one of them shouted at me.

In a haze, I obeyed.

Additional Cancun agents were already waiting for us, and they immediately activated a series of highly coordinated maneuvers. We were at the far end of the building's parking lot, and I lifted my head slightly to look out the window. Ahead of us was the red Jetta, leading the way.

Why so many police officers? I thought to myself.

I peeked behind us, hoping to see my bodyguard following, but the only vehicle there was the white Liberty (which we would later prove belonged to Kamel Nacif). They'd floored it, and we were already turning onto Nichipté Avenue, heading for the highway. It was at that moment that I realized I'd been tricked. A feeling of outrage swelled up inside me. I sat up and began rattling off at the top of my voice, "This is illegal! This is kidnapping! You didn't let me see my lawyer! I need my medicine! I never saw any arrest warrant!"

I could feel my whole head growing flushed. But the agents said nothing. Montaño produced a slip of paper and dialed the number written on it.

"Ready, sir." He gave a quick numeric code. And then, "Everything is in order."

I closed my eyes and thought, *My God, they're going to kill me, they're going to disappear me . . .*

I began shouting desperately, "You're violating my rights, I'm sick, I need my medicine. This is illegal, my lawyer is supposed to know that you're taking me. I want to see the petition, I want to see the arrest warrant. Do you hear me?"

Montaño was speaking quietly over the phone, and the man driving—whose name I would later learn is Jesús Pérez—answered back furiously, "You don't have rights—you don't have shit! Now shut up or we're gonna cuff you!"

Moments later, he pulled up to a stoplight, and immediately he whirled around, pressed the barrel of his pistol into the center of my forehead, and shouted, "Just shut up, bitch, you're with us now!"

I fell silent.

Montaño hung up and, without looking at me, said in that tone I would come to know so well over the next twenty hours, "Just settle down there, or we're going to handcuff you . . . We're going to take you to the Puebla jail, you can ask for your rights there. And see if they'll give them to you."

He smiled calmly, and we started driving again.

HIGHWAY OF HORROR

They stopped at a gas station on a corner, and the white Liberty pulled up on our right. I saw that the driver was a thin man with a mustache and the person in the passenger seat was an older man with gray hair who had just rolled down his window to give the others instructions. He was carrying a gun in a shoulder holster (they were all visibly armed), and sitting behind them was the blond woman I saw when I was first picked up outside of CIAM. The red Jetta was stopped on their right. I started counting—there were two agents in the front seat, three in the car behind us, five, six . . . a total of ten. I looked behind me and saw a green, Suburban-type vehicle fitted with tinted windows, but I couldn't see anything inside except the driver's silhouette. The driver of the red Jetta told the others that they were going to start directly for the highway to Mérida and instructed everyone to follow him. Montaño jumped to the backseat, pulled my hand behind me, and cuffed my hands into a twisted position so that every time I moved, my elbows seemed to pinch. They drove off quickly. We eventually recovered the highway security videos with all the cars and men to be identified properly.

We sped toward the highway, flanked on three sides. The other vehicles accompanied us all the way to the onramp for the toll road to Mérida. As we approached the tollbooth, the red Jetta honked good-bye to the Puebla agents in the car with me. Montaño rolled down the window to wave a friendly thanks, then he quickly shut it again, and the driver laughed.

The pink folder lay before me, between the two front seats. I asked the agent driving to allow me to see what I was been accused of. Although I was speaking in a submissive tone now, his response came in the form of an aggressive shout.

"Shut up! Don't get all hysterical now!" As he looked through the review mirror and said this to me, he gestured to the gun lying next to him. Once again, I fell silent.

It suddenly dawned on me that I was going to be spending the next 1,118 miles or more alone in a car with two armed police agents, and three more in the vehicle behind us. Never in my life had I felt more alone, more vulnerable, more aware of the fact that I am a woman. On many occasions, I'd told women who found themselves in situations of domestic abuse that they needed to come up with a safety strategy; now it was my turn. I would make a mental list of things I shouldn't say in order to avoid upsetting my captors, and I would try to make sure someone saw me wherever we went. I would have to take note of which numbered highway markers we were near when we stopped (if we did make any stops), and I would remain calm.

A question suddenly came to me: *Why would the Quintana Roo attorney general let me go if he knew there had been death threats made against me? If he had an order by the InterAmerican Court to protect me against the mafia? And hadn't Ana Patricia said that the crime they were taking me in for didn't warrant imprisonment?* I'd studied some twenty cases where the killers were State Judicial Police officers or federal agents. *What was to say that these individuals weren't hit men working for the Judicial Police? I can't know,* I thought. I could only wish that

I make it to Puebla alive. That my team would call the right people, that these men would realize there would be a heavy price to pay if they killed me. The only thing I could do now was wait, and visualize myself arriving in Puebla in one piece.

The agents went back to talking amongst themselves. Montaño was now behaving very courteously, and he explained that his boss chose to send him rather than anyone else because he had a reputation for being kind. The man driving—Pérez—laughed at this, complaining that because of me, they hadn't even gotten a chance to go down to the beach while they were in Cancun. He explained that they'd arrived on Thursday, the day before, and that because of me they were going to miss their own attorney general's Christmas party, too. They were talking to each other about how they hadn't even had time to eat breakfast because they'd been so busy coordinating with the Cancun agents. Pérez said that "the boss, the *patrón*"[6] (I didn't know who they're referring to) was making life difficult for them.

"Who's the *patrón*?" I ventured to ask.

Without so much as glancing back at me, Montaño replied, "Why do you have to go poking around in the bosses' lives? What do you want to go writing about their business for . . . ? You're pretty, but you really are a nosy little thing."

There was silence for a while. We passed another tollbooth, and I tried to get the toll taker to look at me without Pérez noticing. I made a gesture of anguish, but the toll taker paid me no attention. Pérez handed over some money, but he told him not to worry about it—it was a "courtesy." The two agents thanked him and commented on how nicely everyone had been treating them in Cancun.

I took a chance and asked who the three people in the white Liberty were, and why they'd sent so many agents to arrest me, as though I were a member of the mafia.

---

6   Translator's Note: As understood here, patrón is a mixture of boss and protector.

"Oh, you know," Montaño replied, "we thought there might be some fireworks with your federal guards." And then, referring to the individuals in the Liberty, "They're here to protect us, ma'am, not you."

Pérez started talking about sexual assault arrestees and how they always give the two of them a lot of trouble and then go on to get raped in prison. They were asking me questions as though they didn't know who I was. Suddenly, Montaño remarked that he went online to find out who I was, and he started chatting me up about my TV show. I found myself answering in a friendly tone, trying to connect with them, to make them understand that a lot of people knew who I was and would be looking for me. From time to time, they stopped listening to me and started laughing, joking among themselves about times when different prisoners had tried to escape from their custody. They kept asking if I liked the sea, if we should maybe swing by the coast, and if I enjoyed swimming. Montaño said that when he was a boy, his father would take him to Veracruz to see the ocean. He asked me if many people drown in the sea. I told them I was a good swimmer. They laughed at this and replied that it was a good thing, too, because, in the words of Pérez, "we might just toss you into the ocean in a little bit."

I thought back to my past, to my sailing trips around the Caribbean, searching within my memory for an inner strength that nevertheless eluded me. The two men started talking about my book, and suddenly I heard, in a casual, offhand voice, the name *Kamel Nacif*.

"Do you want to know why I wrote that book?" I asked them, shifting forward on the seat.

Montaño whipped around and barked, "Get back!" A few seconds went by, and then he asked, "Why'd you mess with Kamel?"

A shiver ran down my spine—the nonchalant way the two discussed Succar Kuri's protector hinted to me that he might be "the boss" they had telephoned. I started explaining to them what my book was about. I asked them if they have any children. Montaño replied that he had two, and Pérez said that he did, as well. Without thinking, my mouth dry, I asked them to imagine that while they were driving along in the car with me, some man had just taken their small daughter or son and was using them to make pornographic films while raping them. Pérez cut me off and gave a detailed, obscenity-filled description of exactly how he would murder anyone who ever tried to do such a thing. He'd slice off his genitals and skin him alive before finally killing him. Montaño said he would do the same, but that no one in Puebla dared confront the pedophiles; in those parts, they were in charge. I tried to say something, but I fell to coughing again. Operating under the false assumption that they wouldn't do anything to mistreat me, I reminded them that I really was sick. Pérez asked me to come closer, to lean forward. I obeyed.

"I've got your medicine right here . . . a little cough syrup, you want some?" he asked, groping his genitals and laughing.

I leaned back in my seat again, my hands to either side of my body to rest my arms. Montaño made a comment every so often to the effect that I had to do what they said.

I asked them why they had wanted to become cops in the first place; I tried to tell them about Succar Kuri and his friends and their contemptible acts. They asked me questions, and then they answered mine. Montaño told me he'd been working as a State Judicial Police agent for twenty years and that his father was an agent, too, back in the glory days of "El Negro" Durazo[7]. I realized they were lying to me. They went into explanations from time to time about how they had been trying to locate me for two months without knowing where to find me. But then they contradicted themselves, remarking suddenly that I'd been out of the country for some time and asking whether I was worried that someone might break into my home when I was away, saying that it was such a nice little apartment, after all.

---

7.   Translator's Note: Arturo "El Negro" Durazo, famously corrupt Mexico City chief of police serving from 1976 to 1982 and protector of the drug cartels.

Montaño's cell phone rang. He answered and quickly hung up again. He told his colleague that the boss was worried, that he asked if there was anyone else with us—witnesses, that is, the comandante clarified. They made a couple of phone calls and I slowly realized they were asking the people in the Liberty if anyone was following us. I was hoping that my bodyguard was tailing us. The Liberty called back; the comandante spoke so that Pérez could hear and confirmed that no, nobody was following us.

"They've left you all alone," Montaño said, and then the two of them took turns telling me how I'd better behave and how I was going to have to perform oral sex on them if I wanted them to give me anything to eat. I sat still and said nothing. The phone rang again. Montaño's voice repeated, "Yes, sir; yes, boss; yes."

All of the sudden they stopped. Montaño moved quickly to the back of the car and sat next to me. He uncuffed me and ordered me to leave my hands behind my back. I shyly smiled. He pulled his gun out, ordered me to open my mouth and proceeded to put the gun barrel inside my mouth. I immediately felt like coughing. I could smell his breath next to my face. "Come on, cough, lady," he said, daring me. I could only feel the bitter metal taste in my mouth. He took the gun barrel out of my mouth and began sliding it downward, using it to open my blouse and maul my breast as he pushed the gun against me in a slow deliberate manner that seemed to last an eternity. He opened his pants, pulled my hair, and pushed me toward him. I could feel the gun barrel on top of my head. For a second there I wished he just shot me dead, but he did not. It took many years of therapy for me to get that image out of my nightmares.

Ten years later, when Montaño was arrested for torture and I had to confront him in court over the course of five hours, I could still smell his breath from a distance. When the judge asked me to explain the sexual torture I had endured on that infamous road trip, I broke down in tears, but Montaño laughed—he had the same smile that had haunted me for a decade.

A few hours went by, and the two agents were explaining what a big mess I'd gotten myself into by writing that book of mine. They alternated comments about how powerful and important Kamel Nacif was with others about how stupid it was of me to think I could get away with defaming him, and still others about how pretty I was. They said they thought the boss was giving them a nice little reward when they were back in Puebla and they were shown a photograph of me wearing a bikini. I felt the stomach acid rising up into my throat; I realized that the last thing I'd eaten was a bowl of fruit at eight in the morning. But I wasn't hungry—I felt queasy. Every now and then I would carefully bring my arms around to the front of me to get rid of the numbness that kept taking over. I tried to keep my mind occupied by observing the agents, listening to their tone of voice. It bordered on the schizophrenic—one minute they might be speaking to me in a friendly, respectful tone, and the next they might just as easily be insulting me or telling me how I was their little reward and we were going to have a lot of fun together on this trip.

In a moment of silence, I went out on a limb and asked Montaño to let me make a telephone call. To my surprise, he said, "Of course, ma'am, we just have to stop somewhere, because I don't have any more minutes left on my phone card." They were using what we call burners, otherwise known as disposable phones, which make it impossible to track calls.

I let out a long, slow breath. Around twenty minutes later, the vehicle pulled in at a rest stop. I asked for permission to get out and use the restroom. Montaño told me to go ahead, but before I could make a move, the two told me that I'd better not try to run away because one time a prisoner they had picked up in Veracruz tried that and they had been forced to shoot a couple of stray bullets at him. They asked each other if they ever did figure out which one of them had ended up killing the prisoner who tried to run when they let him out to go to the toilet. They went over all the details of how the man died and how they had to carry him back into the car, his pants covered in urine, all because he'd tried to pull a fast one on them. And so I stayed in the car, silent. The same scene was repeated with ever so slight changes of script four more times over the following twenty hours, every single time I asked to use a restroom. It was not until many hours later, when we stopped to eat, that they finally consented to my request.

They got back in the car, laden with snacks and sodas. Between jokes, they offered me something to eat, only to go on to explain that if I had any money on me, they'd be happy to go in and buy me the bottle of water I kept asking for. Right then, Montaño's cell phone rang, and when the comandante answered, he spoke almost entirely in monosyllables.

"No, sir . . . we're alone." He hung up and asked me very kindly, "All right, ma'am, what's your family's telephone number?"

Flustered, I tried to recall a number or two, but I was drawing a blank—this damn memory of mine! I was used to having my entire contacts list stored on my cell phone, and so I'd lost the habit of memorizing these things. I forced myself to make a mental effort, and I gave him a number. He dialed it and listened to make sure it was ringing, then he looked at me and said, "Hands behind your back."

I leaned forward with my hands behind me. He held the cell phone to my ear, and when I heard a voice answer, he snatched it away and listened himself. Then he hung up and said simply, "No answer."

Ten minutes went by, and we repeated the same scene all over again. For some reason I was unable to comprehend; every time, overcome with anxiety, I actually believed he was going to let me talk to someone. But he didn't, and after a while the two men chuckled.

"Well, ma'am, now you've had your call. More than one, even," Montaño said.

Then he smiled and settled back into his seat to eat his snacks and sip his drink. He did this ten more times during the trip. Undaunted by his behavior, I continued to give him the real numbers for CIAM. Luckily, this allowed the office's caller ID system to identify Montaño's incoming calls as being from a Puebla phone, and it also allowed those at the office to call the number back. Montaño answered those calls but immediately hung up. Months later, Montaño submitted the cell phone records of these calls in an attempt to substantiate his claim that I had been allowed to make as many phone calls as I wished. But the fact that each call lasted no more than a few seconds ultimately gave him away.

Meanwhile, the entire CIAM Cancun board of directors had gathered back at the office. Because the work we do at CIAM is dangerous and we have received death threats on several occasions, we have an emergency protocol in place. Edith Rosales, our social work coordinator, was also in charge of coordinating our emergency phone tree. José Antonio Torres, my TV producer who sits on the board, came down to offer extra assistance to the coordinators, who, their lists of phone numbers in hand, were making call after call, relaying the same message each time: "Lydia Cacho was kidnapped by police agents, we haven't seen any official documentation, and we fear for her life. Call the Puebla authorities to make sure she isn't murdered." Amnesty International, Human Rights Watch, Reporters Without Borders, and the World Organization Against Torture all sent out emergency bulletins. The CIAM team called a general meeting and made a decision: Given the level of danger, everyone goes on red alert. They've understood the situation perfectly—if what's happening to me is related to the Succar case, then organized crime networks are involved. Meditation and prayer sessions were also held. Meanwhile, in Mexico City, my magazine editor and friend Alejandro Paez worked hand-in-hand with Jorge, my husband, issuing reports on what they knew.

When I eventually returned to work months later they would tell me what the experience had been like for them. To keep their spirits up during the uncertain hours of my detention, they spoke about my character and my ability to face things head on.

"Don't worry," one of them said. "Knowing Lydia, by the time they get to Puebla, she'll have turned them all on to feminism."

They never shed tears in front of each other, but they did go to their individual cubicles from time to time to pray, light candles, and cry. The telephones were ringing off the hook. José Antonio coordinated, while the CIAM team decided to keep the offices open in order to continue assisting other victims; life went on. Araceli Andrade, the head of our legal team, was able to shed some light on the situation. She herself is from Puebla, so Nacif's name was not unknown to her. When she learned at the state attorney general's offices that the defamation charges had been brought against me by the so-called "Denim King"[8], she knew there was a very good chance I would be disappeared or murdered. Claudia, head of our psychology team, had also heard stories about the time Nacif was arrested in Vegas and his links with Nevada mafias. It was clear that as they sat down to analyze the situation, they weren't blowing anything out of proportion by fearing the worst.

Up north, in Mexico City, Jorge was sitting in his office. He had gotten in touch with the CIAM team mere minutes after my arrest. He had seen the quick and muddled message I sent him when I was arrested. The coordinator at CIAM told him, "They took her away in an armed convoy, there were multiple cars; they haven't let us see an arrest warrant; it looks like they're in with Kamel Nacif, the man who's protecting Succar, the pedophile."

Jorge drew on his experience as founder of the newspaper *Siglo 21* and former assistant director of *El Universal*. He and our friend Alejandro Páez, a fellow journalist as well as an editor at the magazine *Día Siete*, wrote to the Committee for the Protection of Journalists (CPJ) in New York and sent urgent cables to all the national newscasts and media outlets. As far as they understood, this was a case of illegal arrest—that is, despite the fact that the individuals who

---

8. Translator's Note: Kamel Nacif, known as "the Denim King" because he sits at the head of an enormous textile empire he has been building up since he was a young man.

took me were State Judicial Police agents and that they claimed to be acting on an arrest warrant, nobody had been allowed access to the detainee (me) or to any official documents, and the manner in which they drove off with me from the state attorney general's building was just as suspect. The news spread like wildfire. A network of journalists from Puebla and all over Mexico began covering my case and gathering vital information about my captors and the corrupt officials who made my kidnapping possible. All the international human rights advocates I had met over the years began spreading the news like fire on the prairie. My friend in the UNIFEM office in New York issued alerts and asked diplomats to call the governor of Puebla (not knowing he was a part of the plot to silence me). He received the calls calmly and listened to many politicians telling him that it was imperative that I turn up in Puebla alive and safe.

No one other than the agents and the other individuals involved could have imagined, as we later learned, that behind the entire episode of my capture were the iron fists of Governor Mario Marín, attorney general Blanca Laura Villeda, and Puebla Superior Court chief justice Guillermo Pacheco Pulido. All they believed at that point was that Nacif had personally hired a number of corrupt police agents to transport me somewhere. Their only hope was that I would reach Puebla alive. And the strategy at this point was clear: Jorge would have to contact people who were familiar with my work both as a journalist and as the director of CIAM Cancun and ask them to telephone the governor and urge him to take measures to ensure that the police agents would not murder me—in other words, to draw his attention to this act of influence peddling on the part of Kamel Nacif. They could have never even imagined that the criminal collusion surrounding the events that were still unfolding had in fact been orchestrated by the governor himself, and that three other governors were involved in the plot to have me killed.

Journalist Carlos Loret de Mola and Florencio Salazar, the secretary of agriculture at the time, tried to locate the governor in order to apprise him of the situation. But it was hours before they were able to get in touch with him, because "he was attending a pre-holiday business lunch in the countryside."

Eventually, each one of them separately would hear Marín tell them that he "was unaware of the situation, but would see to it that everything be carried out in a legal fashion." Marín had no idea that while he spoke—while he was telling one bald-faced lie after another to the people telephoning him and simultaneously holding conversations with Kamel Nacif regarding his knowledge of and involvement in my abduction—someone was recording his voice and the words that would ultimately make him go down in history as "the Precious Guv'."

Additional calls to the governor throughout the afternoon and evening yielded identical results. Josefina Vázquez Mota, who was heading the Secretariat for Social Development and who had visited our shelter facilities and was familiar with the Succar case, was also met with the same response. Even the valiant PRI senator Lucero Saldaña, whom I'd met when she was the president of the national Senate Commission for Gender Equality, became involved. None of them suspected the governor.

And then there was the Spanish ambassador at the time, Cristina Barrios, who had been a patron at the inauguration of the CIAM shelter and just a few days prior to my arrest had attended a meeting with Marín in which they had signed an agreement with the Spanish Agency for International Development Cooperation (AECID) to address the problems of indigenous groups living in Puebla's sierra region. It was Friday night when the ambassador telephoned Marín and asked him to ensure that the arrest be carried out in accordance with the law and that my rights be respected. According to what the ambassador would later tell me, the governor denied all knowledge of my case and promised to "find out what it was all about."

As night fell, Jorge received a call from General Jorge Serrano Gutiérrez, head of the antiterrorist unit at SEIDO and a trusted advisor to SEIDO assistant attorney general Santiago Vasconcelos. Serrano—who was the same man who had logged my reports of the death threats made against me and, upon seeing the evidence, assigned me a security detail—told him that he had spoken to the Puebla attorney general to let her know that her government was now responsible for my life and my safety, seeing as how the Puebla Judicial Police agents had "given the slip" to the AFI agents who had originally taken custody of me. General Serrano was an old-school military man who knew my grandfather, also a general. He had read my articles and when we met several years later, he told me the exact the same thing a head of US immigration agency told me in California: Without the work of good journalists, they would never be able to find so many bad guys. Good journalism is useful to society, but it's also tremendously useful to law-abiding police officers and investigators.

Meanwhile, out on the highway, I continued to sit, completely unaware of all the maneuvering going on around me. Evening was creeping up around us, and Montaño's cell phone was ringing incessantly, but he never spoke more than a few quick syllables in response. Once or twice, I demanded that he let me make a phone call, and he invariably replied sure, just as soon as he got a new card.

It was almost seven at night when we stopped to eat at a small roadside diner outside of Mérida. I checked the name written up on the wall: DON PEPE. We were next to a gas station. We got out, and the agents ordered me to go in quietly and not speak to anyone. I walked as quickly as my numb legs and the pain in my bladder allowed me, and I headed straight for the restroom.

The two men in the Liberty caught up with us, but I didn't see the woman. Walking very close to me, for the first time, was the tall, gray-haired man who had been riding in the Liberty. I opened the door to the small restroom, and he pressed up against my back, rubbing his stomach across my buttocks. I tried to get away, but he grabbed me by the neck and began whispering quietly into my ear, pressing himself against me.

"So pretty, but such a little bitch. Why'd you have to mess with the boss? You want some of this?" he asked, pressing harder against my buttocks to make sure I could feel his arousal. He put his hand on my left breast and pulled me still tighter against him. I felt his gun digging into my shoulder blade; it hurt, and I told him so.

"You like my gun, journalist?" he asked, his mouth on my cheek. I felt his acid breath in my nose; the urge to vomit overwhelmed me.

"Please, let me go in," I said, glaring at him with a mixture of anger and fear.

"What'll you give me?" he asked, pushing his body against me even harder.

Tears filled my eyes, and before I realized what I was saying, I replied, "I'd rather die." Then I raised my voice so that it would be heard in the main dining room: "Are you going to let me go to the bathroom?"

He shoved me ahead of him into the bathroom, where I stepped into a rickety, white, acrylic stall and closed the flimsy latch; I could see his silhouette on the other side of the door and hear his voice telling me to be quick about it. When I came out, I made quickly for the sink, and just then the blond woman walked into the bathroom, but the man stepped between us and hissed in my ear, "Hop to it, journalist."

A moment later, we were all seated together. They ordered me to sit at the head of the table, with Montaño and Pérez to either side of me, while the thin, mustachioed driver of the Liberty and the gray-haired man who had just accosted me took seats at the other end. The blond woman came out of the bathroom suddenly, but she didn't look at me; she was told to sit at the far end of the table. I tried to speak to her, but the man with the gray hair told her to shut up and wouldn't allow me to talk. He ordered three dishes just for himself and spent the entire meal interrupting, complaining, and chastising. All the men were visibly armed (they were wearing their guns in shoulder holsters), and when they began eating, they laid their weapons in plain view on the beer-stained metal tabletop. The truckers coming into the diner all stared at the agents for a moment, but not a single person approached our table. Months later the waitress would recount the story to the federal attorney; they all thought the gunmen were drug dealers because who other than those thugs would dare display their weapons so blatantly.

Feeling as limp as a rag doll, I implored Montaño to get me my medicine, but he told me he has no money and they'd buy it later. The gray-haired man lectured them as though I weren't sitting right there with them and listening to every word they said.

"If she keeps screwing around, cuff her again. She'll get her medicine once we get to Puebla," he concluded with a guffaw. They all laughed.

The agents didn't know which road to take, and they started arguing, because on the way to Cancun they had taken some wrong turn and ended up on a really crappy freeway. Then out of the blue, the man with the gray hair said, "We have to make a stop in Champoton—they've got these fantastic shrimp cocktails there, plus the water's perfect for swimming, and it'll be dark by then."

They exchanged glances and then fell silent. I pushed my plate away; I was too nauseated to eat, and I was feeling feverish. Silently, for the first time in forty years, I said one of the Catholic prayers I had learned in my childhood.

We left the restaurant, and they shepherded me into the car and then stayed standing outside talking to one another. They filled up the gas tank. Once we were underway and back on the highway again, they asked me what I was doing in the bathroom with the "boss" (I understood they were referring to the man with the gray hair). Nothing, I told them, but they burst out with a harangue of sexual insinuations. It was Montaño's turn to drive now, and Pérez was smoking nonstop. My cough was getting worse; I didn't know how long I was going to be able to hold out before the spasms started to make me wretch.

They started talking, wondering whether they'd get a chance to see the ocean in Champoton, harping on about how pretty the ocean looks at night. Montaño glanced at me in the rearview mirror and asked quietly, "Do you know how to swim in the ocean at night? Of course, it's sink or swim, you know."

That cruel tone of his was back; the comandante's abrupt mood shifts were unsettling to me. I remained silent and tried to calculate how many hours there were to go before we reached Puebla.

If they throw me into the sea, how many hours could I keep swimming? I thought to myself.

Trembling not only with fever but from fear, I hugged my arms around my body and allowed myself to become immersed in memories, trying to steal a few moments of solace. I stared out the window. Gazing at the jungle beyond the highway, without turning my head to look at the two agents, I muttered, "I'm a sailboat captain, I can sail, and I can swim."

I realized I'd just spoken these words out loud, and the two men laughed at me. So I tried to keep my mind alert with thoughts of pleasant things—I thought about my family, about my mother. *What would she do in this situation?* I asked myself. I thought about my brothers and sisters, about my father. I wondered if they knew the police had taken me. *I'll be fine, I'll be fine . . .* I knew Jorge and my team were doing everything in their power to stop me from being killed. I directed my thoughts to the window, as though my message might somehow reach someone through the glass.

The silence was broken when Montaño's cell phone rang, but I decided to ignore it and not listen. A moment later, he said, "All right, journalist, you can make a call."

I gave him a number, and Jorge picked up. My eyes held Montaño's gaze; I kept thinking he was going to take the phone away from me. I spoke hesitatingly. I told Jorge that we'd passed Mérida and were now in Campeche. He asked me if I was okay.

I didn't want to waste any time. "Yes," I replied.

Montaño immediately pointed his gun at my face, the barrel touching my nose, and I was suddenly struggling to focus even on this brief conversation. Jorge told me that newscasters had been informed about my kidnapping, that the story was already on the radio, that I shouldn't worry, that they'd told people everything and now the governor of Puebla knew what was going on. "Everyone knows it's because of your book, baby," he said, as if it was a good thing. Then he stopped suddenly and interjected, "But you're being escorted by women, so you're okay, right?"

"Women? No, they're men!"

In an instant, Montaño grabbed the phone away from me and hung up. Then he said, almost sweetly, that he hoped I trusted him now, that he hoped I saw how nice he was. I did, I said. He asked me if I was going to be like all the other prisoners and go running and tattle to the human rights agencies.

"No," I assured him, "I won't." My voice was shaking.

He told me that's good, because now that they knew where I lived, all alone in that apartment, they knew right where they could slip in easily, and it just so happened that one security grille was really easy to open. I was unable to speak. The sense of calm that had been restored to me for a few, brief seconds when I heard Jorge's loving voice vanished, and in its place I felt a cold, granite-like weight settling into the pit of my stomach. My skin was no longer trembling—it had turned to ice, to crystal. Ready to break.

Montaño stopped the car and said, "All right, let's see if you're telling the truth—let's see if you really do like us."

Pérez got out of the passenger seat, walked around, and climbed into the back with me; then Montaño drove off again. With his robust, paunchy build, Pérez moved closer to me, his breath reeked of onions. I slid away from him, and he scooted closer again. Once he'd positioned himself next to me, he directed me to put my hands behind my back. I obeyed. He removed his gun from its holster and said, "You like messing with real men?"

I didn't respond, I was barely breathing. He took his weapon—a pistol—and brought it up to my lips.

"Open your mouth," he ordered, thrusting the gun so hard he hurt my lips. I tried to speak, I wanted to say that my people knew it was the two of them who'd taken me, but I couldn't—I felt the cold metal of the gun on my tongue, a salty taste, and I was overwhelmed by nausea. He moved the gun back and forth in a semicircular motion, easing it further into my mouth.

"If you sneeze, it shoots," he told me.

I closed my eyes, but he ordered me to open them again.

"You're not such a tough girl now, going around with that loud mouth of yours. You're a criminal and the boss is gonna eliminate you." He kept talking, all the while glancing out of the corner of his eye at Montaño, who was watching us in the rearview mirror. Montaño advised me in a gentle voice to do what his partner said, because he was pretty worked up and he wouldn't be able to do anything to stop him.

"I should be at the Christmas party right now; the boss is gonna raffle off presents—cars and things—but here we are, stuck right up shit creek, and all because you had to go blabbing that big mouth."

He played around with the gun in my mouth awhile longer, moving it in and out and making obscene sexual comments. In a moment of silence, my stomach heaved and I felt as though I was about to vomit, at which point he warned me almost playfully, "Ah-ah-ah, easy now, it'll shoot."

He pulled the gun out of my mouth and told me that since I was the one who got it all covered in drool, I had to clean it off, so he stuck it into my mouth one last time. I was frozen. Then he lowered the gun and rubbed the muzzle back and forth. My body tensed, and he asked me if I felt like a tough girl now. I didn't reply. With one hand, he yanked my right leg open. Then he quickly moved the gun down and put it between my legs. He ordered me to open them wider, but I resisted.

"Or perhaps, ma'am, you'd rather take a little swim?" he asked. Right then, more than on any of the other occasions when they'd been similarly polite in their choice of words, it was absolutely mind-boggling to me that they should use such courteous language, even while torturing me; it's something I will never understand.

I was wearing jeans and a red blouse. With a series of quick movements, he lifted the gun out from between my legs, jabbed it into my chest so far it hurt, caught my nipple with the muzzle, and began tugging at the fabric of my blouse. He brought his other hand down to my genitals and pressed hard against my pubic bone, caus-ing more pain.

"You see, this is what you get for going around making up sto-ries about the boss messing around with little girls and all that. Now you see what it feels like."

He kept up a continuous monologue, and all the while, I could feel the pain from the gun being shoved into my breast, and I wor-ried my blouse was going to tear open at any moment, leaving me exposed. I was frantic; I tried to take a deep breath, but I started coughing. Instinctively, I brought my arm out from behind my back to cover my mouth. This startled Pérez, and he reacted by hurling insults at me, believing that I had moved my hand in an attempt to push the gun away. I told him I wasn't going to and I attempted to calm him down. He pointed the gun lower again and pushed it, hard, into my lower abdomen. I asked him not to, because I had to go to the bathroom, and the two started laughing again.

"Oh, yeah? Well, you do as you like—either you wet yourself or you hold it."

Pérez was still holding the gun in the same position. He spoke to Montaño now, telling him, "Don't turn around, partner, watch the road."

He started to unzip my pants. I felt a wetness spreading uncon-trollably across my lap. Pérez snatched his hand away and began shouting that I was disgusting, a pig, and didn't anybody ever teach me that when you need to pee, you're supposed to do it in a bath-room and not in a car. I tried to apologize, explaining that he was pressing against me so it was his fault. He told Montaño to stop the car. As he moved toward the door he slashed his arm back and hit me hard in the ribs with the pistol grip. Pérez got back into the front seat as if nothing happened. Six months later the federal attorney was able to gather all the biological evidence of my account from the car backseat, and the X-rays showed I had a fractured rib.

I took stock of the sensations my body was experiencing. I was shivering with cold; I had a fever. Every muscle in my body was sore, as if I'd just run a marathon. I attempted to meditate, to pray, anything to help me stand having to remain in that car. I crossed my arms in front of me, terrified they were going to order me to put them behind my back again. For a while, they neither looked at nor spoke to me.

As I stared out the window, different pictures began floating across my mind—images of my family, of my mother, everyone smil-ing and hugging me. A dinner party at my Portuguese grandparents' home . . . the whole family together.

So this is it, I thought, *I'm forty-two years old and I'm going to die at the hands of a couple of police agents.*

A curious feeling of calm washed over me, and my legs fell asleep. It occurred to me that this was how it must feel to be at the threshold of death, and I remembered my grandfather. Shortly before he passed, I was at his bedside, and he took my hand and said, "Dying's not so bad when you've lived a passionate life."

My memory filled with different images from my life, and for a moment, I felt at peace, even forgetting for a time where I was, the emotional and physical pain vanished.

I was jolted back to reality when I felt the car stop and then begin to pull along slowly. The two agents started talking out loud again; I emerged from my reverie and realized that my entire back was tense. But I felt strong, as though my fear had dissolved along with my now receding memories. I inhaled deeply, and this time, I didn't cough. It was then that I realized my whole body had fallen numb. I smiled, I breathed . . . I no longer felt any pain. For some reason I silently thanked my grandfather.

"How about a little swim?" I heard Montaño's voice asking happily while his partner lit a cigarette. I was calm again, and I started to explain that their abuse was going to come to light one day, that they were violating my rights. I was thinking about all the phone calls being made and what Jorge told about my fellow journalists and the human rights organizations being involved; I was sure that by now they'd have worked out the identities of these two agents, and their boss. The thought of a reality existing beyond the misery I was experiencing, somewhere outside the four closed doors of that car, was a deeply empowering one. For a second there I was doing something I have been doing for over ten years now: I was reporting on my own case as it evolved. My awareness was back, and the adrenaline kicked in, this time with a spark of reality. They know their names; if something happened to me they would fall; so if I die at least I would not be one more ghost amongst the disappeared journalists and human rights activists of this world. The world would know who had killed me. Writing this now sounds almost absurd, but back then the mere fact that my people would know the names of my assassins was quite an accomplishment in a country where 86 percent of all crimes go uninvestigated and unpunished. I held onto that thought.

The two men, however, were laughing, and Montaño launched into a few anecdotes about the many times they'd been reported to the Human Rights Commission and said that it has never had the slightest effect on anyone.

"They're always going to say whatever the fuck they want in the media; anyways, it's not like they're going to suddenly believe any of it just because of one more report or anything like that. We're just following orders, it's our job, we just do what we're told. The boss says you're a criminal. And in Puebla, what *el patrón* says, goes," said Pérez, now back in the driver's seat and complaining about feeling very tired.

It seemed we'd reached Champoton. It was dark out. The two agents rolled down their windows and asked me a couple of times if that noise they were hearing was the sound of the ocean.

"I think so," I replied.

The Liberty pulled up even with us and the men all spoke to each other through the open windows.

"Here it is, the ocean, it looks pretty calm. We're gonna go get some shrimp cocktails," the man with the gray hair shouted over at them. The street was deserted, and all the seafood joints lining it were closed. I found myself trying to reason with them, pleading with them almost like a small child.

"But everything's closed, seafood restaurants don't stay open in the middle of the night! Why are you all leaving, where are you going?"

Nobody responded. Slowly, it dawned on me, and I thought silently, *They're leaving so the others can throw me into the ocean.* I called in anguished silence to my dead mother. *Please, Mamá, please don't let them throw me into the sea, no one will ever find my body if they do.*

And immediately, I was met with relief as I heard Montaño say, "No . . . we'd better just get going."

But the Liberty ignored him, made a U-turn, and drove off, leaving us alone. I was suddenly more alert than I'd ever been, and something deep inside my body erupted. It was fear. It radiated out from my gut to the very tips of my fingers and toes, and I could hear my heartbeat thumping in my skull. We were in the middle of the town's waterfront, there was not a soul in sight . . . never had the sound of the ocean seemed to me so fierce.

The two men listened through their lowered windows to the crashing of the waves as they sat there in the darkness, surrounded by the salt air and the acrid scent of mollusks suckered onto rocks.

And then in a breath, they turned off the engine, and Montaño got out. From the driver's seat, Pérez asked halfheartedly, "Don't you feel like swimming?" and he motioned toward the door with his gun. He stepped out of the car, leaving his door open. Frozen in my seat, I replied in an almost nonexistent whisper that I was not feeling well and I was not going to get out. They stood looking out over the ocean for a moment; then they exchanged a few words, lit their cigarettes, and grabbed a couple of Cokes out of the car and began to drink.

"Whenever you're ready," Pérez said to me, leaning down slightly in order to peek his head into the car.

From a couple of yards away, Montaño spoke in a calm voice, like someone politely informing another person of the time, and told me, "As soon as the others get back with their ceviche, it'll be time to go for a little swim!"

In a small but now slightly louder voice, I said, "Please, comandante, don't . . . no one will ever find my body . . . please."

I was interrupted by a renewed fit of coughing. I hugged my arms around myself and continue to sit, petrified, refusing to budge from the place where I was sitting in the back of the car. The two men started teasing, tossing out phrases like, "Not feeling so brave anymore, are you, to walk around telling lies and defaming people like that?" or, "Bet you don't feel like writing anything now, do you?"

Pérez raised his voice to be sure I'd hear and remarked, "Do you remember that time the prisoner we were transporting jumped out and started to run? Poor idiot! That one bullet got away from us, and there he fell, all because he didn't do what he was told! . . . Whenever you're ready, Curlylocks! We can wait out here all night."

I kept silent and curled up tighter on the seat. The only thing I can recall from those several minutes I sat there alone in the car is that my body felt heavy and that I kept imagining the weight of a rock tied to my legs. If they wanted me out of that car, they were going to have to drag me out by force. But they were oblivious to this distress of mine as they continued poking their verbal fun. Pérez suddenly spoke more loudly, pretending he didn't know I was listening.

"Like the boss said . . . she was acting very belligerently, she tried to escape, and she ran into the water. We tried to find her, but it was just so dark out."

Montaño remained silent as Pérez kept rattling on, lighting a cigarette between breaths. Perez opened the other back door, and I felt glued to the seat. He pulled my hair so strongly that I moved with him. He pulled me out onto the sidewalk where I fell on my knees, crying. The smell of the ocean, the stink of their cigarettes, and the sand . . . I could smell the brown sand of the ocean, I could hear the waves crashing into what seemed like rocks, or maybe fishing boats. Perez kept his hand crushing my hair, as if trying to rip off my scalp. I felt like an animal must feel in the hands of a cruel master.

Perez kept talking as a teen brat would: "She got hysterical, and we couldn't pull her back out . . . we were just trying to do our duty and bring her in safe and sound."

Just then, Montaño's cell phone rang, and when he answered, he kept his replies short.

"Yes. No. Yes, sir. No, sir. Yes. All right, sir."

As he conversed, he signaled to his partner to climb back into the car. He hung up and spoke to Pérez through gritted teeth.

"Change of plans." Then he spun around to look at me and said sarcastically, "You're famous, ma'am. You're on TV now."

Suddenly Perez helped me up as if I had just happened to fall, offering me a friendly hand. The car doors were all open. I sat in the back, stunned.

He dialed his phone and told the person on the other end that there'd been a change of plans and that they needed to come and meet up with them (he was clearly speaking to the people in the white Liberty).

I asked what happened, but they didn't respond. They exchanged comments about the boss's orders. They were going to have to drive faster now, which was to say to start driving again at all, because they had to get to Puebla as quickly as possible.

Montaño turned to Pérez and said, "Just as well—this way we'll get there early and the boss can take over."

The other replied, as though trying to understand what had just happened, "There's a change of plans—what happened? Are they gonna take her straight to the boss?"

I was overcome with relief at the thought that I was safe now, but after so many hours on this emotional roller coaster, I was trying not to get my hopes up, because having to watch them evaporate over and over was simply too much to bear, and I knew I wouldn't be able to withstand it again. I wanted to distract myself, and so I decided to try to figure out where exactly we were on the highway by looking at the kilometer markers. I was feeling quite poorly, my fever was rising, and as though the conversation were playing on an endless loop, I asked for my medicine for the umpteenth time. They ignored me.

Then out of the blue, Montaño grumpily handed me a couple of mints and said, "Here, for your cough." It wasn't until I put the piece of candy in my mouth that I became aware of the distinct taste of fear and sadness in my mouth—a bitter, rotten taste just like the smell in hospices where people go to die. Months later I became obsessed with washing my mouth several times a day, as if by doing so I could take away the taste of wishing for death. I had tasted the fear of the inhumane, when another human being—embodying the powers that be—takes away your will to survive by scratching your dignity minute after minute until you begin to forget why life is so precious. When tortured, our bodies produce that acid mixture in our blood that I hope I will never have to taste again. I wish no one ever has to taste death and cruelty in the form of State Revenge.

Night was closing in around us on the highway. My cough and fever were getting worse. An idea occurred to me, and I told them that if they wanted me to be in good shape when they turned me in, they ought to buy me my medicine. If they did, I wouldn't say a thing. I made this promise like a little girl begging her captors for mercy. I didn't care; the only thing I was worried about was making sure I didn't suffer a relapse of the pneumonia that had me hospitalized three months earlier.

My will to live was so poor that night on the highway that I feared I might find solace in an illness that forces the organism to stop breathing. I was afraid of losing my fear, the drive to fight, as I realized that my getting to Puebla alive meant only the beginning of a new ordeal, since they had started to say I was going straight to jail.

As we drove along, I recalled the sweet, inspiring face of Rosario Ibarra de Piedra,[9] and I found in her a touchstone for the sense of anguish I was experiencing. I pictured my family searching for me, not knowing whether I was alive or lost, desperate to at least recover my body, searching for years in unutterable despair. The thought that nobody other than a couple of cruel agents of the state might ever know what really happened to me endowed the fear with added depth. But this fear was no longer my own; rather it was the fear felt by my loved ones. When your fate is at the mercy of others, you have room in your thoughts only for the people you love. I pictured Jesús the disappeared student, Rosario's son. His image rose up in my mind's eye, the same image Rosario carries eternally in her breast, and I saw him, I saw the son bidding farewell to the mother, and I was confident that his convictions must have given his departing soul peace. For the certainty of death is far more lofty and elevating to one's being than the uncertainty of psychological torture is woeful.

We passed the Tabasco state capital of Villahermoso and began our ascent into the Veracruz Mountains. Cold came streaming in through the front windows, which were completely rolled down. The

---

9.   Translator's Note: Mexican activist, politician, and four-time candidate for the Nobel Peace Prize who became involved in politics following the forced disappearance of her son, Jesús Piedra Ibarra, in 1974. His whereabouts and fate remain unknown to this day.

two agents smoked in the front seat while I struggled to remain awake, my face now leaning against the glass. Every so often, I remembered that I was supposed to be keeping my hands behind my back; they would have been acting within their rights to handcuff me again, considering I was their prisoner. They conversed only briefly from time to time. I was thankful for the silence; it had become my ally. I looked behind me occasionally—the Liberty's headlights kept a vigilant watch. Montaño clicked on the UHF radio console installed in the front of the car. They tested it out a couple of times, trying to find the Judicial Police frequency, but we were still too far out.

Montaño spoke suddenly, his voice shaking me out of my trance.

"We'll be arriving in a few hours, so don't forget, like we said— you tell them we treated you well, and we won't do a thing. But if you start blabbing, well then, you know how it is, ma'am—we know where you live and we know where you work, we even know what beaches you go to."

Pérez interjected, "We know how much you love to knock yourself back a few beers and we know what bikinis you use . . . the real sexy kind," and he followed this statement up with a laugh. "We know where your father lives, we know everything about you."

"Do we have a deal, ma'am?" Montaño asked.

"Yes, of course," I murmured in reply.

He continued the conversation by himself for a while, speaking in a pleasant tone that was out of place with the subject at hand. He was explaining to me that he was a man of his word, that he always did what he said he would, and that if I went back on my word, I'd have to face the consequences.

"My boss looks after me. What about you? Who's looking after you?"

"Nobody," I replied, in the foolish hope he'd stop talking and leave me alone.

The car slowed suddenly. A call was coming in. Montaño answered.

"Yes, my Comandante Rocha. Yes, yes, all right, we'll see you when we get to Esperanza."

They started grumbling about how Rocha was going to get upset that his orders weren't followed. They switched on the radio, and after a few minutes, they were continuing their conversation with Rocha in short, coded phrases.

As we left Veracruz behind us and crossed the border into Puebla, they exited the highway, drove into town, and pulled up at a pharmacy. It happened so fast I could hardly believe it. Montaño opened the door and told me to get out.

"I'm going to lend you some of my Christmas bonus money so you can get your medicine," he explained.

Slowly, my legs stiff and sore, I climbed out of the car, wary that this might be another joke at my expense. My ribcage hurt like hell but I moved anyway. I didn't understand what was happening, but I was grateful. I walked up to the pharmacy's barred window and ordered my medicine, but I only had enough for the cough drops; the antibiotics were too expensive. Then we all got back in the car.

When we reached the next tollbooth, I saw a large sign on a pink-colored building that looked to be a restaurant of some sort. A big sign hung on the front of the building: ESPERANZA. *Hope . . .* what an irony, that they specifically chose to stop at the entrance of town called Hope. The sun was about to come up. The dawning light had never been so radiant, had never captivated my soul as it did that morning. It was freezing cold; the icy morning dew got into my bones. I felt like crying, but my tears were frozen too, they refused to come out, and suddenly the salty drops of sadness cascaded inside my mouth; they tasted like the ocean. Everything was bizarre. A senseless mockery was being organized around me, and I was so exhausted that detachment took over me; I was a numb witness. They pulled up to a full stop next to a red car. Out of this vehicle stepped a tall, dark man with a mustache. He was visibly exasperated. The others greeted him as "boss," and "Comandante Rocha." He glanced sidelong at me and gave the two men an order.

"Get a jacket on her."

Montaño took off his black jacket with the State Judicial Police initials embroidered on it and handed it to me, but it gave off a pungent odor of sweat and cigarettes, and I refused to put it on. They had brought me this whole way in just a light shirt, not caring that I had a fever and nothing to put on, and now they were hoping to put on this little charade. Montaño shot me an icy look that chilled my blood and told me it was an order. So I took the jacket, but I only hung it over my shoulders. The thick smell of sweat and stale smoke filled my nostrils, and I had to choke back a gag.

Rocha directed two female, plainclothes State Police agents sitting in his vehicle to get into our car. He ordered Pérez to get out and practically shouted his instructions to the two women.

"You two have been in the car with her since Cancun."

My words slipped out almost before I even realized I was speaking.

"I'm a journalist, Comandante Rocha, and they were *not* with me!" I instantly regretted having spoken. With a hint of disdain in his eyes, he gave me the briefest of glances before ignoring me and turning to Montaño.

"Let her use the phone to talk to her family. Nothing happened here, and if she talks, she'll have to pay the consequences," Rocha concluded while the two female agents gathered up their bags and their comfortable-looking jackets and climbed into our car. Pérez drove off with Rocha, and the Liberty followed behind us.

PUEBLA AND KAMEL'S ANGELS

When we reached the Puebla city limit, I broke my silence and asked Montaño to let me speak with my family. He made a call first and told whomever he was speaking to that we were just coming into the city. Then he dialed the number I told him and handed me the telephone—I couldn't believe it. I took it from him, and in a few seconds, I was hearing Jorge's voice. He spoke quickly, letting me know that they were at the Puebla attorney general's office and would be waiting for me when I got there. I managed to tell him, "They're going to take me to the holding area and then to the jail."

Montaño interrupted me, "No, we're not going to the holding area. I just have to pick up a piece of paper and then we're going straight to prison."

Jorge heard what Montaño said, and we hung up.

Once we were in view of the state attorney general's building, the man in the Liberty came on the radio and told Montaño that they were going to go around to the back entrance. A few moments later, they received different instructions.

"No, change of plans, the press is here, go to the main entrance, and make sure they see her with the women."

It was 9:15 AM when we finally arrived at the headquarters of the Office of the Attorney General for the State of Puebla. The two female agents got out of the car and escorted me, one on each arm, as though they had been at my side the entire time. But this was secondary to me at the moment; I looked up at the steps looming before me like a mountain, and I was not sure if my legs would have the strength to climb them. But then I spotted Jorge, and my sister Myriam, standing right at the top, and I saw a throng of TV cameras. And as I was about to start up the steps in the custody of these two new agents, drained of practically all but my last ounce of strength, I let slip to them quickly and quietly, "The tollbooths in Mérida have cameras; they're going to know you weren't with me." The two women made no reply.

Before I'd taken two steps inside the building, Alicia Elena Pérez Duarte, a federal attorney in charge of the Office for Crimes Against Women sent by the PGR to ensure my wellbeing, approached me and inquired whether I was all right. Jorge suddenly stepped forward and held out to me by way of greeting—almost as a butler might—my dark green suede jacket. I let him put it on me, and we embraced for several seconds. I felt as though I was about to break down. A sob rose up in my throat, tears welled into my eyes, and my mouth filled with saliva, as though my tears had found their way out through my tongue, and I savored the freedom of a cry I had been holding back for nearly twenty-two hours. My sister embraced me quickly, but the agents pulled me along gently by the arm and instructed me to keep walking.

They hurried me down to the office area, and we came to a room where the tables were piled high with stacks of documents. Montaño asked a woman there for something, and two men at the back of the room looked up. One of them had blue eyes and elegantly combed gray hair. He was standing some three yards away; he looked steadily at me and began to gesture. Later I would learn that this was Hanna "Juanito" Nakad, the man who ordered that I'd be raped once I reached the prison and who was at that very moment speaking with Kamel Nacif about me.

He began talking into his cell phone, but I was too far away to hear what he said; he turned around and closed the door to the office. A new and very aggressive group of agents burst into the room, and they told Montaño to hold it right there. They argued briefly, and Montaño told them that he had orders to get me to my prision cell as quickly as possible, but the others ignored him, and one yanked me by the arm and shouted, "Get downstairs!"

They signaled to the two female agents to escort me and follow them, and they complied. Everything was happening very quickly, and I noticed a rush of adrenaline coursing through my body once more; I was feeling on guard and utterly depleted, but I found myself nonetheless driven into the state of forced hyperactivity of one who smells fear in the air and is unsure of what awaits them.

They led me down to the holding cells, and I was practically stumbling now over my own feet. They stopped and held me there, and the two young female agents began to show signs of extreme nervousness. I was making an effort to follow everything that was going on, and I saw that there were two distinct groups of agents: Some had been instructed to feign restraint, and others were highly irate and barking counter-orders. Two large agents with sour faces came out of a small side room and shouted at me to walk. A young man came over to me, and I tried smiling at him, hoping to elicit some feeling of compassion; we'd stopped next to the small room where booking photographs are taken, and he was just about finished setting things up inside. He avoided my eyes and shoved me carelessly against the wall as if I were a sack of potatoes. With everyone watching, he pulled the front of my jacket open and, pretending to slip, placed his hands on my breasts and grinned. Then he hung a numbered sign around my neck, stood back, snapped a few photographs, told me in a tired, automatic voice to turn first to one side, then the other, and the next thing I knew, he grabbed me by the hair without a word and slammed my head against the wall.

The three other people in the room forced a laugh. One of them said, "Who does this delinquent think she is?"

Another one, the tall man who had ordered me to go downstairs, yanked me away from the wall and muscled me along in front of him, hissing, "Get in there, bitch." To my left was a metal door, and the flunky opened the padlock. They pushed me in, shutting me inside, closing the lock again, and thumped their hands a few times against the door.

Right away, I realized I was in a Gessel chamber—a confession room outfitted with a two-way mirror. I sensed there was someone watching me on the other side of the glass.

Witnesses, I thought to myself naïvely, *that's good.*

Then I looked down—on the ground in front of me lay a torn mattress reeking of urine and blood. It was covered in multiple dried bloodstains, and some truly sorry-looking, fetid fluff was spilling out of one ragged corner, which had been torn entirely off.

A few minutes passed, then the door opened and the strongest-looking of the men walked in, tossed out a couple of insults, and told me it was time I was taught a lesson, "To see if I really want to go on writing lies."

I couldn't believe it; I no longer had the strength to believe any of this. My family was right there, upstairs, just a few steps away—and they were going to beat me up? I was sitting on a narrow bench with a black vinyl seat that was torn in several places, revealing areas of old, bare wood that had borne witness to who knows how many acts of torture. I was unable to speak; I remained perfectly still, my head leaning against the wall. The man kept up his barrage of insults, repeating over and over again that I was a criminal. I looked at him, and the only thing I could do was wonder how it was even possible for this man who didn't know me in the slightest to feel so much misplaced animosity toward me. For a while I could not remember how many times the man shoved and pushed me around the cell. It was only years after I was able to read the deposition of three witnesses in my torture case that one of the woman said, "We thought he was going to crush her head against the wall so many times." I lost all sense of time, and my fear gave way to desperation. What I wanted most in the world was to break down and cry, but I managed to maintain my composure—I don't know how, but I maintained my composure, or so I think I did.

The door opened suddenly. As though we were bobbing around in some sort of parallel universe where nothing happens in any kind of linear fashion, a man wearing a jacket with the embroidered initials of the state's Human Rights Commission on it was shown into the room. He walked over and stood facing me, holding a piece of paper in one hand and a pen in the other. The overpowering scent of the lavender and wood oils in his body lotion irritated my nose; his slicked-back hair and dopey expression piqued my curiosity. There was something strange about his behavior—he greeted me as though we were acquaintances getting together for a quick meal in a cafeteria rather than strangers meeting for the first time in a torture cell. He didn't ask but *told* me that I had been treated very well by the police and that I should sign the Human Rights Commission document he was holding out to me. He'd left the door open, and just then several people came walking in. Doing my best to hide my overwhelming feeling of joy, I observed as the petite figure of Araceli, my dear colleague and CIAM's lawyer, approached, followed by a young female reporter and her cameraman from Puebla's Televisa station. The reporter positioned a microphone in front of me as if following the orders of the HR commissioner. I gave a clumsy, abbreviated account of the mistreatment I had experienced during my detention. I was feeling far from lucid; I was weak and distraught. There are not many times in my life when I've felt that distinct mortification that comes from knowing yourself to be completely vulnerable, from knowing that your life and your body are at the mercy of unknown hands and there's absolutely nothing you can say or do to influence or change the situation.

Araceli came over to me, and I, struggling to contain my tears, begged her, "Get me out of here, please, they're going to beat me again."

Her face went pale; she shared my fear. And she had more information to go on than I, what's more—by this point, she knew that the governor was supporting the criminal network headed by Succar and Nacif. She is originally from Puebla, she went to law school there, and so she had the advantage of being in touch with some local sources at the courts who knew a little bit about who had orchestrated my arrest, and how.

The reporter left the room, and to my astonishment, the man (who I would later learn was none other than the president of the State Human Rights Commission as well as an employee of Governor Mario Marín) repeated that I should sign the document and then everything—meaning my release—would go faster. I could smell a trap. I refused to sign, and in response the man told me that I looked just fine to him, and that it didn't appear as though I'd been mistreated at all.

I was about to be left alone and locked in again. But before exiting the room, Araceli told me that the local Puebla lawyers she'd secured to get me out of jail had, apparently, already received threats. The threats had come before I'd even gotten a chance to meet them. The last thing she did before leaving the room was to tell me softly, almost in a whisper, "It seems Governor Marín is protecting Kamel Nacif; they don't want to let you walk out of here."

That was the first time I heard the governor's name in conjunction with all of this.

A few seconds later, Adolfo Karam, head of Puebla's Judicial Police force, ordered that I be brought up to his office. I couldn't stop turning over in my head the question of who "the boss" that would eventually hold my fate in his hands was, the one Montaño was speaking to on the phone in the car. When we reached Karam's office, I found myself face to face with the slender figure of Senator Lucero Saldaña. When she saw me, she instinctively held out her arms to me, and I collapsed into them like a child. We embraced, and for the first time in twenty-four hours, I cried, and I did not cry gently—it was an uncontainable shuddering, my whole body weeping in anguish. Lucero clutched me to her like a mother who wants her daughter to know that she can lean on her strong arms, and as she held me, she whispered that God put me in this situation and He would protect me and see to it that I come out of it alive.

"Don't break now, not now," she said sweetly. "You're here now, and you're alive; we won't let anything else illegal happen to you. We're going to get you out of here—this is not a criminal offense."

She spoke a few quick words of prayer into my ear and then stood back. We held each other's gaze, and despite the strained expression on her face, I could tell her eyes were attempting to exact from somewhere within mine a promise of strength. She handed me a tissue to dry my tears.

Seated in a black, leather chair next to the senator, who was a member of the same political party as Police Chief Karam and

Governor Marín himself, I listened to the hollow words of the head of police, and I slowly managed to piece the two scenes together—it was he, it was he who had been down there, smiling sarcastically in the Gessel chamber when the man from the Human Rights Commission had tried to get me to sign that document stating I hadn't been tortured. An icy shiver ran down my spine yet again. *Who could possibly have the power to set all of this in motion, to bring all this pressure to bear on an unknown journalist such as myself?* I wondered. But I didn't have an answer—not yet.

(Years after this happened, Police Chief Karam entered a war against the state general attorney and looked me up. He offered to confess, to explain exactly how and who planned my torture and eventual disappearance. He did offer his statement as a witness, and it is part of my torture case being judged while I work on the English edition of this book.)

Montaño returned, and as he and the other agents hurried me back out of the chief's office, I caught a glimpse of my family off in the distance. Now we were back in the blue car again, driving to the prison. Montaño realized they'd neglected to bring the prison admissions papers with them, which was just inconceivable. It's ironic—I actually feel safe going to jail! Too many people had followed us outside now, the senator included, for them to dare abuse me further.

In the car I began asking Montaño questions.

"Those men were paid to rough me up, weren't they?"

There was silence. I pressed the issue.

"Even you guys were scared. How much do you think Nacif must have paid them?"

The two female agents exchanged a glance over that last query.

"You could tell, too, couldn't you? I can tell from the looks of worry on your faces."

One of them, the younger of the two, lowered her eyes and kept going in silence while the other stared silently out the window.

There were several cars following behind us carrying my family, human rights advocates, and members of the media.

We arrived at the prison, and Montaño turned to me as if we were old travel companions and said that his work here was done; then he handed me over to the guard. His expression baffled me—he looked almost melancholic, his voice friendly, almost giddy.

"So, Ms. Cacho, we have a deal, everything nice and easy, right?"

I nodded, telling him I'd keep my word. A guard asked me to sign my name in a book. As I took up the pen, the agents' words ricocheted back and forth inside my mind. *They know where I live, they know my family and where I work, they're protected.* I shook my head to rid myself of these thoughts, like someone attempting to shoo away a fly buzzing around their face on a hot day.

I heard a man's voice order me to "follow the guard." Ahead of me stood three police agents dressed in black, military-style clothing and holding long guns, who all eyed me carefully before then glancing at one another. A woman wearing a different, navy blue uniform took me by the arm kindly and led me into a small cubicle. The door had an acrylic and aluminum frame with plastic film stretched across it and torn in several places. I could see the agents stationed strategically, directly on the other side of it, and they could see me. The woman asked me to undress; I had barely enough energy to explain by way of refusal that I had bronchitis and was freezing, and that I had absolutely nothing on my person.

"It's mandatory," she responded flatly.

So I began to take off my clothes, trembling, my ribcage hurting like a pinching arrow. The floor was ice cold. I looked over at the door and asked, "What about them?"

The woman stood in front of me, trying to block as much of my now completely naked body as she could with her small figure, and she looked me over. The eyes of the three armed men were on me, but I realized suddenly that it was a moot point; there was simply nothing I could do to avoid their leering gazes.

She touched me lightly to indicate that I should turn around, and as she did so, she asked me in a tone of worry bordering on alarm, "Do you have a fever?"

I nodded. I was feeling humiliated, too depleted to fight. She told me to put my clothes back on quickly.

As I was shrugging on my jacket, the woman asked me if I was the one on the television, the one who wrote the book about Kamel Nacif and the raped children. I raised my eyes to look at her and replied that I was.

"Nacif has some of his people in here," she cautioned me in a conspiratorial whisper. Then she hissed urgently under her breath, "Don't let them take you into the high-security area."

Just then, another guard came into the room. She was a solid woman with short, curly hair and a kind face who looked at me almost sweetly. I asked her her name. It was Griselda, and now she took one arm, the first woman took the other, and we set off together with the three armed agents bringing up the rear.

Speaking under her breath, as if moved by an impulse to solidarity that was beyond her control, she warned me, "They've got it all set up—you're going to be beaten and raped."

I could hardly put my shock into words.

"But how? Who?!"

"Some of the female prisoners, with broomsticks."

I pled with her in a whisper, like someone offering up a prayer before the inevitable.

"Please, please, don't let them hurt me," I repeated in distress.

I could no longer feel my body. I shuffled down the hallway, almost all of my weight being borne by the guards. The three armed agents were trying to convince them to hand me over, saying that they were supposed to take me somewhere else. Everything was flashing by—they walked me down hallways, through doorways.

One of the guards raised her voice at the men, telling them that they were going to take me to the infirmary to get a medical clearance, and the agents accepted the plan.

"But you bring her back here afterward," one of them shouted.

When the final electric door closed shut behind us, a young female guard announced my name, an electric lock was released, and the door opened. Ahead of me was a sunny patio shaded by a white canopy, under which sat a number of women, girls, and boys, all chatting away together. The off-key sounds of a student band could be heard wafting out of a large hall somewhere to the left. The guard explained that Saturday was visiting day at the prison. "No visiting husbands, only women and children. Men abandon imprisoned women," said the guard.

"The cells are over there," she gestured, telling me that they couldn't take me to that area because they couldn't be sure which of the prisoners there had been paid to hurt me. I was confused—wasn't that the police agents? But I didn't dare ask. They escorted me to the infirmary—it was somewhere to hide me, a place where they could keep me safe—and the doctor there offered me two aspirin. I hadn't eaten, and mere moments after swallowing the pills, my stomach was on fire. A young female prisoner who was lying in the infirmary, an IV in her arm, kept up a constant stream of chitchat that she punctuated by directing the occasional question at me. The room was small, and in the air hung a heavy scent of sweat, urine, and medicine. I asked to use the restroom, only to discover that the toilet had no water in it, the seat was falling apart, and the only way to flush the fetid contents of the bowl was by pouring into it some scummy, gray water from a wash bucket kept nearby. The results were repulsive, so I hurried back out, but the heavy odor in the infirmary room itself was little better. The winter air outside was cold, causing them to keep the windows shut tight. I looked over at the other patient. A tattooed sketch of a graceful, stylized dragon made its way up along her left arm. She turned toward me, and I smiled weakly in reply, my mouth dry and my mind clouded from the lack of sleep or food.

"Did Kamel Nacif put you in here? You're not going to get out. He's in charge here; a lot of girls are in here because they complained about abuses at his sweatshop factories."

I responded, beginning to feel somewhat rankled, saying that the charges against me were not a criminal offense and I should be out in just a few hours.

"Neither are mine, they don't even have any evidence against me, and I've been here six months," the young woman replied in a tone that seemed almost compassionate. I swallowed nervously— then silence.

The other guard came in again. Speaking as though she were simply reading out the weather report, she informed me matter-of-factly that it seemed I'd be staying there until January 2. My eyes welled up with fear, swimming in the salty brine of tears I dared not shed, while speech ran terrified, leaving not a single, solitary word in my mind or on my lips—I was an island.

The other women talked about the power Nacif wielded in Puebla, and about his associate, who exploited prisoners by putting them to work in his textile factories. I was feeling claustrophobic, so I asked the guard if there was some other place I could sit; I didn't tell them as much, but I was fast becoming asphyxiated by the smell in the room, by their conversation, and by my own fear. I was shown directly to the library, where a guard spent a little more than an hour with me, telling me all about the many injustices suffered by the female prisoners there, and particularly about what happens to the youngest ones. I was sitting at a small table, and I crossed my arms in order to lay my head down on them. The guard told me that she had to go and that I should try to read a little while I waited.

"Do you have anything to write with?" I asked.

She handed me a small pencil with the tip almost entirely worn down. I stood and scanned my eyes over fifty or so tattered books until I spotted one by José Vasconcelos. I opened to the first page and read a sentence or two, the statement of a prisoner declaring his innocence—it was a story. I picked up the pencil, checked the back pocket of my pants, and pulled out a business card that someone had handed me at some point in the coffee shop the morning before my arrest. I copied down a few lines of the story, and then I read them slowly, gratefully observing that I had my mother to thank for having brought me up to be such a voracious reader. Literature can rescue us from the world; it's a lifeline that can pull us into different universes. I was more thankful at that moment than I ever had been in my life for the chance to immerse my thoughts in someone else's words and thus steal myself away from reality.

The guard returned four hours later and told me that I'd been summoned to a special holding cell. We walked down more hallways and through another electric door. She opened a barred door that looked like something used to cage animals and told me she had to close it behind me, but she'd be sitting right next to me, just on the other side of the door. I grabbed hold of the bars and felt my legs giving way—I could no longer stand upright. I crumpled into a crouching position close to the floor and called to the guard, who graciously brought me a plastic chair. I propped myself up on my knees yet to those on the other side of the door, I appeared to be simply standing. A figure appeared before me, a woman with full lips, short, dark brown hair, light skin, and an anxious look on her face. She greeted me pleasantly and introduced herself as Fifth Criminal Court judge Rosa Celia Pérez González, before going on to state that she ordered my detention at 10:45 AM. I didn't understand all the terminology, but I nodded. She explained that I had the right to a public hearing, and I replied that I would like one. She reminded me cautiously that it was sure to be a very uncomfortable process for me, as there would be a great deal of press and cameras present in the room. But this was reassuring to me, in fact; I *wanted* my colleagues to be there, I wanted them to see everything that went on, to record it. I repeated my desire to avail myself of my right to a hearing, and I could tell she was on edge.

Araceli approached on the other side of the door. She had Jorge with her, and I could feel the anguish slowly flowing out of my chest.

Jorge pulled out his cell phone, pointed the camera at me, and said, "Smile!"

And of course I couldn't help but smile. He has the ability to make me laugh, even at the most wearisome of times. I still have a copy of that picture he took of me through the bars on the prison door, smiling gratefully at him, loving him for managing to come out with such a joke.

A preliminary hearing was held, at which we were informed for the first time about Kamel Nacif's accusations against me and the evidence his team had submitted. The judge read me the entire report and at long last I realized that the whole thing was actually an attempt to defend the pedophile Succar Kuri. Kamel Nacif's report included a document signed by Emma, the young victim who first reported Succar, partially retracting her original statements. I was agog. The adrenaline came rushing back, and with it, my journalistic concerns—if I was made to remain in prison, the American judge that was holding Succar behind bars in Arizona would think that the contents of my investigation were false, and that would contribute to Succar being set free! Then the girls and boys would be brought back into the pedophile's fold. No, we could not allow this to be silenced.

I reserved my right to make a formal declaration and requested to be let out on bail, which was set at an initial sum of US$10,000 to be paid in cash. My lawyers requested that the maximum period allowed to the judge for the final determination of my legal status be extended. It was nearly 3 PM on Saturday afternoon, the few banks that opened on Saturdays were just closing their doors for the rest of the weekend, and my family and friends weren't able to put together more than seven thousand even after emptying their purses and wallets and rushing out to various cash machines. If the judge left and I didn't manage to make bail on time, I would have to stay in prison until Monday. As it turns out, that was the whole point. My lawyer later explained that in cases similar to mine, the largest amount of money that had ever been required for bail in the entire history of the Puebla courts was slightly less than fifteen hundred dollars They knew nobody carries that amount of cash.

My lawyer asked the judge to reconsider and lower the bond amount. She agreed to do so, although not without first making a few calls from the official court telephone, and thirty minutes later, her discussions having come to a successful conclusion, the seven thousand dollars in cash was deposited at the court.

Later, as a result of the investigations carried out by the Office of the Attorney General of Mexico and the Supreme Court of Justice, we would discover that the Fifth Criminal Court judge had called the cell phone of the chief justice of the Puebla Superior Court of Justice, Guillermo Pacheco Pulido, who in turn telephoned Governor Marín and Hanna "Juanito" Nakad, as he called Kamel Nacif. In other words, the different networks of public servants and criminal collusion put in place by and answering to Kamel Nacif had worked exactly as expected.

The press quickly surrounded the judge, listening intently and recording everything; I felt protected, and I suddenly had a clearer understanding than ever of the power that journalism has to give voice to those who have been silenced by the crushing weight of violence. I was grateful for the barrage of insistent, sometimes overlapping questions, and I tried to respond to every one of them with what little energy I still had. I was informed that I would be released on bail that afternoon. The guard told me that I should go back inside.

"No!" I responded, turning pleadingly to special attorney Alicia Pérez Duarte, who had been sent by General Serrano at SEIDO. She told me that it was all right, that I'd be out in just a couple of hours.

It would not be until later, during my private therapy sessions, that I would come to understand why I felt so instantly overcome with panic at the idea of going back inside. Over the course of the previous hours, every time things finally appeared to be dealt with and settled, some new torturous episode would present itself, and the effects of all this trauma were taking root in my memory, which was working at full tilt to register all the ups and downs of the violence being meted out to me. The invisible elements of torture can only be understood by those who have experienced it. It is precisely this type of succession of starkly contrasting events that ends up "breaking" so many people who find themselves in prison, that end up making them beg forgiveness and plead for freedom. Only those who have experienced such torture know how minutes are experienced as hours, and hours as days, and how life itself is felt as something miserable, obscure, and undesirable.

I was taken back into the jail, back to the infirmary. For some reason, the female guards were taking great care to protect me. They said nothing, but my intuition told me that something was going on. I, too, remained silent. Eventually, the afternoon rolled around, and I was summoned once more. I nearly fainted when I was told they'd be taking me to the office of the prison warden. Two police agents filed in silently, and my female guard left me with them. Then the Puebla State Human Rights Commission official entered the room, the noxious smell of his lotion trailing behind him, and one of the agents exited. The Human Rights official pressured me anew to sign the document.

"Look, you're getting out of here—the press already saw that everything is fine and that we didn't hurt you. If you sign this now, you can leave. Just write that we treated you respectfully."

But I refused, and the remaining agent told me it was simply a formality that would allow me to be released faster. I realized that I was shut in an office room with an armed police agent and the Human Rights individual. I was unable to gauge if the situation was dangerous or not.

The Human Rights man smiled as he waved the paper around in the air and said, "If you don't sign, you're not getting out today—the judge will be leaving in just a few minutes on Christmas vacation."

I grabbed the paper in desperation and signed. At that precise instant, the warden walked in, a moment too late. He introduced himself with a theatrical display of goodwill, shook my hand, and asked the agents what they were doing there. They replied that they needed me to sign a few things, at which point he reprimanded them and offered me his apologies. It was clear to me that there were two opposing forces at work here: Some of the people around me were there, apparently, to protect me, and others had orders to abuse me.

The agents hurried me out, and I was escorted from the building by several armed men. In an instant, I was outside. Free. I looked around me—I was standing in a desolate dirt parking lot, but I couldn't see my family. Then I spotted them in the distance, some five hundred yards away at the opposite entrance. We ran toward each other while my colleagues from the media stood by. I embraced my sister Myriam, and Jorge, and my friends who were there, as well.

The nightmare is over, I thought.

And I smiled as though I'd been reborn. I felt happy, whole, alive, and cared for.

4

THE "PRECIOUS GUV'"

The feeling of freedom lasted only a few hours, exactly the time it took to share a meal with family and friends. In that short space of time, we went from a sense of euphoria at my having been freed to a feeling of silent anguish at the then still incipient suspicion that the powerful strings Kamel Nacif was controlling were more numerous and far-reaching than anyone could imagine. By the time the coffee was brought out, the shadow of a remand order had settled firmly over the table.

When I left the prison, I learned more about how the local lawyers who had originally taken on my case lasted only a few hours before stepping down, fearing reprisals from Marín and the Puebla state police apparatus. As a result, we were forced to start looking for a new team of lawyers, and the nightmare started up again. The judge had warned me on the Saturday I was released that I only had until Tuesday to gather all the necessary evidence if I wished to avoid being remanded. So there we were, stuck in Puebla with no criminal defense team, the evidence I needed was back at my apartment in Cancun, and a large portion of the clippings I had been storing there in a cardboard box were lost when Hurricane Wilma buffeted the city, leaving my apartment flooded for over a week along with hundreds of others in the area, before I was able to return to it. Moreover, Christmas was only a few days away, so no one was returning our calls.

Araceli leapt to my aid. She came over from Cancun, bringing as many pieces of evidence as she could get her hands on overnight, but her area of expertise is fiscal and family law, which meant we were still in need of one or two experienced criminal defense attorneys. The first such expert to agree to work with me never showed up at the court on the day of the hearing, claiming to have been afflicted with a bout of diarrhea that rendered him unable to leave the house. The person who had recommended his services later admitted to me that the lawyer had in fact spent all night going over my book and the evidence for the case and simply didn't have the courage to tell us that he was so scared by the whole thing that he felt completely in over his head and worried sick.

We moved our "defense encampment," as Jorge jokingly called it, to Mexico City. My brother José Ernesto, Jorge, and I waded through the entire complicated, years-long story of the Succar case that had led to my arrest. The effects of the tortures I had undergone combined with recurring attacks of adrenaline made it impossible for me to sleep. I felt as though I were locked in a race against the clock. I knew I had the evidence necessary to support what I had written in my book, and the panic caused by the thought of having to go back to prison and spending the next four years there was my most effective motivator. Finally, three days after walking out of the prison, this horrible period of uncertainty ended when we concluded that we did indeed have enough to go on for the initial defense. Araceli came to Puebla to submit the required documentation and request that I be set free on grounds of lack of evidence. There would be plenty of chances for me to break down later, but for the time being, I would have to hold myself together in order to appear in Puebla on the day the judge issued her resolution to either remand me to prison or absolve me for lack of evidence to support Kamel Nacif's allegations.

SEIDO assistant attorney general José Luis Santiago Vasconcelos asked me to let him know what time we would be leaving for Puebla. He didn't share any information with me but simply informed me that he would send a couple of armored vehicles for us to use on the drive to Puebla, as well as a specialized, six-man unit to accompany us. Under no circumstances were we to travel the highway alone.

Two days before Christmas, a convoy made up of myself, my family, the lawyer, and a handful of supportive friends left Mexico City for Puebla. We reached the outskirts of our destination and stopped for the night at a local hotel in order to appear bright and early at the courthouse the next morning. Jorge and I hardly slept, our arms wrapped around one another. We didn't say much, but from time to time we spoke little words of encouragement, each assuring the other that we were going to make it through this.

In the morning, we went down to the hotel's breakfast room, where after a few minutes we greeted the arrival of my brothers and sisters. Araceli was standing by with all of the documents, and Jorge—professional journalist and information junkie that he is—got up from the table to bring everyone copies of the day's newspapers. We flipped through them, and I came across a full-page spread sporting a one-word headline: "Criminal." Puebla governor Mario Marín Torres had given a statement denouncing me as a criminal, and it had been reprinted in several of the local papers. I took a sip of my coffee and spoke slowly to those gathered around the table.

"They're going to remand me."

My sister Sonia said that I was wrong and lovingly urged me not to be so pessimistic. But I knew this: If the governor was already daring to publicly denounce me as a criminal, long before the judge even issued a remand order, that clearly meant that this had all been orchestrated from the get-go.

In another paper, Puebla state attorney general Blanca Laura Villena declared unreservedly that if the judge failed to find me guilty, she would "see to it personally" that I be "locked away." We stared at the array of papers spread out before us, unable to believe what we were reading. The state attorney general had made this statement with an unusually venomous attitude for one charged with safeguarding the constitutionally binding principle that "every individual is innocent until proven guilty." You didn't need to be a journalist to understand that Kamel Nacif had the governor and the state attorney general in his pocket, but the question, as my eldest brother asked, was, *Why? What did they owe him?*

We left the hotel with plenty of time to spare and drove to the courthouse outside the prison. An inordinate number of journalists were waiting for us when we arrived; we made our way toward the building in silence, and the only statement I gave as we approached was that we would all have to wait and see. I was still holding the newspaper that had printed the governor's statement, and I brought it into the courthouse with me.

At the door, surrounded by my family and with Jorge at my side, I said, "Let's go get the remand order."

I needed to be prepared—I didn't want to allow myself any room for hope. It had been four nights since my torturous highway journey had ended; I couldn't sleep for the nightmares, but I wasn't willing to let this pedophile's accomplices know that. I fortified myself with thoughts of the brave girls back in Cancun who were still undergoing therapy to help them survive the horror of having been subjected to Succar Kuri's pornographic crimes. *My book is for them, for those little girls,* I reminded myself silently. They're the reason we're here, and the various forces at play in this case are trying to silence me in order to silence them.

We walked into the courtroom, and the judge was there to greet me and my lawyer. She held her hand out to me; it was sweaty and trembling. The eyes of the media were on her, and the courtroom's large observation window left no place for secrets to hide. I spoke to her without hesitation.

"I know that you'll do the ethical thing—I'm innocent."

The judge gave me an inscrutable grimace of a smile, and then rather than sentencing me herself, it was a bailiff who read out the verdict. With no further preliminaries, without even so much as glancing at me once, his eyes firmly set on the paper he was holding in his hands, he read the sentence for the ravenous media to hear.

"A remand order is issued for the crimes of defamation and libel."

A murmur of collective gasps and groans filled the room. I felt a wave of icy energy wash over my body. The reporters and cameramen stepped aside slightly as we began to slowly file out of the courtroom. I took a single deep breath. Araceli looked at me, her eyes brimming with tears because she felt responsible; she was my lawyer and my colleague, and she thought I could count on her. She would eventually come to accept that this went far beyond any of us, that the plot had been hatched ahead of time and the only thing in our power to do was to attempt to defend ourselves in a dignified manner.

Upon exiting the courtroom, almost without thinking about what I was doing, I held the newspaper high above my head and declared for the first time that Governor Mario Marín was involved in some way with my illegal arrest and that an investigation should be made to look into what had prompted a governor to cast himself in the role of trial judge for a case ostensibly involving two private individuals—Kamel Nacif, associate and protector of the pedophile Succar Kuri, on the one hand, and myself, the journalist who had published the truth of the story as narrated by the two men's victims, on the other.

The next day marked the beginning of an interminable whirlwind of statements and declarations that would end up lasting more than a year as many more pieces of the story came together, most of them incomprehensible for the wider public until a series of recorded telephone conversations surfaced two months later revealing that while all of this was going on, Kamel was phoning Marín and addressing him warmly as "my hero, my precious Guv'" for having granted him the favor of mobilizing the justice system to have me jailed and tortured.

We began systematically gathering copies of every newspaper, video or radio recording, and interview in which the Puebla authorities and Kamel himself were making statements against me. Among them was one particular jewel—an interview given by Kamel Nacif to *Reforma*, published on December 20, 2005, in which he "publicly thanks the governor" for having ensured that justice be done, because, as he himself had told Marín, "This lady is libeling me, and then boom, out comes the arrest warrant."

Nacif would later make several attempts to retract his direct revelation of the governor's involvement, and Marín would also submit press releases through his spokesman Valentín Meneses denying any such participation—but to little avail. The demons were on the loose. Having grown accustomed to flexing their abusive muscle, all of them—from Nacif to the governor and the state attorney general, and the head of the State Judicial Police force, to boot—predicted with a sneer of pride on their lips that "this crazy, lying journalist," as Nacif once referred to me on the radio, wouldn't be able to do a thing to prove the existence of the criminal collusion they had organized for the purpose of protecting Succar Kuri, the pedophile *par excellence*, through the intermediary actions of his right-hand man, Kamel Nacif.

I told the story of my trip to Puebla and the hours I spent in jail countless times. The state attorney general declared to TV Azteca of Puebla that my human rights had been handled in an absolutely respectful manner and that it was a shame that I had decided to make up such a story. A year later, it would be proven that I had been telling the truth.

The judge had ordered that I check in at the Puebla jail once a week. But I live in Cancun, and the jail is 930 miles away from my home. How could I afford the weekly travel costs of US$6,000 just to sign my name to a few papers? I was still continuing to search high and low for a criminal defense lawyer, and in the meantime, I was in communication with Random House, publisher of *The Demons of Eden*, the book that had ended up landing me in prison. The publishing house's director told me that people were now snapping up my book left and right. But although my account of my investigations was selling well, I still hadn't seen a cent of the royalties from it. Most authors are content to draw their advance, however little it may be, and when the royalty checks start to come in a year later, they're never for as much as they imagined at the start. And my case was no exception. The publishers had agreed to pay for some of my legal fees, but only up to a limit, all of which amounted to an added source of stress for me, as the question plaguing me at the time was the same question that plagues millions of people who find themselves suddenly involved in court cases: *Where am I going to get all the money I need?*

In January, I finally succeeded in locating a lawyer who was willing to defend me. The media had managed to shed some light on the Puebla governor's corruption and involvement in my case, and that had in turn brought the State Superior Court under scrutiny. Because the Court's hand in my case had been revealed—and not because the latter believed the decision to be just, although in theory that should have been sufficient reason—my lawyers managed to get the trial moved to Cancun, on the argument that if a crime had indeed been committed, it would have taken place either in Mexico City, where the book was published, or in Cancun, where I had written it. On January 13, the Superior Court of Justice for the State of Puebla's Second Criminal Court gave its ruling, ordering me not guilty on the charge of libel but upholding the defamation charge. Later I learned why: Libel consists of propagating a falsehood, while defamation means simply to cause a person's reputation to become negatively affected, the negative transformation determined according to the opinion of a judge. And there's no way to defend against that.

I also learned that the crime of defamation for which I was now the "likely culprit" involved several subjective elements, such as the honor and good name of Kamel Nacif, and the supposed "deceitful intent" I had demonstrated in the writing of my book. I put it to my lawyers that in the case of "the Denim King," there was no good name to protect in the first place, much less any deceitful intent to slander him by writing the book, which I had approached as a work of investigative journalism, pure and simple, backed by a legitimate public interest to protect Succar Kuri's victims. Moreover, it just so happens that freedom of the press and freedom of expression are constitutionally enshrined rights in Mexico and that this consideration, according to multiple theses on jurisprudence, trumps the protection of any one individual's honor, given that honorability is a highly subjective concept. My lawyer, who made me learn and understand legal terminology despite my resistance to the idea, explained the following example to me: If a bank robber assaults a financial institution and is taken to prison and then a journalist writes about his life and the facts of his case, the thief can sue the journalist from prison for having damaged his honor, even if there is video evidence of the robbery, "because his family and friends had not previously been aware that he was a criminal." It may seem like a bad joke, but it's true—just as long as the thief in question is lucky enough to have an official from the Attorney General's Office in his corner and a judge willing first to allow the accusation to stand and second to issue a remand order. This tends to happen in situations where influence peddling is involved, as it was in my case and is in the cases of thousands of others in Mexico.

We learned that the accusation had been brought before the Office of the Attorney General's specialized electoral crime section in order to ensure that it go unnoticed, and we also discovered documents proving that the judge had refused at first to accept the case because "a crime allegedly committed in another state could not be tried in Puebla." Nevertheless, after being pressured by the president of the Court—Guillermo Pacheco—and Hanna "Juanito" Nakad, the judge agreed, the second time around, to order my arrest. We uncovered forged signatures on the detention record and a series of other data that pointed to a seeming enigma. The idea that practically the whole of the Puebla justice system as well as the state's governor were conspiring against me seemed absurd, and I for one refused for a time to believe it was true. But the reality of the matter turned out to be unfathomably shocking.

"YOU'RE MY HERO, DADDY"

On February 14, the nation of Mexico awoke to a spectacular piece of news. The daily *La Jornada* and the renowned radio and television reporter Carmen Aristegui presented the public with a series of recorded telephone conversations in which Kamel Nacif is heard offering Governor Mario Marín a bottle of Cognac to thank him for the "smacking" I would be getting. Immediately, all the media outlets that had been giving me a voice fell to analyzing, reprinting, and studying the calls. Everything I had been saying since I left prison was now laid bare, including the plot devised between Kamel Nacif and Hanna "Juanito" Nakad, operator of the prison textile factory, to have me raped with broomstick handles and beaten while I was in jail.

Joaquín López Dóriga was unsparing during his extraordinary interview with the governor, which aired that very night, as was Carlos Loret de Mola the following morning. The story of the telephone conversations was even picked up in the United States by ABC News in Bryan Ross's *20/20* report, by the *El País* newspaper in Spain, and by *The New York Times* and *The Washington Post*. Press members and pundits, especially those outside Mexico, expressed incredulity that Governor Marín should still be occupying his post after these calls came to light, and even greater disbelief that Kamel Nacif and his accomplices had been neither arrested nor even investigated by the Mexican authorities.

My case had taken a step forward, and the consequences were almost immediate: The death threats multiplied; my home telephone started ringing off the hook; the Puebla state attorney general stepped up her attacks against me in the press; and I received communications from third parties operating on the governor's behalf and wanting to know "how much money" I would need "to let the whole thing drop."

Every time I received any sort of threat, I turned around and informed the press, and every time Marín's and Nacif's teams tried to negotiate with my lawyers, I publicized their clumsy attempts to smooth things over. I got together with my lawyer and decided to file a report against Governor Marín and his entire team, Kamel Nacif, and Hanna "Juanito" Nakad for criminal association, attempted rape, influence peddling, and other crimes. My lawyer was clear in his forewarning that I had no chance whatsoever of winning the case, or even of having anyone investigate it properly.

I was not unfamiliar with the phenomenon to which he was alluding; every time the Office of the President wishes to scuttle some case, or series of cases, and silence the public's calls for justice, it creates a new special attorney to deal with the matter. And sure enough, the office of the Special Federal Prosecutor for Crimes Against Journalists had just been inaugurated.

I knew all of that, but I thought it would be better to demonstrate with hard facts, rather than assumptions, that even when a Mexican citizen can prove her or his constitutional guarantees and human rights have been violated, the institutions of the state offer neither protection nor the right to a prompt and speedy trial. And so we would put these institutions to the test. That way, if I did end up losing my life, at least I would have done everything I possibly could to defend myself from the actions of an official state that was hell-bent on protecting such elements of criminal power. The decision to go ahead with a formal accusation is one I made in conjunction with my family and Jorge. On the day of the actual filing, for the first time in a long time, I felt happy. The agents who'd kidnapped me had told me several times that reporting them would do no good; after all, it was my word against theirs as men. But they were wrong, because in addition to my own word, we now had their bosses' words—uttered loud and clear over the phone and captured on tape—to back me up.

A few months later, I learned that my lawyer had not submitted all the required evidence. The Quintana Roo judge was doing everything in his power to make things easier for Kamel Nacif and stymie my cause. We were unable to prove this corruption existed, however, because to chronicle the sum of subtle machinations being used to back me into a legal corner would have required that an expert sleuth spend all day, every day sniffing around the courthouse. I couldn't do it myself—I had to work for a living, plus I had to gather evidence for my accusation against Marín, Nacif, and their accomplices, and I had to fight back the nightmares that assailed me with visions of my kidnappers coming into my apartment in the middle of the night, pressing a gun to my forehead, and saying "We told you we'd come for you if you reported us." I was determined not to allow my tormentors to see how much I was suffering on their account. I gave interviews, and I took care to choke back the sobs that would rise up when certain questions were asked. If we took a step forward, the authorities would drag us three steps back. Evidence would go missing, and the judge was insisting that the items from the Succar case that we were submitting as evidence for our defense in the defamation case brought against me by Kamel Nacif had no bearing on this latter suit.

There were some weeks when my distress was so marked that I would wake up in the mornings unable to do anything but sit alone in my house crying. Then I would force myself to get up, do a little yoga, have some breakfast—in short, to keep going. My cell phone was constantly ringing as people from all over invited me to attend a plethora of different events; their outpourings of solidarity were inexhaustible, but so were their demands on my energy and time. I was receiving between 150 and 200 emails a day; there were people offering moral support, readers of all ages—women and men alike—expressing their indignation or sending prayers or well-wishes, invitations to attend various events and receive all manner of recognitions. People were stopping me on the street to take photos with me, to ask for my autograph, or to tell me what a big impact my book had had on them. My three-agent security detail—two men and one woman—found they now had to step up their vigilance; we couldn't be sure whether one of these people approaching me with a smiling face might not also be carrying a gun. I never gave them leave to mistreat anyone, but there were a few occasions when some unknown individual would approach me at a public event, frantically trying to hug me, and I had to ask for my bodyguards' help.

Amid the chaos of this new life, I fired my lawyer. In the four months since my detention, I had spent close to half a million pesos on my defense, with the aid of my publishers and the financial solidarity of people who were buying my book as a way to support my cause. Over time, I would come to spend nearly three million pesos on legal fees. Different feminist networks had taken up collections to help offset some of the cost of my defense, and they were joined by Sylvia Sánchez Alcántara—the president of the International Women's Forum, Mexico Chapter—and all the other wonderful women belonging to this group of female business leaders. And people weren't just making small donations and walking away; on the contrary, they remained by my side, they followed the news of the case, and they renewed their moral support every time some new problem would arise.

Without my realizing it, the image of me as a heroine had begun to swirl and take form in the minds of some. Many people came to have certain expectations about me that I myself never encouraged and that I'm quite confident I will never be able to live up to. But my country was in such need of hope that it was possible for a single brave woman standing uprightly in defense of her principles to be viewed as something exceptional. I spent my days trying to cheat fear, spurred on by the hope that I would one day be able to get my old life back. But as reporter Nino Cancun remarked to me one day at the end of a radio interview, "You'll never go back to your old life." And he was right.

CRIMINALIZING TRUTH

When I was a girl, my mother used to tell me that the truth is far lighter than a lie, and that a lie will always end up collapsing under its own weight, for to cover up one falsehood, countless more are needed, and they become stacked, one upon the other, until the burden is eventually too large to bear without someone noticing that you're carrying it. The truth, on the other hand, floats effortlessly upward for all to see.

It is abundantly clear that nobody ever warned Governor Marín of what the consequences of maintaining his fallacious stance in the face of the mounting evidence against him could be. Perhaps that's why he and the most trusted members of his cabinet decided to pursue a strategy of implacable revenge against anyone who came out in support of my cause and against his corruption.

When I walked out of the Puebla jail on December 17, one of my closest friends was there among the group of concerned, caring people waiting to greet me: Mónica Díaz de Rivera. A Puebla-born writer and former coordinator of the Lafragua Library at the Benemérita Universidad de Puebla (BUAP), Mónica is a well-known feminist who has dedicated her life to promoting women's rights through her work in academia. She has earned a great deal of deserving praise since founding the Instituto Nacional de las Mujeres [National Women's Institute] and, later, the Instituto Poblano de la Mujer [IPM; Puebla Women's Institute]. From the very moment of this latter institution's inception, she sat on the citizens' council tasked with providing it with structure and a sense of purpose as it worked toward its goal of promoting equality and eliminating all forms of violence against women and girls. As a reward for her commitment, Mónica was invited by the IPM's president to accept an official post with them, where she would be working to ensure that Puebla women truly receive the protection and assistance they need. And she did an exceptional job—until, that is, Marín ordered her termination as an act of retaliation for having hugged me upon my release from jail. Mónica knew just how far the governor's repressive power reached, but she remained by my side regardless, allowing herself to be photographed by state attorney general Villeda's hatchet men. Just days after I was released on bond pending trial, the president of the IPM summoned Mónica to her office. Her cheeks pale and her expression skittish, she informed Mónica bluntly that she had no choice but to demand her resignation. When asked the reason for this sudden decision, the only explanation the president—a PRI supporter—offered was, "It's an order from above."

Mónica was followed by some twenty individuals from various professional walks who all spoke out against the violence and injustice in my case. For a year and a half, the IPM's work was brought to a forced standstill by the constant outflow of the employees needed to keep the organization afloat, and the consequences were suffered by all the female citizens in Puebla who were seeking support as victims of gender violence and no longer finding it.

But they were not the only ones; many are the lives that have been affected by Marín's retributive efforts. Former senator Lucero Saldaña, who had served as president of the Senate Commission for Equality and Gender as well as president of the Bicameral Commission Against Femicide, also paid for her moral rectitude. A member of the PRI like Marín, and with a thirty-year political career to her name, Lucero was positioned to eventually take over the mayor's office of the city of Puebla. She is an intelligent woman known for her strong political credibility and ethics, but her life changed after her appearance during my detention prevented the beating that had been planned for me from taking place. On the orders of the governor and the president of the local PRI chapter, Saldaña was blocked from appearing on the party's closed list of candidates running for a plurinominal deputy seat.[10] Later, during the primaries for the mayoral race, sources at the PRI's political council confirmed that Governor Marín's orders had been clear: "Anyone supporting that journalist Cacho has no place in this state." For having been consistent in her defense of women's rights, Lucero found herself exiled to a state of political ostracism.

Shortly after the public circulation of the "Precious Guv'" telephone calls, the governor's advisors had bracelets and decals made up displaying the words "I believe Marín." I received more than a dozen emails from public servants explaining that their bosses had warned them that if they failed to stick the decals on their cars or wear the bracelets, they could expect to receive an immediate dismissal. Puebla society was fast becoming polarized. Those who didn't previously have an opinion either way about my case decided they'd better find out more about the repressive discourse to which they were being subjected without understanding why. The Puebla media were scrambling to uncover the truth, not only because they finally had a real story on their hands but also because when Governor Marín came to power in Puebla a year prior to my arrest, he gave a stern warning in the local press regarding his determination to criminalize freedom of expression. Now the state media had the chance to show Marín in his true colors, for many of the large, national media outlets

---

10. Translator's Note: The Mexican electoral system is based on a parallel voting arrangement in which senators and congressional deputies elected directly are called uninominal and those elected by proportional representation are referred to as plurinominal.

shared and supported them in their love of freedom of expression. To add to their joy, many local outlets were even managing, a year after Marín's unwelcome announcement, to resolve their financial difficulties thanks to the millions the state government poured, and continues to pour, into their coffers to pay for a campaign to whitewash the image of the governor and that of his team.

The governor's hard line and the extent of his desire for retribution began to border on the absurd. Low-level employees of the "Precious Guv'" set up support networks at the middle-management level of every government department, to the point that heads of schools and even universities were mounting attacks against their students' freedom of expression. Two examples will serve to illustrate the phenomenon.

Macondo Jiménez, a model student fifteen years of age, received three days' suspension from the Venustiano Carranza secondary school for having put two stickers—one in the school's restroom and the other in the library—depicting a caricature of Governor Mario Marín Torres as Kamel Nacif's accomplice. The teenage student was informed by the school's director, Fortino Castillo Alvarado, that he had violated the Secretariat of the Interior's anti-graffiti codes. The director had originally intended to expel the student permanently, but public outrage in the community prevented him from doing so.

A second notable case is that of the president of the Universidad de Las Américas, Puebla campus (UDLA), Pedro Ángel Palou, a writer belonging to the self-styled *crack* group of Mexican literature (a superb assortment of five writers who challenged an entire generation of women and men of letters). Palou had served as Secretary of Culture under former governor Melquiades Morales, and he maintained a close friendship with Mario Marín. I was invited by the students of the journalism department and the editors of the school newspaper, *La Catarina,* to give a conference during UDLA's Communication Week. The students were told that "conditions were not ideal for Lydia Cacho to speak at UDLA." When *La Catrina* made mention of the "Precious Guv'" and published a couple of caricatures of him, the university's president sent in a security squad to handle the issue in full-blown police style—all of the paper's computing equipment was taken, their electricity was cut off, their website was shut down, and the newspaper's staff was forced to quit the premises. In the months that followed, the most renowned academics at both UDLA and BUAP were persecuted and intimidated for calling for Marín's resignation.

Meanwhile, in a closed-door meeting held in early 2006, Governor Marín and State Attorney General Villeda, together with the former's most trusted associates, met with two women who were long-standing PRI-party activists and knew me well. Both were women who had spent years promoting my writing in Puebla. The request put to them, according to one of the two, was a specific one: Investigate every last detail of Lydia Cacho's life, and try to find some former friend or lover willing to talk about the journalist's "dark side." During the meeting, the governor's spokesman at the time, Valentín Meneses, said that they already had taps on my telephone lines and were hoping to find out "who Lydia Cacho is working for." The orders were to start a rumor about my (nonexistent) direct participation in candidate Andrés Manuel López Obrador's campaign.

"López Obrador is known," one of the women in the meeting explained to me, "to be having an affair with a woman from Puebla; we're supposed to start a rumor saying that his mistress is really Lydia Cacho, the journalist, and that will distance her supporters in the PAN[11] from her and at least take some of the local heat off. Plus, we can tie her to the EPR guerrilla group."[12] The announcement to the press of my supposed ties to the guerillas was given by the state spokesman himself.

---

11. Translator's Note: Partido Acción Nacional, National Action Party—one of Mexico's three main political parties, it is a conservative-leaning, Christian democratic party.

12. Translator's Note: Ejército Popular Revolucionario, Popular Revolutionary Army—a leftist guerrilla group operating in southern Mexico.

Months later, several witnesses came forward—the majority of them women—and provided me with information that would prove key to understanding the extent of the ill will borne against me by Governor Marín and his people. The former lover of one of the governor's most trusted public servants showed me copies of faxes and reports sent by two "investigators" who had been dispatched to Cancun to follow me and install a wiretap on my home phone. As I went through these documents, I was astonished to find accounts about people with whom I had gone out to lunch or dinner at one point or another, with special attention being paid to the names of men who ought to be investigated further. (My AFI security team never acknowledged the fact that we were being followed.) My kidnappers had been staying and had spent almost two months at a hotel whose name sounded vaguely familiar to the woman who brought me all this information. "Solymar Villas," the report read. My blood turned to ice—that was Succar Kuri's hotel.

"But is it possible they could be so obvious?" I asked the woman.

"I don't think so," she said, "Nacif is helping them. It must be like a safe house for them, somewhere they won't be found out, because they're careful not to leave any sort of paper trail—the only thing they pay for is their meals, and they do it in cash."

A week after this meeting, I met with my therapist to analyze the sudden return of my nightmares, and she recommended that I stop receiving any direct information about my case.

"Have all of your sources talk to your lawyer," my therapist advised. "You can't live with all this mounting stress—you're going to end up in the hospital."

I did as she suggested. I was already experiencing anxiety-related health problems. I had realized by then that all the persecution and constant uncertainty were feeding my anxiety and that if I went on as I had been, I would eventually wake up one day to find I had no other choice than to turn tail and admit defeat.

I left my session and headed home, somewhat more calm now, determined to find some emotional anchors that might keep me safely tethered to a state of inner peace. I sought refuge in books, in the sea. It was Wednesday afternoon, and I found a rock on the deserted Puerto Morelos beach, where I sat and wrote in my diary:

> Now that my eyes have seen so much human misery, I search within my heart—as though it were a basket of red apples—for some piece of fresh, sweet hope. And I find it. Though I am persecuted out there, here in my soul there is peace, a peace that draws its strength from my persistence, my determination. Truth will endure, fear will pass. My strength and my power lie in my ability to accept reality and to show things as they truly are.

Little by little, a sense of tranquility returned to me. I remembered that hope cannot survive on bitterness toward what is already past—rather it must be fed by the dream of building a new future, a future free from violence, for all those who will come after us. I, too, shall pass away, but my life will not be defined by this handful of malevolent characters. My life is the people I love, it's music, it's literature—it's far more than any single dark episode. My life is the luminous causes I believe in, the same causes millions of peace-loving people believe in. I would rest easy, at least for tonight.

5

THE NATION REACTS

While we were searching far and wide for new lawyers, our fellow reporters had managed to get the federal authorities to acknowledge not only the importance of the Succar case but also the fact that the case did indeed—as I had said in my book—involve organized crime, child pornography, sex tourism, and money laundering. Security experts advised that I keep up my press appearances; my visibility was my most effective life insurance policy.

One afternoon, Christian Zínser, a lawyer I had met at a forum on freedom of expression held in the congressional building in the capital, came to me and offered to help me in any way he could. At the time, he was defending Olga Wornat, who had been sued by none other than Martha Sahagún de Fox, wife of the now former president Vicente Fox. I took him up on his offer and told him I needed him to recommend a good lawyer, a firm that wouldn't shy away from taking on Marín and Nacif. A few days later, he telephoned to say that a friend of his, Xavier Olea, had been following my case and was prepared to defend me.

I met with Xavier and his son, Xavier Jr., at a restaurant in the Condesa district. Jorge was with me, too. The two of us gave them a brief overview of the case, and I presented them with a copy of my book. His voice raspy from the effects of thousands of cigarettes smoked over a lifetime, Olea assured us he had no problem going up against powerful politicians like Yunes, Emilio Gamboa, or Mario Marín, and much less against businessman Kamel Nacif. He gave us a quote for how much it would cost to secure his legal services. Jorge and I blinked at each other in silence for a moment; then we agreed to think it over and call to let him know.

I paid a visit to the head of Random House the following day and told him that I had finally located a good lawyer—a proper one this time—but I needed money. The royalties from my book weren't due for another year, so they agreed to cut me a check for an advanced portion of them, but it wasn't enough. The truth was that all the royalties in the world couldn't cover such fees.

I was beginning to understand that one aspect of the concerted, strategic efforts being employed by Governor Marín, Kamel Nacif, and Succar Kuri's lawyers—a total of half a dozen law firms working against me—consisted of wearing me down physically and financially. Each one of them individually threw the entirety of his legal resources into multiplying the number of summonses, psychological evaluations, and submissions of additional evidence I had to juggle. They were so good at it that on one particular week, I was under obligation to appear before courts in Cancun, Mexico City, and Puebla—all on the same day. Kamel had said it on one of the recordings: "I'm going to sue her over and over again, until she begs for forgiveness."

Olea's firm calculated they would need four lawyers working my case full-time in order to deal with the avalanche of legal requirements. That meant purchasing four round-trip tickets once a week for the eight or nine months they estimated the trial would last. In addition to their fees, we would have to cover the cost of their meals and lodging. I rented an apartment in downtown Cancun for them to use. On top of all of this, I had my innumerable trips to the capital city to make. The special prosecutors for crimes against women and for crimes against journalists were asking me to appear practically every third day, in addition to the many appointments I had scheduled to sit for psychological and medical evaluations, give testimony, verify information, and present witnesses. The litany was never-ending, and so were the costs. But after meeting with my older brother, Jorge, my sister, and my father, we came to the joint decision that if I agreed to see this thing through, they would help me pay for my defense as well as my case against the governor. I telephoned Olea and explained my financial situation to him, and we reached an agreement. I finally had a new lawyer, one who wouldn't allow himself to be bought or intimidated. I slept very soundly that night.

Xavier Olea Peláez had risen to fame in Mexico as a result of his work on "the Braun case," which dealt with the murder of Merle Yuridia Mondain, a girl barely seven years of age. The case had rocked the nation in October 1986 when reports surfaced that Alejandro Braun Díaz, alias "The Jackal" and now a fugitive from justice, had kept the child chained up in his apartment, where he beat and raped her repeatedly for months before finally killing her.

Olea Peláez acted as guardian of the little girl's case. He was originally hired by her parents before continuing to work on a pro bono basis after the latter withdrew, and he became the first litigant to ever bring a criminal accusation against a Mexican Supreme Court justice. In 1988 Justice Ernesto Díaz Infante Aranda had pressured judge Gilberto Arrendondo Vero to rule favorably in the suit brought by Alejandro "the Jackal" Braun Díaz after he was accused of the minor's homicide. Olea successfully demonstrated that the judge received US$500,000 from Braun Díaz's lawyer, Enrique Fuentes León, in exchange for helping the girl's killer flee the country. The judge spent eight years and six months in prison on charges of corruption.

Justice Díaz Infante died in 2007 at the age of seventy-seven while under house arrest, where he was residing in accordance with Mexican laws allowing individuals over the age of seventy to serve out their sentences in their homes. It was the most notorious case of corruption involving a federal judge in the entire history of Mexico . . . up until then.

And that was what I needed—to make sure that if Marín or Nacif attempted to buy off, or had already bought off, the authorities, we could follow the trail wherever it led without finding ourselves on the losing side in the corruption case, as happens to millions of Mexican women and men who end up being chewed up and spat back out by the criminal justice system every year.

The country's criminal justice system is organized on the assumption that all victims lie; as such, they are forced to jump through a disgraceful series of hoops, including long, tiresome evaluations—psychological testing, in other words—in order to determine whether the individual filing an accusation against someone is speaking the truth. The first evaluation to which the Attorney General's Office subjected me was carried out by a young, inexperienced psychologist. She showed up in Cancun one day with no warning, and I was taken to an office where I was kept from ten o'clock in the morning until after nine o'clock at night with no access to either food or drink, as though I were a delinquent rather than a victim. Ostensibly, the idea behind these psychological evaluations is to determine the victim's level of emotional stability. The authorities use all means necessary to make sure victims fear and distrust the expert specialists conducting the tests, so that the latter can then report that "the victim was uncooperative, because he or she was unable to establish a relationship of trust with the examining psychologist" who had been sent to rout around in the victim's mind using a series of outdated analytical methods. My first evaluation was inadmissible, because the examiner had failed to adhere to the specifications outlined in the Istanbul Protocol, which is used to establish whether an instance of torture has taken place. I was told that I would have to submit to a second evaluation. At each of the sessions, I was asked to describe in ever greater detail not only the facts of what had happened to me but also the emotions I had experienced, in order to evaluate the extent of the emotional damage caused. I was, as I confessed to my own therapist one afternoon when I couldn't stop crying, no longer able to tell which was more traumatizing for me—what the agents had done to me, or the systematic abuse on the part of the authorities who were trying to prove that no crime had in fact been committed. Meanwhile, stacks of overwhelming evidence were lying patiently upon the desks of bureaucrats for whom the mere mention of the name Kamel Nacif was enough to set them quaking in their boots. I discovered something new with each evaluation, and I sought comfort in my diary. On my own, in my home, I would write and write until physical and emotional exhaustion got the better of me and I fell asleep.

It wasn't until one Friday evening, after having spent eight hours in the company of a criminologist and a victimologist sent by the PGR, that I finally understood where I had gotten the strength I needed to go on.

The experts required me to go over and relive every second of the illegal arrest that took me across five states in twenty hours, my mind accosted all the while by two ever-present questions: *When would they kill me? Where would they dump my body?* I finally realized why I had survived the repeated, cruel torments of those two Judicial Police agents who were carrying out the orders given to them by a businessman and a governor intent upon teaching me a lesson and giving me a good smacking to force me to shut my mouth; I finally realized why I had come through it all with as much sanity as I had.

The criminologist was questioning me with pointed insistence about every humiliating detail of my torture—*Why do you say that you were tortured? How are you going to prove it? Why are you crying?*

What are you so afraid of—tell me, what is it? Are you aware that there are even crueler tortures whose effects are visible on the body? What are you so afraid of? And it was at this point that I burst into tears and shouted, "That my body might never be found! That my family might never be able to come to peace with my death!"

To conclude the evaluation, the victimologist asked me how I had managed to maintain my sanity in the face of all the pressure and fear. When I got home later that night, I spent twenty minutes standing under the shower, my sobs lost amid the sound of the fresh water falling all around me, and finally, suddenly, I realized how it was that I was able, at least for a few hours, to sleep at night, when demons rouse themselves and roam.

It was the presence of loving arms, that precise, warm crook of space between my partner's collarbone, his shoulder, and his beating heart, that small patch of skin waiting for me and welcoming me on sad nights. It was there that I found peace every time the moon shone down disquietingly. My head and my body nuzzled up against him in order to find the tranquility to dream that someday soon, I would wake up and find the nightmare had ended. My lover's arms became a ship, carrying me to that safe harbor almost nobody in my country believes in—the hope of a shared cause.

And throughout those 270 days there were other arms, too: the arms of fraternal affection; the arms of feminist supporters; the arms of a stranger in the middle of the street reminding me that I wasn't alone in this fight; the virtual embraces of readers sending me their prayers; the bracing words of journalists who, out of solidarity, have never allowed my voice to fall silent. There were the arms of my thirteen-year-old niece, Paulina, who caresses my cheeks with her soft, young hands, who is untouched by fear, who speaks to me with innocent wisdom in her voice and tells me that everything is going to be fine, and the bad guys don't always win.

Before going to bed at night, I turn over the words brought to life by Eduardo Galeano, and I will appropriate a wise phrase of his to use here: "Torture is not a means of wresting information, rather it is a ceremonial confirmation of power." I smile as though the Uruguayan writer had personally offered me one of his warm embraces. I was able to understand, then, that I was the victim of a comity of criminal and political powers. And I slept for a few hours in peace, surviving the nightmares brought on by the memory of the armed agents and the state of uncertainty into which they plunged me from that day on.

The victimologists keep asking me, *Have you been sleeping?* And I respond to them truthfully: If I hadn't been sleeping these past nine months, even if only for a few hours each night, madness would have killed me long ago. But, you know, if a person is managing to sleep at night then it must necessarily mean that they have been lying all along about being tortured. And I, my eyes brimming with my soul's salt tears, calmly reminded them that the loving arms that encircle me—the people I love, the individuals I share my life and my dreams with—had given me the peace of mind I needed to become a survivor rather than a perennial victim. But the system doesn't like survivors; they want us to go on being victims, to remain subjugated, in order to remind us who holds the reins. I told them that the power to transform oneself is found in love and hope, but such displays of sentimentality ultimately have no place on official reports, because the uncanny strength of police torture and state-sponsored violence belongs to those who choose to employ their power to silence and wear people down, rather than to discover the truth.

My dear friend and poet Ángel Petisme wrote, "It's no fair crying without learning." And that's precisely what we're doing in Mexico—shining light on the wreckage, and crying. All in order to wrench from the rubble of life a lesson that will give us at least some small indication, some sign of hope that we might one day succeed in shrugging off this yoke of corruption, and that future generations might know what it is to live in a country where justice is possible.

CONGRESS STEPS IN

On April 4, 2006, American judge David K. Duncan authorized the extradition of the pedophile Jean Succar Kuri to Mexico, and by the 18th of that same month, the Mexican Congress had requested that the Supreme Court of Justice of the Nation exercise its authority to assert jurisdiction and investigate the alleged violations of my human rights. A multi-partisan group of congressional deputies came to me and asked that I help them collect evidence in order to draw up a document with which to petition the Supreme Court. I went without sleep for a week as I rushed to get my evidence together, and I was then ushered by David, a young congressional lawyer, to the capital.

A few days later, I was awakened by a telephone call—it was David. He informed me that the nation's highest court had taken on my case, and I immediately start crying upon getting the news. I phoned Jorge and told him, "The Supreme Court has accepted my case! The deputies in Congress say there's a chance the 'Precious Guv" could be impeached!"

We celebrated this development as a small, partial victory, for we had been craving some progress and good news in the case. The Court had accepted Congress's petition and ordered the creation of a preliminary investigative commission. The commission's goal, as I was informed in the offices of Justices Emma Meza Fonseca and Óscar Vázquez Marín at the Supreme Court building, is to ascertain whether there is enough material to justify initiating impeachment proceedings against the governor. Now I would have to divide my time between even more courts, gather yet more evidence, and convince my witnesses from Cancun and Puebla to give testimony at the Supreme Court in Mexico City, as well. It would not be easy task.

On the night of July 5, Jean Succar Kuri was extradited to Mexico. I received a phone call from a federal agent who had become a good source for me in the case.

"They're bringing him over right now in a PGR plane; you can notify the press if you like."

I was at Jorge's apartment in Mexico City. We switched on the television and saw Succar Kuri, looking older than ever, making his way down the steps of a private jet. Surrounded at all times by an escort of agents, he was questioned by my colleagues in the press. The phone rang—the media wanted my opinion. How did I feel now that the subject of my investigation was back in Mexico? I saw him wave a kindly good-bye to the federal agents as he disappeared through the door of the Cancun prison, a low-security facility.

Then in the last days of July of that same year, in the heated days of battle, Quintana Roo state attorney general Bello Melchor Rodríguez Carrillo stated that, "during Governor Hendricks's term of office, his public servants were known to have aided Succar in his escape, and appropriate response measures were never taken." Telephone recordings made public by Carmen Aristegui, *La Jornada*, *El Universal*, and *Reforma* in September included one particular conversation between Nacif and Governor Hendricks, still head of the state of Quintana Roo at the time when the recording was made, in which the latter asked the former to do him a favor and help director Alfonso Arau film a movie in the town of Tulum. And sure enough, Arau filmed his *Zapata* in that very Riviera Maya town, thanks to the good offices and financial investment of a Lebanese associate and friend of Nacif's.

One Saturday around lunchtime, I was finally, for once, back in my own home, sitting in front of the balcony door, writing in my diary, when I received a call from reporter Carlos Loret de Mola. He told me that he had just conducted an interview with Succar from the jail and that it was going to air on Monday. It's not one to be missed, my friend advised me.

Seated before the cameras, Jean "El Johnny" Succar Kuri, in a sorry imitation of Joaquín Pardavé's Baisano Jalil,[13] acknowledged

---

13. Translator's Note: *El Baisano Jalil* is a film from the golden age of Mexican cinema, and director Joaquín Pardavé's most famous work. It tells the story of a family of Lebanese immigrants living in Mexico. The misspelling of the term paisano ("countryman" or "compatriot") in the title is meant to reflect the Lebanese protagonist's accent when speaking Spanish.

that Miguel Ángel Yunes Linares, who had now been appointed Secretary of Public Security of Mexico, was a friend of his and that the two had known each other for fifteen years. He also admitted that Kamel Nacif financed his defense to the tune of US$300,000. The details of the story were coming together, but the Cancun judge was still refusing to allow that my case and the Succar case be related in any manner.

Almost immediately after the interview was broadcast, a cascade of events stripped me of the small amount of peace of mind I had managed to recover. In early August, four individuals stole my case file, which had been created just a few months earlier, from the National Human Rights Commission (CNDH). It was the most complete, extensive dossier regarding my case in existence, and if it were to fall into Marín's hands, he would have access to the names of my key witnesses. The commission filed a criminal report with the Mexico City Attorney General's Office (PGJDF) in order to request that the robbery be looked into. One of the commission's lawyers asked that I meet him in secret at a café. He revealed to me that the thieves had broken into the offices of Guillermo Ibarra and taken a single item— his laptop computer—before making off in a taxi, but that the offices had gotten the whole thing on tape. He also explained that the police had recovered the computer, its hard drive now missing, from a garbage dump in Puebla, thanks to information given to them by the taxi driver who had been forced to drive the thieves there.

In a baffling move, CNDH president José Luis Soberanes admitted to the media that the story of the laptop's theft was true, but his office tried to downplay its importance weeks later by saying that the theft had nothing whatever to do with my case. Nonetheless, the laptop's owner assured me that all the information pertaining to my case was, in fact, on that computer. Every time we succeeded in shedding a little light on some aspect of the case, the authorities would begin contradicting themselves and foil any forward progress we believed we might have achieved, dragging us backward again.

For example, on Thursday, March 2, Alicia Elena Pérez Duarte, the special prosecutor for crimes against women, acknowledged in an interview with *La Jornada*'s Gustavo Castillo that Succar Kuri's network was operating internationally. An extract from that interview, transcribed below, serves to illustrate the incoherence of the country's judicial system—I was living with countless death threats and an accusation against me, guarded day and night like a criminal by federal agents, and the individuals about whom the authorities knew every last detail went about their business in the world with absolute impunity, smiling free and easy, buying up officials and ad time in order to protect themselves while openly revealing their ties to powerful politicians.

INTERNATIONAL CONNECTIONS IN THE SUCCAR KURI CASE
La Jornada, Thursday, March 2, 2006
By Gustavo Castillo García

Jean Succar Kuri fulfills his humble role as head of an interconnected web of pedophilia, sex tourism, and white slave trade networks operating in the Mexican states of Baja California, Mexico, Puebla, Chiapas, Veracruz, and Quintana Roo, as well as in the nation's capital, Mexico City.

"These are not Mexican networks designed for Mexican consumption," as "multiple international connections" have been identified, in the words of the special prosecutor. This same public servant, who works under the Attorney General of Mexico (PGR), explained that the journalist Lydia Cacho "never realized just how far-reaching the network was," and that Succar Kuri's detention "does not mean that anyone can declare victory" or even that his networks have been dismantled, as it is impossible to rule out the prospect that some women may have been taken to such places as Taiwan or Singapore, after having been deceived into believing they were going to be offered work as models, for the purpose of forcibly prostituting them. Pérez Duarte confirmed that there are details in the Succar case that point to involvement on the part of the executive secretary of the nation's Secretariat of Public Security, Miguel Ángel Yunes Linares.

CASTILLO GARCÍA: Does a large-scale pedophilia network exist in Mexico?

PÉREZ DUARTE: More like a series of networks. One large-scale network was already uncovered. It all starts in Cancun, or rather, in Tapachula.[14] The girls are taken from there to Cancun, they're exploited there, but they come to Cancun from all over the world, and apparently there are some other connection points, as well.

CG: In Tijuana, Veracruz, and Juarez?

PD: Precisely. There's another in downtown Mexico City. We're talking about the central region of our republic.

CG: Are they all working together?

PD: Very probably. And not only at the national level, but on an international scale, as well.

What we need to do is to appeal to all the people who think it's 'normal' that high-class escorts are being offered at our country's tourist resorts, but it's nothing more than prostitution, and when the escorts in question are particularly young, it's most likely pedophilia.

CG: Does any of this have to do with Succar Kuri and the accusation filed against him by Lydia Cacho?

---

14. Translator's Note: Town on the southern border of the Mexican state of Chiapas with Guatemala, located to the southwest of Cancun.

PD: Absolutely, this is one of the large-scale networks regarding which the PGR has put together very thorough documentation. In the Succar Kuri case, specifically, multiple international connections have been shown to exist. More than were previously thought.

CG: And Tijuana, Veracruz, Juarez, and Cancun form part of that larger network Succar Kuri is involved in?

PD: Correct, or rather, that network of networks, because although links exist, we can't say with absolute certainty that they are all part of the same network with one single head. If that were the case, it would mean that if we caught that one person, we could dismantle everything. I'm wouldn't declare victory just yet.

CG: Are you referring to some sort of interaction between economic and political powers?

PD: That's exactly what I'm referring to. Very "upstanding" businessmen consider it "normal" that they're being offered these services [sexual services] in hotels, and they're using them.

CG: Do you have any information connecting Cancun and Juarez?

PD: There are significant similarities between the two. I've been receiving some meaningful information coming out of Mexico State.

CG: Is it true that after being tricked into believing they are going to be given work as models, these underage girls are later murdered or disappeared and their families never hear from them again?

PD: Exactly, that's how it works.

CG: Does that also include the possibility that some of them left Mexico, "convinced" that they were going to work as escorts, and that they were sent to Taiwan or Singapore?

PD: I don't even know why you're asking me, you have more information than I do. That's part of our work. It's part of what the Assistant Attorney General's Office for Special Investigations on Organized Crime (SEIDO) is investigating, because these are not Mexican networks designed for Mexican consumption, we should be clear on that point.

CG: Is Succar the head of the larger network?

PD: What we have is a visible head, we could say that we have one of the leaders, but I'm still not convinced that he's the head of it.

CG: Is that why the Lydia Cacho case is so important?

PD: Yes. Moreover, in my opinion, the case isn't about Lydia Cacho, in my opinion the real case is Succar Kuri. She's being persecuted because there are those who wish to cover the whole dirty thing up, and Lydia isn't allowing them to do that.

CG: Are you investigating financial operators working for Succar in the central part of the country? Might we be talking about operators and recruiters in Juarez with connections in the Cancun area?

PD: That's what it's looking like, and that's the side of things that falls outside of my area of operation, it's in SEIDO's hands.

CG: You are in possession of information regarding these networks of collusion, is that correct?

PD: Not in the Juarez cases, but in others. We are certainly receiving information.

CG: Some names have started coming out in connection with
this pedophilia network, like Miguel Ángel Yunes, Kamel Nacif,
even the governor himself, Mario Marín. Is your office going to
investigate them?

PD: The Supreme Court is looking into the matter. It's true that
what we're seeing is the governor of Puebla and his relationship
with Nacif, and how they affected Lydia Cacho, but, naturally, the
investigation the Court has underway will necessarily have to cast
a wider net than that. The rest of us officials should be carrying
our notebooks around, taking notes, seeing what's going on, doing
our work, but we have to wait, necessarily, for the Court to release
its results.

CG: Is Miguel Ángel Yunes's name mentioned in any of the files
being used to request Succar Kuri's extradition?

PD: Some of the victims mention him as being one of the people
who visited Succar Kuri. That's how his name comes up.

Gustavo Castillo García's interview launched an avalanche of follow-
up interviews. "Now we're really getting somewhere!" my colleagues
said to me. Kamel is sure to be arrested, and Marín will be brought
up on impeachment charges.

But I had other concerns—anonymous calls coming in on my
cell phone from unknown numbers, and rumors coming out of the
Cancun prison, which had now grown too numerous to ignore, to
the effect that Succar was planning a jailbreak. Pedro Flota, the
Quintana Roo secretary for public security, had alerted the PGR to
the fact that the Cancun jail was not the ideal place to be holding

such highly dangerous prisoners. And so on August 17, in complete secrecy, the authorities transferred Succar Kuri to the Chetumal Correctional Facility. A week later, after completing an evaluation of the prisoner, Quintana Roo criminal court judge Sergio López Camejo asked that the Federal Preventive Police (PFP)[15] admit Succar to the Altiplano prison in Toluca, as the inmate had been determined to be extremely dangerous. According to the request filed by Camejo, following an investigation conducted by the state Secretariat of Public Security (SSP), Succar Kuri was discovered to have been involved with a dangerous extortion ring operating inside the Chetumal and Cancun prisons. The media revealed that Emma, Succar's victim, paid him several visits over the course of those weeks, and that she was accompanied on every occasion by his lawyers. My uncertainty grew, as did my sadness.

FIRST WARNING: ATTEMPTED MURDER

I had been receiving calls on my cell phone from an unknown number; the person on the other end would breathe heavily for a few moments and then hang up. Then the calls began coming in on my apartment's landline, until I eventually had to unplug the phone every evening upon arriving home. In the final days of October 2006, I got a phone call from Chetumal—a special agent at the prison there asked for my fax number. He said he was an admirer of mine and had read my book; he respected my bravery and needed to warn me that my life was in danger. I gave him my office number, and he faxed over a document explaining that inmates Armando Bocanegra Priego and Juan Ramón González had admitted to having been hired by "El Johnny" at the Chetumal prison to assassinate several witnesses, myself among them. Succar had given them a drawing of my home in Cancun, sketched in blue ink on the back of a napkin. That same morning, when I went out to buy the day's

15. Translator's Note: The Policía Federal Preventiva, under the direction of the Secretariat of the Interior. It was replaced by the Policía Federal (Federal Police, PF) in 2009.

press, a reporter at the local paper *Que Quintana Roo se entere*, had published the document. My security team asked me to leave Cancun for a few days until they could evaluate the threat level. But I refused, because I was sick and tired of having my life continually held hostage by these individuals.

On November 16, 2006, Succar Kuri was moved to the Altiplano high-security prison in Toluca, and a few days later, he orchestrated the biggest jailbreak in the history of Quintana Roo. Nearly one hundred inmates fled the Cancun municipal jail, and three were killed in the commotion. I heard the news from the voice of David Romero, the broadcaster on the most widely followed radio news program in the state: "Authorities have confirmed reports that Succar was involved in planning the prison break, in which he had also hoped to make good his escape."

A deathly silence fell over the vehicle in which my security team and I were riding. Nobody dared speak a word. Things were shaping up worse for Succar Kuri, and better for his victims and for us.

A few days afterward, three more underage girls appeared at SEIDO to report crimes committed by Succar Kuri. We learned that they belonged to a separate group of girls who had never met Emma, the original accuser. Two additional female witnesses came forward to give testimony regarding the trafficking of minors to the United States, and they also provided the authorities with new names of businessmen involved in the scheme. While the media continued their coverage of the story, bills were being debated in the lower chamber of Congress that would require more severe punishments for pedophiles and producers of child pornography. A few bills were likewise proposed to decriminalize different journalistic efforts, and a new law to that effect was eventually passed.

In the midst of this whirlwind of activity, exhaustion took hold of me, and sadness, as well. My therapist told me that I had to stop— my body was revolting against the enormous quantities of adrenaline I was constantly producing in order to maintain my current level of activity—but I couldn't. Both my freedom and the lives of the girls were still at risk. I felt that the moment I stopped responding to each blow, the moment I stopped denouncing the new outrage of the day or stopped filing counterclaims in response to irregularities in the legal process, the "demons" would know that the time to attack me had come.

With the constant comings and going across the country, I came to view every return home as a momentary respite, an oasis. Seeing my friends, having dinner together, and sharing in moments of laughter brought back another side of my humanity to me. But then something happened that filled me with deep sadness. I had arranged to meet at a restaurant with a group of my closest male friends, a handful of influential businessmen and journalists who, behind their masks of power, happen to be lovely human beings. I arrived late to the meal, as I had to come straight from the airport following a trip I had made to receive an award. From the very first moment of my arrival, the references to the great fame I had acquired were constant, to the point that I was forced to make a joke in order to put an end to that particular topic of conversation.

"Fame is a burden; what I have isn't fame, it's notoriety for continuing to be alive, for refusing to negotiate my dignity. Fame is what artists have."

But one friend in particular wouldn't let the issue drop.

"Oh, come on, Cacho," he countered, puffing on his cigar, "the truth is you've got fame and fortune, you're even on CNN, and you've won a ton of awards!"

My throat tightened as tears welled up inside me. *What the hell is going on here?* I wondered. I couldn't speak, and I didn't want to cry, not there, not in front of my friends, my friends who were supposed to be supporting me and after so many years of friendship should have known by then exactly what kind of person I am. And now here I was, suddenly having to defend myself, to explain how it feels to fear you'll be murdered, to explain the fear that rises out of bed with you each morning as though it were some kind of unshake-able shadow. And *fortune?* I had never lived for money; that was a personal choice made long ago. I lived modestly off the money I earned from the articles I wrote and from the occasional conference given here and there over the years. The royalties from my book had gone entirely toward financing my trial, and the money from all the donations and awards went to cover the staff members' salaries at CIAM. It was more than I could bear; I got up from the table and announced I was going home.

As I took my leave, I held my friend's gaze and asked him, "You do understand that this isn't some soap opera, right? It's a never-ending battle against organized criminals protected by the Mexican state. When some new fashionable topic comes along and all of this is no longer in the spotlight, *those guys* aren't going to forget about me."

My friends urged me to stay, but I was feeling overwhelmed with sadness, and I preferred the solitude of my home, and silence. That night, I wrote in my diary:

> That idiotic Mexican capacity for the trivialization of serious mat-
> ters like this one, like corruption, is what reinforces the dehumaniza-
> tion, lack of compassion, and mediocrity in which Mexico is mired.
> Everything becomes a joke in the end, a punchline, everything is
> eventually accepted as normal, its importance is downplayed, or
> denied, and then it disappears, dissolves away into our unwillingness to
> transform ourselves; I pity my country. I weep for myself and for those
> who have the power to change it but instead choose to perpetuate the
> status quo.

People were dancing to songs about the "Precious Guv'" in fashionable clubs, there were online video games about him, and snippets of the original, ghastly telephone calls between Nacif and Marín were selling in the form of cell phone ringtones. I would occasionally hear them going off in restaurants, and I would feel instant shivers up and down my spine. At times, people would go so far as to ask, "What, don't you have a sense of humor?" The parodies were slowly crowding out the real issue that lay behind them—the trafficking of women and young girls, organized criminals acting in concert with the political powers that be. Some people actually began confusing me with a soap opera star.

My lawyers informed me that I had to go to the capital city; the Supreme Court would be holding a session and we were required to be present for it. I prepared myself to hear the bad news; it was all I had the energy to do. I was fed up with how the case had been trivialized. And so one early September morning, we took our seats in the first row of the Court's session chamber to hear Justice Ortiz Mayagoitia explain that insufficient evidence had been presented before them for the highest court in the land to take my case under consideration. Deliberations were initiated, and then to my complete surprise and that of my lawyers, the Supreme Court ruled seven to three in favor of widening the scope of the inquest for the "Cacho-Marín case," in order to investigate the so-called "Precious Guv.'" To that end, a second special commission was created, to be presided over by Justice Juan Silva Meza.

"Very good," Olea concluded. "Now you'll have to testify face-to-face with Kamel again. You need to prepare for this—it'll be the last chance you get. You'll have to answer hundreds of questions, and the session will last between five and six hours. The idea is to wear you down, to break you. It will not be a time for tears," he pointed out, as though I weren't already aware of the fact. I left my lawyers' offices that day in a stormy mood.

KAMEL AND SUCCAR SHOW THEIR TRUE COLORS

I think back to my first encounter with the "Denim King." On the morning of May 23, I hung up the phone after a long conversation with my lawyer (at this point, it was still Cuén, the lawyer I had immediately before Olea). I had to be ready—it had just been confirmed that Kamel Nacif would be coming down to the courthouse to face off with me before the judge the following day. I would be face-to-face with the man who had turned me into a hostage of the judicial system. I set the telephone down on my desk, paced around my small apartment, sat down in the living room, and lit a white candle. *How do I feel?* I asked myself, searching in my breath for an honest answer. What I found were mixed feelings. Mere feet away from me would sit the owner of that gravelly voice and its vulgar, pernicious language; practically at arm's length would be the man who, while I was being transported by the State Judicial Police agents from Cancun to Puebla, had snickered the words "Vengeance is a dish best served cold." And not only him, because Hanna "Juanito" Nakad, the mastermind behind the plan to have me raped and beaten in jail, would be there, too. Part of me wished never to have to be near them, but another part of me was experiencing a feeling of solid certainty that the only way to exorcise the fear I had of my tormentors was to face them head on, with the truth acting as my shield.

I'm ready, I told myself. *This will be a chance to show them that a woman can stand up to them without fear, to remind them that they are not the masters of the world.*

I thought back to the indigenous women of Acteal, Chiapas, whom I had interviewed following the massacre that took place there. They had faced paramilitary assassins, and when I spoke to them, I asked them if they'd felt scared.

"We have nothing to lose other than our lives," one of them replied with the purest sincerity.

At the time, her response struck me as brutal; now I couldn't agree more. For several days now, professional colleagues from different states across the country and international correspondents, as well, had been calling to find out my opinion on the proceedings and to let me know that they would be in attendance on my court date. And not one failed to ask whether I felt scared. I replied honestly—I said that even stronger than my fear was my desire to remain alive and free.

As I write these lines, I can recall every event as though it were yesterday. A few days earlier, Paty—one of the girls who had survived the abuses of Succar and his accomplices—told me that if she had the opportunity to face the man protecting her rapist, she would tell him that we don't want any more corruption. With this idea in mind, we at CIAM immediately had T-shirts made up bearing the slogan "No more pedophiles, no more corruption, no more impunity." On the morning of the 24th, after meditating and taking a bath, I donned the shirt; when I looked in the mirror before heading out the door, I felt armored by these three simple demands shared by tens of thousands of people. I felt as though the forty thousand people who had taken to the Puebla streets to march in protest and all the other people following the news of my case day in and day out were with me, somehow, in those three phrases. I felt prepared.

I climbed into the armored SUV, and we pulled up outside the courtroom, located inside the Cancun prison, at 10:05 in the morning. The media were already there waiting when I walked in with my lawyer. Journalists and cameramen crowded around the table in the room; the judge stepped out of his small chambers and warned them all two or three times that if they didn't maintain order, he would have them sent out.

"This is a public trial," one journalist declared in a challenging tone, and a few beads of sweat trickled down the face of the judge where he stood not two yards away from me.

The look on Nacif's face was one of a man wild with rage and struggling to maintain his cool. I glanced at him calmly, head on; then I turned my torso so that he could see my shirt. His eyes fixed on the words, and a bright red flush burst across his face. When the time came for his statement, he said that I had been lying about everything, and he reaffirmed his accusation.

I had submitted the evidence from the Succar case, along with the victims' testimony, to the federal authorities, but the judge, avoiding my eyes, stated that no connection existed between my case and the Succar case. How could I possibly defend myself for having written an account of my investigations into a child exploitation ring if the judge would not allow me to corroborate the contents of the book? That's Mexican law for you, my lawyer explained. But by that same logic, I argued, a drug dealer could bring defamation charges against any journalist who happened to be following his case while he was in jail awaiting sentencing after having been extradited. Exactly, my lawyer replied, although he would need a judge to accept the case and issue an arrest warrant—which is precisely what had happened here.

Nacif and his lawyers smiled with self-satisfaction. "The Denim King" persisted in his assertion that he was telling the truth.

When my turn came, I asked him calmly, watching as his eyes darted away from mine every time I attempted to hold his gaze, why his defense was being funded by the pedophile Succar Kuri. And though the judge would not allow the question to stand, the businessman's lawyers couldn't stop their client from leaning forward toward me in his seat, like a panicky bull readying himself for the charge, and whispering in a snarl, "Goddamn you fucking lady."

The judge trembled in his perch but spoke not a word of rebuke to Nacif.

Later, Hanna "Juanito" Nakad took the stand. He stated that his friend Kamel Nacif is an upstanding man incapable of committing the "disgusting acts" he is accused of in my book. At last, staring him straight in the eye, I got my chance to ask him if he considered it an example of *upstanding* behavior to have ordered the prisoners at the jail to beat and rape me. To the utter shock of all those present, his white skin turned crimson as he spat despotically in reply, "That rape was never carried out in the end."

His lawyers gaped in horror, but his words had already been taken down by the court stenographer. I felt like a soccer player who'd just managed to slip the ball past the unbelieving eyes of the goalie, right straight to the back of the net, in a single, clean, glorious shot.

Five more hours went by before the session came to a close. Nacif had already behaved abusively with the journalists who had tried to interview him earlier, as he entered the courtroom, and the scene as he exited was very similar. Coming out to show their support for me that day were members of various Cancun NGOs, the feminist activist and actor Jesusa Rodríguez, and Julio Glockner and other representatives of Puebla's civil society. A public prosecutor had warned us that the judge had received veiled threats from Nacif's lawyers, as well as from Nacif himself; this information seemed credible in light of the judge's refusal to admit that my detention had been a ploy dreamed up by Nacif to protect Succar Kuri. If the evidence proceeding from the testimony of those who had been victims of the pedophile and had specifically named Nacif and other associates of Succar was not deemed admissible, how was I to defend myself? As if this weren't enough, their defense strategy consisted of trying to prove that because I don't hold a university degree from a journalism school, I cannot be considered to be a journalist and, therefore, I had no right to appeal to the principles of public interest or freedom of expression.

I would later come to believe that this first lawyer of mine was intentionally "letting the case go." There were threats and corruption everywhere we turned. The feeling of anxiety produced by not knowing whether your defender is going to give in to corruption is something that is impossible to describe. A few nights after learning that the judge would not be allowing any further evidence because my side had not submitted it in time, I had a clear vision of my lawyer seated with Nacif and Mario Marín's people and handing over my documents to them. More than angered, I felt deeply saddened and emotionally drained.

In late September of that year, I had my second and final face-to-face session with Kamel Nacif, this time with Olea defending me. Nacif had new representation, as well. He showed up at the courtroom in the presence of a legal team from Farell, an influential Mexican law firm. When I entered, while the Public Ministry official was finalizing preparations and everyone was getting settled in their seats, I walked straight over to Nacif, who was leaning up against one of the walls. I positioned myself directly in front of him, standing very close, and informed him quietly, "Kamel, every time you look in my eyes, all those abused girls will be looking back out at you."

I retired quickly, and he fixed me with a look of wide-eyed disbelief and hatred that was captured perfectly by the several video and still cameras in the room.

As the session was drawing to a close, when it became clear that he was going to be unable to prove the "millions in losses" his textile factories had, according him, suffered as a result of the words I had written, Nacif flew into a rage. His lawyers, frantically chewing their gum, could do nothing to calm his furor. At one point, the judge whispered to me, "Step over there, you don't want to get yourself beaten up."

My lawyers and I couldn't believe our ears—instead of alerting the livid Nacif to the inappropriateness of his actions, the judge was making me responsible for my own protection from any possible act of violence inside the courtroom. As though he were not the authority figure in the situation!

Then, when Nacif realized he had run out of arguments, he began to shout at me, "Prove it in courts, lady, not in the media. You come off more like the Virgin of Guadalupe."

With his characteristic lack of verbal skills, what he was trying to say was that the press had painted him as a monster and me as a saint.

When the session was over, I returned to the office and met with some of the pedophile ring's victims. They had been following the news of my battle for months. We offered each other encouragement and strength. For years, these girls and women believed their rapists to be untouchable, all-powerful beings; now their tormentors were humans, plain and simple, and standing up to them was a woman just like them.

"It's true, we are all Lydia Cacho," the mother of one of Succar's survivors observed with a beautiful, pearlescent smile.

I could only respond, "And Lydia Cacho is all women. We're in this together."

The days went by, and it was a veritable three-ring circus of activity. First, I had the case against me—I had to defend myself against Kamel Nacif and go head-to-head with him in long, six- to nine-hour sessions marked by intense tension and aggression, while simultaneously gathering evidence and remaining vigilant to any possible acts of corruption on the part of the authorities. Second, in the case I had brought against the "Precious Guv'" and Kamel Nacif—I had to put together materials, interview people, and try to locate witnesses willing to testify. Finally, there was the Succar case, also sometimes referred to as "the Cancun pedophile case"—more and more girls and mothers had been coming to CIAM Cancun seeking help, and although my colleagues were doing an extraordinary job of fielding all their requests, it still fell to me to deal with certain complicated formal procedures and to help coordinate everything, for no one understood better than I the intricacies of the case and the dangers involved. After holding his own meeting with one young victim who had been abused by Succar Kuri from the age of twelve, Xavier Olea agreed to defend the girls, as well. Ms. Acacio had long since given up her defense of the victims, having herself received kidnapping and death threats, not to mention the fact that she had other cases to defend.

Faced with this panorama, I had an urgent need to carve out some time for myself—to work, pay my electricity and telephone bills, earn enough to keep CIAM going, and take care of my physical and emotional health. Then one afternoon, my lawyer told me that I would have to give testimony in the Succar case. I had been subpoenaed three times after similarly preparing myself to face Kamel Nacif's associate and accomplice, but each of those times, the judge had ruled to accept the petition made by the pedophile's lawyers to postpone my appearance. The day finally arrived, however, on May 3, 2007.

I had only ever seen him in photographs and video footage. Like millions of others, I'd watched the video in which Jean Succar Kuri, with a sadist's cruelty, describes how much he enjoys seeing five-year-old girls bleed when he penetrates them. I arrived at the El Altiplano high-security prison—more commonly known as Almoloya—at 9:30 in the morning, accompanied by the underage girls' lawyers, and we spent fifteen minutes at the entrance checking in and undergoing various screening processes. There is no cell phone coverage in a two-kilometer radius surrounding the prison, and the initial sensation upon entering the isolated area is strange. The most dangerous prisoners in the country are held here. No one is even allowed to bring in food or drinks; you walk in and walk out with nothing more than the clothes on your back. I never imagined I would end up spending twelve hours there without eating or drinking a single thing.

The hearing rooms are small. When I walked inside, my gaze settled immediately on a clear glass window reinforced with two-inch-thick bars. Through them, I glimpsed the gaunt, pallid face of the man who was looking more than ever like his friend and protector Kamel Nacif. I was wearing my shirt that read "No more pedophiles, no more corruption, no more impunity." I stepped forward and stood in front of Succar Kuri where he sat, and the expression on his face became distorted; he eyed my shirt carefully, then immediately gestured for his attorneys. A few minutes later, Wenceslao Cisneros, the pedophile's lawyer (who would step down several months later after viewing one of Succar's pornographic videos), requested that the judge order me to cover my shirt, as it was "offensive to the prisoner." The complaint was logged in the court record. The hearing was exhausting, and it wasn't until eleven o'clock at night that we were finally able to leave. It was above all a chance to understand how all the pieces fit together and gave rise to corruption and the creation of the network protecting the pedophile.

It was clear to me that his lawyers lacked a coordinated strategy. In reality, Succar Kuri is indefensible, considering the vast amount of pornographic videos and photographs that had been uncovered in his villas several years back. And on top of that, there is the testimony of those brave creatures, like Margarita and Cindy, who had just barely ceased to be girls when they sat in Succar's line of sight and explained before the courtroom how he had raped and filmed them. Not to mention the work of a handful of professional, honest police agents who had managed to gather a sufficient amount of evidence and testimony for him to be arrested. Nevertheless, three whole years after having first been accused, he was still awaiting sentencing.

Succar Kuri spent his time during the session glaring at me with intense rancor. From time to time he would screw up his face so tightly that his pale lips all but disappeared from sight. We were seated a mere six feet from one another, face to face. The man for whom Kamel Nacif had ordered that I be imprisoned and tortured, for whom Mario Marín had sold out justice itself—and me. At other times, such as when his lawyer insisted that I am not a journalist because I don't hold any sort of professional credential, Succar would raise up his arms and pound them against the barred window before bringing them down to beat his own chest, like a gorilla marking its territory. I stood directly in front of him; he is a small man—at full height he comes up to my chin, just like Kamel. The judge would order him to control himself whenever he made such scandalous gesticulations. He had my book brought out again and again for all to see; since he was not able to touch it through the bars, his lawyers would hold it up for him and he would point at something written on the pages and pose questions to me about whatever it happened to be. From one moment to the next, my appearance, which I was ostensibly making in the capacity of a witness, had morphed completely—now it was almost as though I were the one who was on trial. How clearly I recalled then the utterances and arguments that Kamel Nacif, "the King of Denim and Cognac," had been aiming at me for a year now! There was one particularly critical moment when I even found myself asking the judge if I was making this appearance as a witness who knew the raped girls or, rather, if this was a trial being held against me for having published *The Demons of Eden*. For nearly four hours, Succar's lawyers persisted in their ferocious attacks against me; faced with the impossibility of defending their client, they had turned to attacking me.

I did manage, despite all this, to tell the stories of the terrified girls, to tell how the pedophile's lawyers had offered some of the victims' mothers 200,000 pesos and others 500,000 in exchange for their silence—offers that were accompanied by threats, naturally. Succar insisted that the reason Emma—just one of his many victims—had filed a civil lawsuit against me was that she wanted to demand a portion of my book's proceeds go to her, on the grounds that I "had told her story." The detailed knowledge the pedophile had regarding that suit confirmed our suspicion that it was he, together with Nacif, who was paying for the lawyers she was using to sue me. I remembered how Kamel had promised in one of the recorded telephone calls that after I got out of jail, he would sue me until I "beg forgiveness," until I go "crazy," in his own words. The pedophile and his lawyers were doing their utmost to skirt the main issue under consideration at the trial: namely, the girls and boys who had been raped and used by this man to produce child pornography. I pressed the issue as best I could. Finally, after more than eleven and a half hours, his face contorted and his eyes wild with rage in an expression reminiscent of Hannibal Lecter, Succar let it be known that he was going to end me.

We overheard him with perfect clarity as he instructed

his lawyers to sue me for having published *The Demons of Eden*. Unfortunately, the judge had already left the room by that time. We waited around a short while for some documents requiring our signatures to be printed. Succar was reiterating that it was all my fault he was imprisoned. As he saw it, since he had already managed to use threats and money to ensure some of his victims' silence, I was his only remaining nuisance and obstacle. I, for my part, replied out loud quite simply, "You're not in prison because of my book but because of your own deviant acts. My book exists thanks to the bravery of the girls whose souls you left shattered for life; my book merely tells the truth about why you were almost allowed to walk free with the help of your powerful friends."

We eventually left the main prison complex, ready for the long trek back to the parking lot. As we walked through the beautiful gardens leading out to the main gate, a security van pulled up alongside us. The agent driving it asked, "Are you the reporter?"

With a greater sense of pride in my heart than I had felt at any previous moment, I replied that I was indeed. Behind me, several feet under the ground, sat the man who had possessed, like some amoral demon, the souls and bodies of who knows how many girls and boys. Ahead of me was the fresh, free air, and I breathed it in deeply, happy to find myself in this position that was allowing me to work to recover some small shred of dignity for Mexico.

The agent driving the vehicle offered to give us a lift to the parking lot; then he remarked casually, "Those guys over there are the devil's lawyers. They can walk."

Back in the SUV, for the almost two hours it took to drive back to Mexico City, I sat next to my bodyguard with my face turned toward the window and cried inconsolably. Nobody but those young souls who had lived under this man's cruel yoke could know what it was like to submit to his psychological tortures. I was acutely moved by these young girls and their bravery. *If they're not giving up, nobody else has the right to give up, either,* I thought.

A few months later, that same lawyer who had called me crazy in the press was to give a live interview on the news with Carmen Aristegui. During the broadcast, the lawyer explained that he had quit Succar Kuri's employ because he had seen a video that had been submitted into evidence in which the pedophile, naked from the waist down, sets up a video camera and orders two small girls to undress and lie down on a bed. The video goes on to show explicit footage of their rape.

In the midst of trials and a sincere attempt to take back my life—going out to dinner with my friends, talking about things that had nothing to do with the dramatic unfoldings that occupied so much of my time—I, like one who has traversed the wide ocean and, unable to remain submerged, lifts her face above the surface for a breath, was seeking out spaces where there was happiness and laughter, places far away from the many people beseeching me to help them with their cases, as though I were the country's attorney general. Wherever I went, people would ask me to tell them about the case. I traveled to receive awards, which on the one hand afforded me protection, but on the other hand forced me to publicly narrate the entire disgraceful story of Mexican corruption and impunity again and again. *Who is Lydia Cacho?* and, *Where does she get her strength?* were the two questions I was constantly asked, and I was at a loss for compelling answers. The truth is, to say that I was brought up to never surrender, to explain that I act conscientiously and consistently when translating my principles into thoughts and actions, convinces no one; it's not a heroic argument to say that I'm a woman like any other who has simply decided to defend herself against what she considers to be unjust.

While the Succar case proceeded and we awaited the imminent sentencing of the pedophile in Puebla, "Precious" Marín and State Attorney General Villeda, still refusing to acknowledge the existence and importance of the Succar case, declared again and again that they considered me a liar. They claimed that I was using the episode of my kidnapping as an excuse to garner fame and fortune for myself. The state attorney general even went so far as to say that the contents of my book amounted to mere exaggeration, as the pedophile's guilt had not yet been proven. Not once did she mention the rights of the girls and boys who had been raped and who later reported him, or the fact that in order to proceed with "El Johnny"'s extradition, Judge Duncan had seen with his own eyes several of the child pornography videos Succar had filmed, according to information published in *Proceso*, *La Jornada*, and other outlets.

After I won the case against Kamel Nacif, Marín's team decided to modify their strategy. Their new watchword? Refuse to answer even a single question about the Cacho case, distance themselves publicly from Kamel Nacif, and pretend nothing had happened. Popping up in the press with greater and greater frequency were ads endorsing the Puebla governor, photographic inserts of the "Precious Guv'" in the company of foreign heads of state. His team even published a doctored photo in which Marín is seen apparently sitting between the Secretary of the Interior and the Secretary of Finance. To create this version of the snapshot, published in Puebla's daily *Milenio* newspaper, a designer switched the Puebla governor's head with that of a different governor, the one who had in actuality been flanked by the two secretaries, in order to make it seem as though Marín were the center of attention in the scene. But the ruse was uncovered. Ever since, he has been paying to secure slots for himself on various political speaking tours in order to increase his visibility. The most noteworthy moment came when he was photographed with President Felipe Calderón, who just months earlier, while still on the campaign trail, had proclaimed ecstatically that if elected president, he would see to it that Marín be brought up on impeachment charges. His promise was so full of passionate conviction that he and his local Puebla candidates were seen brandishing red cards, in a soccer-inspired rebuke, to demand that the "Precious Guv'" be expelled from the political game.

Slowly but surely, the powers that be were gaining ground. PRI members that had spoken out strongly against Marín's immorality and corruption were now heard referencing my "exaggeration of the case" instead. Beatriz Paredes, a career politician who had spent a long time moving actively among different feminist groups, who had fought tooth and nail to defend the rights of women, and who had demanded in all manner of forums that gender violence be more adequately addressed, finally rose to the post she had been dreaming of for years: president of the PRI. As soon as she took office, she closed ranks with Emilio Gamboa, who in one of Kamel Nacif's telephone conversations published in the press had called Nacif "Daddy," informing him that the nation's Senate was about to pass a bill dealing with betting at racetracks. In the phone call, Kamel chastises him, telling him no, he doesn't like that law. Gamboa, obsequious and affectionate, says that's fine, he'll "block it," and that if he, Kamel, says so, "that shit's not getting through the Senate." Even Beatriz herself—who had once told me, while seated at my side in a public forum, that she believes ethics are non-negotiable—now chose well-known feminists to relay the message to me that I should leave Governor Marín alone already, claiming that what they did to me wasn't so bad. She, too, had forgotten the girls.

"But thousands of people are tortured in this country—what is this woman complaining about? What makes her so different or so much more important that the Court should trouble itself with one individual case?" Justice Aguirre Anguiano of the Supreme Court of Justice of the Nation had dared to ask.

Eight months after I was released from prison, the nation had become desensitized to my case, had come to see it as something trivial. In a country where the abetment and perpetuation of corruption by political and economic actors is widespread and commonplace, society's only escape valve is moral outrage. But organized crime and the connections between the criminal world and powerful politicians cannot be combated with mere indignation. And so the powerful have only to recur to the simple strategy of shelling out a couple of millions to rebuild a corrupt figure's public image in the press. Some media outlets sign pacts promising to give preferential attention to the whitewashing of a corrupt figure's image over any real news coverage about them, so that whatever topic they had been in the news for falls further and further by the wayside, until the public has completely forgotten about the case. This was, and still is, the tactic employed by Marín's team.

Meanwhile, I continued submitting evidence and gathering witnesses for the Special Prosecutor's Office for Crimes Against Journalists, the Special Prosecutor's Office for Crimes Against Women, and the Supreme Court, while at the same time rehashing my evidence from the Kamel Nacif case in order to defend myself in the civil suit brought against me by Emma, one of the victims being manipulated by Succar. The argument used by the young woman's lawyers in this latter case is identical to that used by Nacif's and Succar's defense teams: I am not a journalist; therefore I had no right to publish my book *The Demons of Eden* in the first place.

6

THE END OF THE LINE

B y the beginning of 2007, it seemed as though I had managed
to put the nightmare behind me, for at the outset of January,
I won my case against multimillionaire Kamel Nacif. In March,
I set off on a sixteen-day tour of the United States, beginning in
Milwaukee on the 23rd of the month, where I received Amnesty
International's Ginetta Sagan Award for my work in defense of the
human rights of women and children.

But there was still a long road to travel. The wheels had
begun to turn at the Supreme Court after an initial investigation
had come to a premature close when suspicions arose that a plot
existed to "cover up" for Governor Marín. Now a second constitutional investigation was underway, headed by Justice Juan
Silva Meza, a respectable, highly ethical lawyer who also served
as a judge at the Criminal Court for many years. On May 3, I
went face-to-face with the Cancun pedophile in a session that
lasted nearly thirteen hours and culminated in yet another death
threat. Despite this, I felt stronger than ever. Over the course of
the last several months, the demons had shown their true colors,

and I had faced them successfully. It appeared the winds were finally in my favor.

Then, barely five days after I had sat with Succar in the session chamber, as I was returning to Mexico City from Juarez with a group of fellow journalists, we were attacked.

My bodyguards were waiting for me at the airport; the PGR had sent an SUV for our use during my stay in the capital city. Journalists Alejandro Páez and Jorge Zepeda, along with director general of *Nexos* magazine Rafael Pérez Gay and his wife, were heading to the same general area of the city, so I offered to give them a lift. Just as we were picking up speed and preparing to pull onto the Viaducto freeway, the SUV began to fishtail, and the driver, who was one of the agents assigned to protect me, instantly slammed on the brakes, swerving to the curb in order to bring the vehicle to a stop. When we got out of the car, we saw that the tire had been blown out. Everything changed, however, when we saw the face of Agent Nuño, my head bodyguard, go pale as she exchanged a series of quick glances with the driver. In her hands, she held the wheel's lug nuts, or fasteners. She hadn't even needed a wrench to pull them free. Everything moved very quickly after that. Agent Nuño told us to step away from the vehicle, that we had to get out of there, and that we should flag down a couple of taxis as quickly as possible. The lug nuts glinted in the light as she held them in the palm of her hand; they were stripped down and scratched, as though they had been gone at with a hacksaw. The wheel was not correctly attached but rather shifted from its proper position on the axle, and the whole thing was about to fall right off, rim and all. We hailed a cab and drove to a colleague's house. Agent Nuño asked me to avoid going outside until they could determine for sure what had really happened.

"Do you think this was intentional?" I asked, still incredulous.

"Yes, ma'am, it may have been an attempt on your life. Please, stay inside—I'm going to report this to my superiors."

It was not until that precise moment that I began to feel worried, and my friends even more so. I decided to telephone SEIDO, but no luck. Then I dialed José Luis Santiago Vasconcelos, the former assistant attorney general for SEIDO, a man with deep knowledge of the Succar and Kamel Nacif cases. I told him what had happened, limiting my comments to a strict description of the facts; at the time, I expected him, an expert in organized crime, to tell me that my security team was overreacting and that what had happened was most likely nothing. I couldn't have been further from the truth. He instructed me to call my lawyers and file a report immediately. Now that Governor Marín was colluding with Nacif and Succar, all three of them stood to lose much more if I persisted in my efforts to bring them to court. Moreover, although Succar's threats had been made from prison, they could not, as Santiago Vasconcelos reminded me, be taken lightly.

At this point, he put me through to a special agent at the AFI, an expert trainer in driving and high-speed chases. I explained once more, in full detail, what had happened to our vehicle, and he responded with the warning that a "job" of that nature, if carried out properly, could have easily killed us. The idea, the expert explained, is for the rear wheel on the driver's side to come completely off its axle. The Suburbans put out that year were notoriously unstable, and had the wheel detached fully, the vehicle would have flipped, and at eighty or ninety miles an hour, the speed at which we had been driving, the accident would most surely have killed us. The following day, I went down to the PGR offices with my lawyers and we filed charges—yet again—with the Office of the Special Prosecutor for Crimes Against Journalists, this time for attempted murder.

In a further act of confirmation of our blighted state, the Special Prosecutor's Office took more than three months to react to our report of the attack. Then one Friday night, as I arrived home, my bodyguards spotted a car parked outside the building, with someone sitting at the wheel. They approach the individual, who said he'd been sent by the PGR to deliver a summons for me. *Ten o'clock at night on a Friday, and the PGR is out delivering summonses?* we marveled.

I took receipt of the document and read in amazement that pursuant to my having filed charges of attempted murder, the PGR was convening me for the very next day—a Saturday, and without the presence of my lawyers—to undergo a psychological evaluation in order to provide further explanations on the attack against me. They did not request to see the vehicle's lug nuts, nor did they ask to interrogate my security team or the other material witnesses, or petition that the PGR immediately hand over the SUV for analysis in order to verify whether or not it had been tampered with. The Special Prosecutor's Office only wanted to determine whether I was in my right mind and telling the truth. I telephoned my lawyers in a fit of outrage. I did not respond to the summons. At the time of this book's publication, the special prosecutor has still not analyzed the vehicle we were traveling in, which remains to this date parked outside the PGR offices, and the lug nuts are still safely tucked away. Meanwhile, a female PRI-party congressional deputy allied to Marín declared mockingly in the press that she herself had filed down the lug nuts, that it was she who had attempted to kill me. A Puebla radio station gave me a cassette with her full statement. I turned it in to the Special Prosecutor's Office—a civil servant there told my lawyer that it was no big deal, that the congresswoman was simply making a joke.

Thankfully, it wasn't all bad news. On June 21, one week before the Supreme Court was expected to present its findings, a group of filmmakers, intellectuals, artists, and social activists ran a full-page spread in the big national newspapers entitled, "Once Upon a Time There Was a Pedophile." With the names of multi-award-winning film directors Alfonso Cuarón, Luis Mandoki, Guillermo del Toro, and Alejandro González Iñárritu heading the list of signatures, the spread quickly became a sounding board for moral outrage, a rallying point for international solidarity, as it called upon the Supreme Court justices to listen to the public's concerns over the case:

> We urge the justices of the Supreme Court to return to the citizens of Mexico our right to trust the courts. So far, the reprisals dealt to Succar's victims and the campaign of persecution against Lydia Cacho would appear to confirm the views of eight out of every ten Mexicans, who believe the reporting of crimes to be useless because the institutions of the state will not afford them the proper protection. If the Puebla authorities are cleared of all responsibility, if the obvious existence of networks propagating child pornography, child abuse, and the trafficking of minors in Mexico is not recognized, it is highly unlikely that any other citizen will dare to step forward and challenge in court those men who use the power of the state to corrupt society and strengthen criminal activities in Mexico.

Among those who lent their names to the text were Noam Chomsky, Ana Claudia Talancón, Sean Penn, Ashley Judd, Milos Forman, Benicio del Toro, Blue Demon Jr., Ángeles Mastretta, Bridget Fonda, Carlos Reygadas, Ana de la Reguera, Charlize Theron, Clive Owen, Susan Sarandon, Woody Harrelson, and Salma Hayek. More than three thousand signatures were gathered, a mixture of the usual, well-known supporters of causes as well as newcomers. The text was sent to the Court. The dedicated, loving solidarity of individuals representing the entire spectrum of religious beliefs and political leanings made us feel safer than ever.

The findings of the Court's investigative committee were finally communicated to the public on June 26, 2007. I was there at the Supreme Court when the session was called to order, with Jorge and my lawyers at my side. For an hour and a half, we listened to Justice Silva Meza. And what a surprise was in store for us! For the very first time in Mexican history, a full and thorough investigation of human rights and women's rights had been conducted by the highest court in the land, without any intrusive meddling by a president and his iron fist.

When Justice Silva Meza presented his conclusions and explained how he and his investigative team had arrived at them, tears welled up in my eyes. For nearly two hours, I managed to abstain from crying in public. Not because it is my belief that tears are demeaning to people in general or to women in particular but because, on the one hand, there are those in the media who will always seek to highlight the dramatic in any situation—the same ones who insisted in response to every single interview I gave that I was playing up my role as the devastated victim. But I wasn't. I was defending my dignity as a woman and my work as a journalist. I had also come to understand by this point that my battle was the battle of millions of Mexican women and men who had been following my story every step of the way, and not because of anything I was doing as an individual, but rather in order to see for themselves whether it was true that the Mexican state, despite all the evidence, could possibly be capable of such complicity. On the other hand, when I chose at times to control my tears in the presence of my colleagues, it was due to the fact that I often feared that if I began to cry, I would end up drowning in my own sadness and become unable to ever return to a position of strength from which to continue the fight. In order to remain brave, to be able to see each act of corruption for what it was, and to respond to every move in this bitter, protracted battle with the indispensible clear-sightedness of a chess player, I needed the inner calm and peace that my daily meditations, together with my convictions and unwavering sense of solidarity, provided.

This time, I told myself, it was different—my country's Supreme Court was acknowledging the crimes committed against the young girls and boys, as well as those committed against my own person for having given them a voice in my book. In underlining the seriousness of the problem of child exploitation in Mexico, Silva Meza remarked, "Journalist Lydia Cacho did not go far enough in her book." For a single, shining moment, I felt I could finally let down my guard and cast off my protective armor—the truth was there for the whole nation to see. What more could we ask?

But then came what felt like a slap to the face, and it instantly checked my tears. Chief Justice Ortiz Mayagoitia gave the court clerk leave to read a statement supposedly written by Justice José de Jesús Gudiño Pelayo, who had lost his voice and was unable to read the statement himself. The stage was set. In his statement, Gudiño called on the Supreme Court to withhold its ruling on the case "until such time as the rules for reaching a determination have been decided upon."

If we compare this to a soccer game played in front of a full stadium of fans, it would be like the referee declaring that there was "no winner" until they conducted a review of the rules by which goals would be defined. Several constitutional lawyers assured me that if the ruling had been in favor of the governor, no one would have asked that the rules be reexamined *a posteriori.*

Justice Silva Meza was visibly taken aback; the media representatives present in the room couldn't believe it, either. But attorneys Aguilar Zínzer and Fabián Aguinaco, two members of the seven-man team defending Governor Marín, stood behind us, unflustered, while the justices cast their votes one after another and agreed to postpone their ruling.

We walked out of the court, and the governor's lawyers, ecstatic and smiling, told the press that they were very satisfied because the Supreme Court justices had heeded their request to protect the rights of Governor Marín. One of them later denied having made the statement, but thanks to a reporter on the scene, his words were recorded for all posterity.

Various analysts concluded that a politically motivated negotiation had taken place between the PRI (Marín's party) and the

PAN in order to smooth the way and set the stage for some difficult agreements on fiscal reform, agreements that the president needed secured, being as they were so instrumental for his economic plans for the country.

But the truth had been spoken that day at the Supreme Court, and the media reflected society's outrage faithfully. And near the end of September 2007, hope came and peeked its head around the corner once more.

After keeping us in suspense for thirty days, the special commission upheld the Court's investigative methodology. The results of Silva Meza's team of justices and lawyers will remain forever in the annals of the Mexican justice system. Below, I have transcribed some of the team's findings, taken directly from the public reading of them made in Silva Meza's own voice.

LAST RECOURSE:
THE SUPREME COURT OF JUSTICE AND JUAN SILVA MEZA

First. That there did exist a coordinated effort between the authorities of the states of Puebla and Quintana Roo to violate the fundamental rights of the journalist Lydia María Cacho Ribeiro, and that the democratic principles of federalism and separation of powers were likewise violated, in particular the principle of judicial independence.

Second. That there did exist repeated, systematic violations of fundamental rights to the prejudice of minors.

Third. That the definitive decision regarding whether or not to proceed with the impeachment charges that may in such cases be brought against high-level servants of the Federation such as graduate of law and Constitutional Governor of the State of Puebla Mario Plutarco Marín Torres shall fall to the Congress of the Union.

Fourth. That as concerns the responsibility on the part of the authorities that participated directly or indirectly in the governor's dealings with the businessman he was aiding, it shall fall to the legislature of each federal entity[16] to analyze the question of whether to initiate the corresponding procedures against the chief justice of the Superior Court of Justice of the State of Puebla, Guillermo Pacheco Pulido, as well against the attorneys general for the states of Puebla and Quintana Roo.

Fifth. That it shall fall to a plenary session of the Superior Court of Justice of the State of Puebla to decide, without the participation of those individuals in question, upon the nature of the conduct of its judicial servants, particularly that of Fifth Criminal Court judge for the State of Puebla, Rosa Celia Pérez González.

Sixth. That it shall fall to the Offices of the Attorneys General for the states of Puebla and Quintana Roo to carry out the penal actions corresponding to corruption of authorities and to crimes against the administration of justice.

Seventh. That it shall fall to all institutions dependent upon the Office of the Attorney General of Mexico, as well as to the Offices of the State Attorneys General, to combat and pursue with all the strength and ingenuity of the State any and all acts of pederasty, child exploitation, and child pornography. To this end, and given that this is a segment of the population whose incomplete development prevents them from understanding the damage caused to them or from participating in its solution, it is suggested that a periodic, public presentation of the findings of such investigations be made, the secrecy or confidentiality of the victim and of the aggressor being justified only when, for reasons

---

16. Translator's Note: Mexico is divided into thirty-two "federal entities," which include the nation's thirty-one states and its single so-called "federal district," Mexico City.

of degree or manner of participation, the victim's identity is apt to become known.

Eighth. That it is hereby recommended that the jurisdictional
courts, when acting to gather proof elements for conviction,
give preference to the rights of the victim, ensuring inasmuch as
possible the full right to participation of the latter's progenitors,
professional advisors, and legal representatives.

In order to arrive at these findings, the public servants working in Marín's administration were investigated, and by judicial order, twenty-one wiretaps were authorized on telephones belonging to the following individuals: Governor Mario Marín, Kamel Nacif, Margarita Santos (Marín's wife), Irma Benavides (Nacif's ex-wife), judge Rosa Celia Pérez, Chief Justice for the Superior Court of Justice of the State of Puebla Guillermo Pacheco Pulido, and others. Taps on the phones of several secretaries and others receiving orders from Marín were also authorized. In a 1,205-page document, which was analyzed with extraordinary meticulousness in issue number 87 of the political magazine *emeequis*, the Supreme Court's special commission unraveled and laid out, step by step, all of the lies and accusations that had formed part of the criminal conspiracy against me.

Justice Silva Meza concluded as follows:

The work of the Investigative Commission revealed that the report
filed by the journalist [Lydia Cacho] provides but a small picture
of the very serious situation in which a large number of minors
find themselves, for in order to confirm the existence of the sexual
abuse of which some of the individuals mentioned by the journalist had been victims, the Investigative Commission was prompted
to verify, with all the resources at its disposal, the various rights
violations that might be affecting a portion of the population. To
that end [. . .] the Investigative Commission requested information

from diverse public and private institutions, especially from those concerned with the prosecution and administration of justice, as these latter constitute the best source of information to which the Supreme Court of Justice has access.

The current Special Prosecutor for the Detection of Crimes Against Sexual Freedom, Its Normal Development, and Public Decency, which operates under the Office of the Attorney General of the State of Quintana Roo, reported the initiation of 1,595 prior inquiries into sexual crimes committed against minors. The delegate from the Special Prosecutor's Office for the Defense of Minors and Families provided sixteen files corresponding to cases of minors who are in their protective custody and in situations of risk, fifteen of them as a result of child sexual abuse and commercial sexual exploitation.

The file containing these findings was submitted to the Congress of the Union's Subcommittee for Initial Analysis. The document was carefully reviewed, and sufficient material was identified to justify a request that Mario Marín be stripped of his political immunity and denied the right to stand for election in the future. Nevertheless, a number of PRI and PAN deputies refused to vote against the "Precious Guv'," among them Diódoro Carrasco, a former PRI-party activist and now a member of the PAN, the party to which President Calderón belongs.

Some of Mexico's most powerful politicians, including the chairman of the Congressional Committee on Finance and Public Credit, Jorge Estefan Chidiac Charbel, have defended the governor fiercely. Chidiac served as Secretary of Social Development for the State of Puebla, and he maintains a close relationship with the "Precious Guv'." Others have taken sides depending on the potential usefulness of "the Lydia Cacho case" in helping them to attack their political enemies. The truth of the matter is that despite the Supreme Court's having carried out an impeccable investigation, despite its findings' having already been translated into legal frameworks for dealing with such issues in the future, and even despite extra time having been granted to the governor's seven lawyers for the submission of evidence in support of his defense, the Congress of the Union still does not seem to understand that every person who votes in favor of and defends the governor is using the power of the state to perpetuate corruption and is indirectly protecting the pedophilia networks. The nation's legislators parade around with an utter lack of scrupulousness, as though it were not part of their purview to behave ethically.

On October 16, 2007, leftist senator Pablo Gómez, one of those to originally present the impeachment request against the governor, stood at a press conference with the Puebla Civic Front.[17] He explained that he was at a loss to understand what was going on within the PAN, because "if PAN-party deputy Diódoro Carrasco Altamirano fails to convene the Subcommittee for Initial Analysis, as corresponds to his role as president of said subcommittee, it will not be possible to go ahead with the impeachment process against the governor of Puebla, Mario Marín Torres." Carrasco was a member of the PRI until a short time ago, when he decided the right-wing PAN party offered him better opportunities for wielding power.

A few more months would have to pass before we would learn the outcome of this whole affair; in the meantime, we had been provided with a snapshot of our nation's criminal justice system and the extent of the far-reaching pacts made by corrupt elements of political power to the detriment of the average citizen.

The lessons learned are countless. Never before have I possessed such a clear understanding of why Mexico has not yet become—and will not easily become—a country governed by the rule of law.

---

17. Translator's Note: A citizen's association with ties to the Party of the Democratic Revolution (PRD).

7

A NEVER-ENDING STORY

On the evening after the SUV I was traveling in was attacked, I paid a visit to the office of Justice Juan Silva Meza. I had requested the meeting some time previously, and, like my counterparts in the case, I had been scheduled for an audience. I rode up in the elevator, and when I reached the reception area, a man kindly showed me into a waiting room. On each of the room's walls there were doors, and on each of the doors was written the name of one of the Supreme Court justices. I couldn't help but imagine them seated in their offices—going over documents, making decisions, debating whether to adopt a juridical position colored by political concerns or a political position backed by juridical arguments. *How do they handle all the pressure?* I mused in silent wonder.

When Silva Meza read the ruling that found Marín guilty of criminal collusion, Justice Mariano Azuela had shown himself to be the perfect embodiment of that attitude of brazen defense of the governor. The Court cleared the governor in that first instance, because the investigators decided that "Mr. Governor," having already been sworn in to public office, neither could nor should be comprehensively investigated. What was the thinking that guided that first commission? The ancestral fear of confronting state governors, who for more than seventy years have been considered untouchable? Could it represent some new form of collusion among public servants? Is it possible some of its members might have been bought off? I once again recalled the case where a Supreme Court justice was jailed after having been accused by the man now acting as my lawyer, Xavier Oléa, of accepting money in exchange for allowing the man who raped and murdered a little girl in Acapulco to walk free. Why should this time be any different? I was at a loss.

I realized that as I sat waiting, I was leaning forward, my elbows resting on my knees and the palms of my hands pressed together, like someone about to utter a prayer. An overwhelming realization came to me: *The battle does not end here.* Although this is the final institution of the Mexican state to which I can appeal in order to defend myself, the demons are out there, and they won't rest until I am dead. The events of the day were a reminder of that. Will I spend the next twenty years effectively held hostage by a team of bodyguards in order to avoid being murdered? Eventually, worn down by all the threats, will I become just another emigrant violently forced out of the country? And my life, the lives and suffering of the girls and boys abused and disappeared by this network of child traffickers—will it all become just another anecdote among the millions of cases inevitably destroyed by corruption? Sadness erupted and flowed over my body, a sob rose up uncontrollably in my throat, and I closed my eyes in a useless attempt to check it.

And yet this is a daily sensation for millions of Mexican citizens. Never before had I been so keenly aware of a feeling of orphanhood from one's country; there is no fatherland, no motherland to protect us, there is a merely a void, and in order to avoid admitting that fact to ourselves, for fear of tumbling into the abyss, millions of individuals who feel themselves to be defenseless submit to the designs of those in power, they join the ranks of the corrupt, they silence the truth.

A young man's friendly voice broke into my thoughts.

"You may go in now."

I took a deep breath and quickly stepped into the restroom to dry my tears and regain my composure. Once again, it was time for the public Lydia, the one who perseveres and never breaks, to spring into action, while the private Lydia felt too exhausted to go on participating in this endless game—perhaps I should call it a farce?—with the Mexican state.

Seated at his desk, Justice Silva Meza welcomed me into his office with the same warmth and politeness with which he greets everyone. In a kind, professional tone, he gave me a recap of where things stood and explained that Governor Marín would have access to the complete case file in order for his defense team to prepare their arguments.

"But this isn't a criminal trial," I protested naïvely. Wasn't this supposed to be an investigation in which all parties had to submit evidence and give testimony, and then the Supreme Court would make an assessment of all the concrete facts and circumstantial evidence?

Silva Meza explained to me that, in light of the findings, the Court had decided in its plenary session to give the governor a second chance.

And if the situation had been reversed, would I, a citizen with no political power, have been given a second chance?

The justice sat silently for a few moments; then he went on to explain that it would be another few months before the Supreme Court would convene in plenary session again to vote. An old, familiar feeling ran down my spine. A picture of that drive along the highway in the presence of the Judicial Police agents flashed through my mind—all those moments I found myself feeling grateful toward my captors because they weren't following through on their threats to kill me, the incessant, electric buzz of adrenaline when they would raise my hopes by allowing me to make a phone call before immediately snatching the telephone out of my hands, leaving me to listen helplessly to my family's voices as they asked, "Who is it . . . ? Hello . . . ? Hello . . . ?"

I can't do this anymore, I thought to myself, and as I looked into the justice's eyes, I found my pupils were suddenly swimming in a salty sea of despair, farewell drops running indecorously down my cheeks. Words abandoned me; I had run out of arguments. There was nothing left to say. I took a tissue out of my purse, and I was able to slowly regain my composure.

The justice was moved, and his reaction was very respectful toward me. He did not ask me not to cry; on the contrary, he told me how he himself had once been threatened, while he was serving as a criminal court judge on a case involving a man of great police and political power.

"I was not thinking of myself, but of my son. If someone was looking to hurt me, it was possible they might do something to him. But I stayed the course, because demonstrating fidelity to one's principles is the only way to preserve ethics, to attain justice."

I observed him, transfixed—his gray hair, his round face, and, beneath his glasses, two eyes completely free of dissemblance. His thick hands gestured in the air as he spoke.

"I read somewhere," he remarked, and I thought I almost detected a sparkle of mischief in his voice, "that no one is allowed to give up, because the abused girls need to be protected."

This Supreme Court justice was quoting me! I smiled. I pictured the shining eyes of the two abused girls, who, while waiting for their psychologist to arrive for their appointment, sat coloring in my office, happily showing one another their drawings, their children's wisdom instinctively reclaiming their right to happiness.

I stood to take my leave. The justice explained that the upper and lower chambers of Congress had already requested the case file in order to study the possibility of an impeachment.

"Let us hope that justice will be served, but you must not give up, for the country is not giving up, either."

As I climbed back into the SUV, my security team on more heightened alert than ever, I mused on the fact that the moral outrage unleashed across the nation as a result of my case had not been enough to crack even the facade of institutional corruption in Mexico. What were needed were human beings, real people willing to transform the system and its institutions from within. But who? How many people are there who would be willing to never give in? How many would be able to stop themselves from repeating, day in and day out, that "that's Mexico" and there's nothing for it, and that it's for that reason they make sure they always "take a little something for themselves"?

Just how big is this institutional monster? How are we to understand this hellhound, this Cerberus, topped—as in the *Theogony* of Greek mythology—with more than fifty heads and charged with blocking the exit of all those souls that have been dragged into the inferno of impunity? The heads of the Cerberus are many, but if we examine them closely, we will be better able to understand Mexico. On one of those heads we see the effigy of that large portion of society that allows itself to be perverted or led down the path of least resistance every chance it gets, thus feeding a generalized state of corruption. It is the police agent who asks for a bribe, and the driver who gives it to him; it is the person who makes a pirated copy of a film, and the person who buys it. It takes two to dance this national tango.

"Mario Marín has cost the people of Puebla more money than any other governor—184 million, to be exact," declared federal deputy Francisco Fraile. He was referring to the public funds the "Precious Guv'" funneled through his administration's Social Communication Office beginning on February 14, 2006, the day when the telephone conversations between him and Kamel Nacif were first made public. These funds were used to improve his public image, nothing more. But could money be all that was buying Marín his impunity? I don't think so. In order to understand why some congressmen, or even a governor, who find themselves at the center of a public scandal in the United States or Spain or France will be pressured by members of their own party until they step down, while in Mexico such individuals are protected as if they were victims being crushed by an uncomfortable truth, we need to understand the political and social mechanisms of Mexican corruption.

A woman currently serving as a PRI-party deputy stopped me one day at the airport. Behaving like someone on the run from the KGB, she drew me quietly into a corner and explained in hushed tones that her admiration for my cause compelled her to warn me that her party was unwilling to vote in favor of impeaching Marín— although she herself would vote to impeach. To do so, she explained, would amount to opening the door to the possibility that they, who are also protected by immunity, might one day be judged for their own corrupt acts.

"They see themselves in Marín; their alliances with the business community may be moral or immoral. They support the corrupt system, and they've managed to float this idea around in Congress that you've exaggerated matters, and that women are just hysterical crybabies. You've become a threat to them, an omen that there are potentially millions of us women out there that might one day reveal them for who they truly are; plus, Gamboa's told everyone you're not a real journalist."

Before going our separate ways, she asked me not to give up. This woman huddling in a corner to speak the truth represents the human side of things, the small acts of solidarity that can be undertaken by those who belong to the system. The other side of things, the political side that works to maintain the status quo, is something far simpler to grasp, and it rests on a combination of historically strong presidential rule, the power of state governors, the country's economic model, and an inoperative criminal justice system.

In the past, Mexico's governors exercised control through meta-constitutional mechanisms, a practice that was made possible by the country's particular system of presidential rule. For more than six decades, presidents were known to make frequent use of their clout in order to resolve crises and eliminate rival groups. It would not be until Ernesto Zedillo's administration that Mexico would witness the first failed attempt on the part of one of its presidents to "remove" an undesirable governor (the case involved Roberto Madrazo, who was accused of electoral fraud in the state of Tabasco in 1995). Prior to this episode, the case of the Aguas Blancas massacre—which ended up reaching the Supreme Court and was revealed in full thanks to the journalistic efforts of Ricardo Rocha—was eventually resolved not out of a desire for justice to be done in the face of proven crimes but on orders given by the president to the governor who had ordered the killings. History provides further evidence of this presidential authority: Luis Echeverría dismissed Armando Biebrich from his post as governor of the state of Sonora via a message left on the latter's telephone; when Ramón Aguirre Velázquez was dubiously declared victor in the elections for the governorship of Guanajuato, Carlos Salinas removed him when the former was still governor-elect (which is how Vicente Fox's career got its first big push, as Aguirre's removal paved the way for Fox to be elected governor of this same state four years later); and following the moral outrage over a series of gas explosions on April 22, 1992, in Guadalajara—which were reported on by the journalists at *Siglo 21*—it was Salinas again who forced Jalisco governor Cosío Vidaurri to step down.

But then, in 2002, along came Vicente Fox, a PAN-party president with scant notions of how to govern. His election was a political watershed, albeit a circumstantial rather than an intentional or strategic one; it shattered the paradigm of dictatorial, all-powerful presidential rule. Previously, presidents based their decisions not on ethics but on tactics—they sought to secure the PRI's hold on power and contain any possible social rebellions that might surface in response to the moral outrage of a Mexican society mired in a state of criminal impunity, poverty, and increasing violence. And while all of that was going on, the television was keeping public opinion distracted with soap operas and soccer.

But the country's system of presidential rule did not limit its controlling tendencies to state governors; its area of influence extended to the masters of money and the media, as well. For instance, when Bailleres, one of the five richest men in Mexico, died, the heir to his fortune was summoned to a meeting with President Gustavo Díaz Ordaz, who asked him what he planned to do with the windfall, before going on to offer him a few of his own "good ideas." And the founder of Mexico's most powerful television network, Emilio Azcárraga, famously known as "The Tiger," once declared proudly, "I am a PRI soldier." Thus the connection between media and political monopolies was kept strong, with all necessary measures being taken to tell the stories it was in the interest of the system to tell, to create and present to the public a picture of a Mexico that was conveniently false—everything calm and under control. Everything perfectly under control as the country sat and watched episodes of *The Rich Also Cry* and *Den of Wolves*.[18]

The masters of Mexican political and business monopolies grew up side-by-side, like all "good" families do, and the resulting atmosphere of secrecy and pact-making fed a feeling of intimacy and created bonds of complicity among them. The country's big businessmen did not necessarily build their fortunes on a foundation of criminal activity, but they did build them with the help of their close ties to political power and the facilities to which this privileged position gave them access. In some cases, such as that of Quintana Roo (home of Cancun and the Riviera Maya), a portion of the domestic and foreign business investments made in the state for the purposes

---

18. Translator's Note: *Los ricos también lloran* and *Cuna de lobos*, popular Mexican soap operas originally airing in 1979–1980 and 1986–1987, respectively.

of money laundering are backed by high degrees of structural corruption and, at times, concrete ties to organized crime.

Currently, the twenty richest families in the country not only represent a proportion of the national wealth far in excess of 10 percent of the country's GDP, as well as controlling more than half of the value of the Mexican Stock Market, but they also enjoy a considerable amount of sway over political decisions—much more than they did during the era of strict presidential rule. Now they can buy politicians by the truckload, to the point that men like Jorge Mendoza, the head of TV Azteca, can easily become congressmen in order to look after the interests of their businesses and their party, the PRI. Their news broadcasts reflect the deals, pacts, and tendencies of their party. New times, new strategies—same results.

Numerous specialists agree that Vicente Fox headed the last PRI government. For although his office of the president belonged to a different party—the PAN—the country's financial and tax infrastructure as well as the administrative portion of its public safety organisms were still made up of PRI figures who were familiar with the old system and amenable to the use of the same tried and true mechanisms that had been supporting their own economic, political, and judicial models for so many years.

Felipe Calderón attempted to keep the PRI in the opposition, but his fractured arrival in office forced him to return to the arms of the system's old operators in order to secure stability and control for his presidency. The political debt he owed to the business community, together with his own personal worldview, made him a strong ally of big capital.

The system did not undergo any process of democratization; there was no gradual social transformation by which the government and society broke with the previous paradigm. It's the same old cake, baked in the same old, circular mold, in the same old oven— the same old opaque elections. The decoration on the cake is the only thing that's changed; now the icing's blue, and the little plastic figurine on top is a man called Felipe, who's been making up his notion of presidential rule as he goes along. But now that the PRI is in the opposition, their political negotiations allow the public to glimpse, better than ever before, the full power of the state bastions. In a country of 104 million inhabitants spread across thirty-two states, each governor acts as the PRI presidents once did, reproducing the same model on a smaller scale. Marín in Puebla and Ulises Ruiz in Oaxaca provide a faithful illustration of the fact that the nation lacks flexible instruments with which to unseat "undesirable" governors. Such a step would necessarily have to go through the Congress of the Union and every state legislature. Even when there are powerful legal arguments in favor of an ouster—as in the cases involving the Atenco and Oaxaca disturbances of 2006[19] as well as my own case, among many others—a governor will always be able to negotiate with the state's various parties in order to defend his post. Impeachments are not the product, therefore, of ethical debates and considerations. And such processes will of course never be initiated from within a governor's own region, because governors like Marín are in effect holding their state legislatures hostage by placing deputies of their choosing into their congresses, thus securing total impunity for themselves during their "reign."

The governors have countless instruments at their disposal with which to act against the wishes of their own state legislative and judicial branches, even when their party does not hold a clear majority in the state government. Take Arturo Montiel's legal "pardon," or the media and public relations strategy employed by Enrique Peña Nieto, the governor of the State of Mexico who has recently been thrust into the national spotlight thanks to the work of several enormous groups supporting and promoting him. Or recall, too, the millions Marín has spent on publicizing the fact that he has held

---

19. Translator's Note: Two separate episodes of particularly violent confrontations between state security forces and civilians, both involving an excessive use of police force that resulted in the deaths of protestors as well as various other documented abuses.

more than ten meetings with President Felipe Calderón, an outlay designed to send the message that he has since been forgiven by the man who while campaigning for the presidency called for—and promised to get—the former man's head on a stick, "for the girls and boys of Mexico."

Never before have the governors acted with such a large degree of autonomy, and in that sense many of them have become political actors with power of their own. And Mario Marín is still one of them. For despite having lost some of his public credibility, as governor he enjoys the unconditional support of his congress, he has the ability to spend millions of pesos on publicity, and, most importantly, he is dealing with a business community that has no qualms about using his weakness to extract deals from him that favor the accrual of wealth to a handful of individuals in exchange for promising to withhold political pressure against him. Among these business leaders are the vice president of Coparmex—the Mexican Employer's Association—and Rogelio Sierra Michelena, who tactlessly confessed to Álvaro Delgado of *Proceso* and to Puebla's *Quinta Columna* that the "Cacho-Marín case" had in fact been useful to him and other members of the local business community in that it had made their negotiations with the Puebla governor easier. Sierra Michelena—a contractor for the Puebla government—had been an outspoken critic of Marín, but now he says he has forgiven him because "he is shaping up to be the best governor in the history of Puebla, having shown himself to be *deeply regretful* [for the Cacho case]." A few of Coparmex's members have remained true to their ethical principles and hope the Supreme Court's decision will be complied with; unfortunately, they are but needles in a haystack.

The best illustration of federal impotence in the face of the almost monopolistic power a governor can wield in his own state is the case of Oaxaca and Ulises Ruiz. Despite the overwhelming number of obviously aggravating circumstances, the federal government's attempts to get rid of the governor kept coming up against one legal wall after another, and against the hard reality of gubernatorial autonomy itself. A governor's power is, in theory, checked by that of two additional, separate powers, namely, the state's legislative and judicial branches. But only in theory. In the case of Puebla, the Supreme Court's investigation has provided us with what amounts to a clear map detailing the patterns of collusion on the part of its public servants, from Guillermo Pacheco Pulido, the chief justice of the Superior Court of Justice of the state, to the judge, the state attorney general, and some thirty others who are publicly perpetuating a lie at the behest of their boss—the governor—who in turn is at the beck and call of multimillionaire businessman Kamel Nacif. According to the recordings and hundreds of testimonies gathered throughout the course of this whole affair, Kamel Nacif has three state governors at his feet; they ask him for money, they do him favors, and they refer to him affectionately as "Pops," "Daddy," and "my hero." His telephone conversations revealed his influence over one of Mexico's most powerful politicians, Emilio Gamboa Patrón, who was referenced by the girls who had been victims of Succar Kuri's pedophilia ring and even named by the pedophile himself as his friend and protector.

How many more politicians does Nacif have in his pocket? How many public servants, how many attorneys general, how many Public Ministry workers? Only he and those who have prostituted themselves for his money know the answer to that question. Several dozens of newspaper articles and radio programs had publicized details of Nacif's track record—his arrest in Las Vegas, his ties to the Nevada mafia. But former president Vicente Fox still pointed to him as "a model citizen." He had invested a small amount of money to open a factory in Chiapas—a state whose governorship was held at the time by his friend Pablo Salazar Mendiguchía (also mentioned in the recorded telephone conversations), who had come to power as the head of a coalition pacted by the Party of the Democratic

Revolution (PRD)[20] and the PAN, among others—while the bulk of the financing came from public funds. The factory was later closed, with reports of exploitation at the plant having been investigated and denounced by national and international workers' rights organizations alike. But the most important thing for all of these individuals is "job generation," even if that means workers being exploited or falling ill, or environmental contamination running rampant, or millions of workers' rights being violated. As long as their model continues to sustain itself, the social repercussions are inconsequential. The country's growth is not fueled by ethical principles and a long-term vision for the welfare of the majority but rather by the fulfillment of the personal agendas of a mere thousand or so individuals who are controlling the rest of the country.

A Supreme Court justice remarked to the cameras in one particular plenary session that in the old days, the Court had to take its orders from the president and that things are different now. They are indeed different, it's true. But what will we do now that there is no one tyrant who can order that justice be done in whatever manner he sees fit? Whose hand will swing the gavel and deliver fair sentences? Does anyone truly know how to exercise freedom? A handful of individuals have demonstrated that it is in fact possible, Justice Silva Meza among them, but one swallow does not a summer make. What this affair reveals is that the nation's corrupt system is not perpetuated in a vacuum; it requires real people to feed it, to build it up, and to use their willingness to prostitute themselves to close the doors to transformation and democratization.

The final piece of the puzzle is the disfunctionality of the Mexican criminal justice system. Guillermo Zepeda Lecuona explores what he calls "the investigative victim" in his essay *La investigación de los delitos y la subversion de los principios del subsistema penal en México* [Criminal Investigation and the Subversion of the Principles

---

20. Translator's Note: Partido de la Revolución Democrática—one of Mexico's three main political parties, it is a leftist party created in 1989 as a breakaway movement from the PRI.

of the Justice System in Mexico]. Criminal law, says Lecuona, has given rise to the conception of the Public Ministry as a specialized legal institution, an agency charged with investigating crimes, a body responsible for gathering evidence and representing both society and the victim/accuser in the legitimate expectations of their rights. However, because it is impossible for the Public Ministry's workers to fully investigate all the cases assigned to them, in practice the victims are inappropriately saddled with many of the costs of their own cases. And so victims must locate evidence and even deposit it themselves on the corresponding authorities' desks if they wish to see their cases prosper. In fact, undue, unconstitutional barriers exist for the reporting of crimes and the participation of victims in their own cases. In addition to long waiting times, it has become commonplace to see such practices as the required "corroboration" of accusations, as well as high participation costs during the prior inquiry and the trial period. It is for this reason also that victims (whose rights have been constitutionally enshrined since the year 2000) and society at large have become relegated to a position of such secondary importance as to be rendered all but invisible—their rights are not legally protected, and they do not receive sufficient support from the authorities.

The Public Ministry was created and remains to this day within the administrative sphere of the executive branch of government. And this in a country where, for decades, the office of the presidency was subject to no real checks or counterweights. The reaches of the Public Ministry's power can be summed up in a single phrase: free discretion without effective control. The existence of this unchecked power is not accidental; it corresponds to a vision of public power in which the executive wishes to keep the investigation and prosecution of crimes—as well as the chance to impose its decisions absolutely upon judges in order to secure guilty convictions—firmly within the bounds of its sphere of authority while also retaining complete discretional powers and avoiding any external oversight. This power turned the nation's various attorneys generals' offices into just another node in that vast network of control that has been placed at the service of hegemonic political interests. A large part of the rationale behind the current institutional design of our criminal justice model can be found in the selective application of criminal law—in ensuring that dissidents are punished and allies are guaranteed immunity. The case described in this book is the perfect proof—the pedophilia ring, despite being made up of individuals whose full names are perfectly known, remains untouched. The only person to have gone to jail over the entire affair is Succar Kuri. The Office of the Special Prosecutor for Crimes Against Women (FEVIM) has had arrest warrants against my torturers prepared and waiting since 2007, but those warrants have been blocked by orders from above.

Millions of Mexican women and men are crushed or beated by their nation's justice system. My case is by no means unique. I am just one among millions. But my case *has* been useful, because I have managed, with perseverance and a great deal of national and international backing, to stay strong while preserving two of humanity's most precious commodities: hope and solidarity. My dear colleague Ricardo Rocha told me years ago that "no one can be a good reporter without good luck." I was lucky enough to survive in the face of torture, first police torture and then institutional torture. I was able to follow my case as a reporter would: compiling evidence and hard data, comparing different versions of things, keeping tabs on hundreds of small and large-scale acts of corruption. I was able, together with other journalists, to take a snapshot of Mexican impunity and corruption. I was able to do all of this because my will to fight this battle is not fed by anger or spite but by the conviction that those who violate the law and human rights must be held accountable to society. I have managed to work with a warm heart and a cool head, aided in no small part by my support networks.

I am now completing my work on this book from the city of New York, where in just a few days I will receive the Courage in Journalism award from the International Women's Media Foundation (IWMF). As I prepare to give my acceptance speech, I would like to reiterate that I have viewed every recognition I have been granted throughout the course of my career, and during the last two years in particular, not as a chance to boost my ego but as an opportunity to spread knowledge about the true situation of journalism in Mexico and the systematic violation of human rights by the Mexican authorities. At the same time as American and European media outlets have been giving me a platform from which to shed light on these topics, Marín has been shutting me out of the media in my own country.

My close friend, journalist Mariane Pearl, insisted a year ago that I write this book. She had written the story of her husband, Daniel Pearl, who was assassinated in Pakistan while on a newspaper assignment there.

"Don't wait," she told me with that sort of frank realism one only sees among journalists. "You carry the entire story within your memory, and you're the only one. Get it out there, before the media forgets about you."

8

THE FINAL VERDICT

We weren't sure when the Supreme Court would deliver its final verdict, so I decided to attend the Guadalajara International Book Fair (FIL), the most important literary event in all of the Spanish-speaking world; I would present the original Spanish edition of this book, my fourth, on the afternoon of November 29, 2007. On the night of the 28th, my lawyers called me and said, "You should prepare yourself—the Court is convening tomorrow, and they're going to make their final decision."

It was to be broadcast live on television. Before going to my presentation, I met with a group of friends, authors, and journalists in the lobby of the Hilton hotel where we were staying. Fifteen of us sat there in the bar to watch the Court's deliberations. The whole thing was like a scene out of a police drama.

With beers or tequilas in hand, perched on stools around the small, round bar tables, we sat looking up into the corner where the television set, normally switched to a sports channel, was transmitting the first images from inside the large session chamber of the Supreme Court of Justice of the Nation. There were carved mahogany walls, high ceilings, and a long, U-shaped podium, also made of fine mahogany, behind which we were able to glimpse the impeccable black gowns of each of the justices, along with the Supreme Court shield and the Mexican flag at the back. My lawyer was there in the chamber alongside the governor's seven and the human traffickers' five. The solemnity and tension in the room were palpable even on screen. The court crier announced the order in which the justices would speak and then proceeded to explain that this was one of the most closely followed Supreme Court sessions for the media and society at large in recent memory. A colleague seated near our table was listening to the radio broadcast on his laptop and relayed to us what one journalist was saying: "Those little girls are going to win, and all of Mexico along with them; they have to win, the evidence on their side is incontrovertible. The people are watching this public session on televisions in their homes, in restaurants; this is historic."

Then we all fell silent, the camera focused on Justice Silva Meza, and after the chief justice gave him the floor, he said:

> The violation of the human rights of the journalist Lydia Cacho as a result of the concerted actions of the governor of the state of Puebla and the authorities of the State Attorney General's Office and the Court of Justice of the same has been irrefutably established.

He then read out the names of the accused.

We let out our breath. I grabbed Jorge's hand as tightly as I could, and he squeezed mine back; his eyes and the eyes of all of us there listening to the decision were brimming with tears. Other friends, among them Cristóbal, my editor, stood and laid their hands on my shoulders, their gazes still riveted on the television set. The huddle around us grew as more and more people filed into the lobby bar.

Slowly, each of the justices took their turn to speak, in a scene that looked like something out of a 19th-century British trial: Genaro

Góngora Pimentel, José Ramón Cossío, and José de Jesús Gudiño Pelayo declared that crimes had been committed that required prosecution and that the child pornography networks I had denounced, as well as the governor, judges, and other individuals involved in my arrest, should be fully investigated. When the turns of the two female justices came around, we all froze. The first, Olga Sánchez Cordero, a blond-haired woman who adjusted her glasses repeatedly as she read her statement, began to stutter. She said that crimes had indeed been committed, but that said crimes were not very serious in nature. She contradicted herself several times, and in the end, to the utter astonishment of those watching, she exonerated the governor and his accomplices. She, the pro-feminism judge, had bowed to political pressure. Then Margarita Luna, a conservative justice with close ties to the PAN, did the same. Our sources had warned us beforehand that Governor Marín's former lawyer, now an advisor to President Calderón, had lobbied her, pressing her to avoid provoking a breach in relations between the PAN and the PRI. None of us could speak; the only sounds in the lobby were the uncomfortable sighs of some and the slight, exhaling groans of others. The remaining PRI-aligned justices voted in the same fashion, one after the other, all couching their protection of the governor and his accomplices in pseudo-legal speak. Silence filled the bar, and I realized that every single person there was staring at the television screen. Then, here and there, people hung their heads, buried their faces in their hands, and more than one journalist began to offer up insults; everyone expressed their dismay as best they could. I knocked back my tequila in a single gulp. The mafias had gained control of the Supreme Court.

I was devastated. My friend, journalist Denise Dresser, hugged me at almost the exact moment that my cell phone began to ring.

"Lydia," said the small voice on the other end of the line, "we lost—the judges say what happened to us was nothing. Now they're going to kill us all." The girl was crying softly; I tried to contain my own sob, but it was almost impossible.

"No!" I managed to reply. "We can still beat them. Succar is still in jail."

I promised to call her and the rest of the trafficking network's victims the following day. Reporters and correspondents, writers and poets all looked at each other, hugged one another; we were in a state of collective shock. A significant portion of the national press had written not one day earlier that this time, justice was really going to be done.

We were wrong. We repeated it over and over again, speaking dazedly, as survivors of some sudden building collapse might. Radio commentators spent the evening analyzing the Court's decision. The public—everyone outside the PRI's upper echelons, that is—was indignant, furious even. My telephone was ringing off the hook. In one interview after another, I dove into analyses of the legal consequences of the ruling and the importance of ensuring the well-being of young girls and boys not currently protected under our legal system.

I had no room for anger. At some point, I slipped away and went up to my room to be alone. Once there, I collapsed onto the couch; I can only remember that I was crying and that I wished my mother were alive. The desolation I felt was immense; the emptiness inside me was an absolute abyss. In my mind, I heard the echoing voice of that young girl who had been abused by the politicians and Succar. She was right—we were more unprotected now than ever. Four years after I first reported them, society was on my side, on the side of the victims, but the power of the state was on the side of those who were as corrupt as it was. I called my sister Myriam. We cried together, and she told me that it wasn't over yet.

"Don't break now, little sister, we're going to win, you'll see."

I washed my face and composed myself. I was supposed to present my book in half an hour inside a three-hundred-seat auditorium. The whole country had heard about the Court's verdict by now. I meditated briefly and went down with Jorge, who had been waiting to accompany me to the presentation.

"Be strong," he told me, squeezing my hand just briefly so that I could make my entrance and go up on stage.

The room was completely full, and the lobby outside was packed, too; there were more than five hundred people in all, and giant monitors had been set up outside the auditorium to allow everyone to see the presentation. The air was thick with anxiety. I made my way in from the entrance, and the audience began to rise; they clapped and called out my name in a clamor of sadness and support. When I stepped on stage, the people applauded for nearly five minutes. *This is Mexico,* I thought, *and the feeling that resounds here is indignation, indignation on behalf of all the girls and boys abused in silence, on behalf of all the mothers and fathers who took to the streets and marched to demand that these pedophiles being tried today receive their just punishment, that their punishment serve as an example to others.* This was not applause in recognition of glory or fame. It was applause like that of my friends in the Congo, who taught me how to stand in a circle in the forest and clap together with them to ward off evil spirits, pain, and fear. With palms together and the sympathetic accompaniment of echo and air, the sound evokes the suffering of the entire tribe.

When the presentation was over, a young man about eighteen years old who had remained standing throughout the presentation took the microphone and, his voice faltering, asked a brutally honest question.

"Why go on, Lydia, now that you've lost at the Supreme Court? Corruption triumphed—again—and I don't believe in anything anymore. How can we believe in Mexico?"

His question set my skin bristling; it had been only a few hours since we'd heard the verdict of the six Supreme Court justices in support of the so-called "Precious Guv'" and Kamel Nacif, the pedophile's protector and partner. I looked the young man in the eye and told him that when I was his age, I had asked myself the same question, and that now, twenty-six years later, I knew it was worth it to keep trying. I couldn't help but recall that when I was a girl and my mother was at university, there was only one female student for every fifty or sixty male ones. I was five years old when the Tlatelolco massacre[21] took place, and then there were the forced disappearances of the 1970s. In high school, when I chose to take woodshop instead of sewing and then an electrical wiring class instead of baking, there was only one other girl with me, and a great deal of teasing and disdain from the boys who told me that such things weren't proper "women's stuff" and that I "must be a lesbian." By the time I was eighteen, I had become aware of the fact that there were just a handful of journalists in the entire country who managed to escape the government's crushing yoke. A few—very few—refused to accept money in exchange for placing their reports and columns at the service of the powerful, putting positive spins on stories and even inserting personal messages when asked. Scarcely any editors were able to resist the temptation of an expensive gift from a politician, and many fewer still dared to refuse the Secretary of the Interior's inevitable request for a meeting if they were known to be working on stories considered "inconvenient" for the Mexican government. And by the time I was twenty and working as a production assistant at Estudios Churubusco, I had learned that the Secretariat of the Interior made a practice of censuring important topics while at the same time turning a blind eye to the promotion of sexual exploitation and violence against women in cinema and the press.

I came to understand that this hypocritical discourse was simply the voice of the patriarchy and that those who hoped to belong to the system and to move through it easily were essentially prostituting themselves by submitting to its designs. The first time I applied for a job, the head of personnel insinuated—as though

21. Translator's Note: An episode in Mexico's Dirty War that took place ten days before the opening of the Mexico City Summer Olympics, on October 2, 1968, in which an as-yet-unconfirmed number of civilians (estimated variously at anywhere between thirty and three hundred) died at the hands of security forces near the National Autonomous University of Mexico (UNAM) in the Tlatlecolco district of the nation's capital city.

it were the most natural thing in the world—that I should pay him sexual favors in exchange for a good salary. I discovered that machismo and sexism pervade every last corner of our lives and that those who do not rebel against them end up submitting to them, accepting them as the social norm, and eventually go on to propagate these values themselves.

When I was a child, single women had no access to bank loans and single mothers experienced three times more social discrimination than they do today. When I was twenty, everyone said that machismo and violence against women were "normal" and "a private matter."

Then when I was twenty-two, a friend of mine had an illegal abortion and called me in the middle of the night, gushing blood and terrified. I took her to a hospital, where her father, who was a doctor, treated her in secret in order to save her life and prevent her from being arrested. That night, we dreamed together of a day when abortions would be legal and such large numbers of women wouldn't have to die from them.

The first time I ever told a press director that I wanted to be a journalist and specialize in women's rights, the man told me, "You're better off doing society news—you're pretty. All this *rights* business isn't newsworthy."

Before I turned thirty, I wasn't aware that the word *femicide*, or a whole category of analysis called Gender Perspective, even existed. When my mother gave conferences during my teenage years, she said that universities would one day have as many female students as male, and that is the case today. Back then, there were no shelters for abused women, and nobody spoke about pedophilia at all, whether aloud or in hushed tones.

When I was nine, my mother listened to Alaíde Foppa on Radio Universidad de México, on a program that was to become the window to the world—to our world—for millions of girls and women in my generation. When I did my first radio show in Cancun, I dedicated it to Ms. Foppa. It was Alaíde who inspired me to seek out wise women, to discover Susan Sontag, Kate Millett, and the three Marías of *New Portuguese Letters*. At the time, we young Mexican women knew that there were millions of us who shared this vision of a different reality. We knew that a conspiracy of freedom was brewing, a collective urge to create a world where we would have a vote, a voice, and human rights.

Despite the momentary sadness brought on by the terrible news out of the Supreme Court, I knew that Mexico had in fact changed, that important aspects of Mexican life were continuing to change, and that there are just as many changes yet to come—that is why we can hope. That is why rage and anger don't get the better of me, why I instead feel happiness at the small battles fought and won as moral and ethical triumphs, if not judicial ones. That's why I continue to do what I do, because every time someone at an event or even simply walking down the street shouts, "Lydia, you're not alone!"—as hundreds of people had done that night at the Book Fair—I take it as a cry of support from equals, from individuals who see in me the bravery and the voice of *all* people. I recognize that the exercise of freedom requires some minimum measure of bravery, because accepting the consequences of our decisions requires that we hold firm convictions and not allow ourselves to labor under illusions or act on temporary impulses.

The next day, Denise Dresser, doctor of Political Science at Princeton University, published her column in the prestigious daily *Reforma*:

> "There are blows in life, so powerful. Blows as if from the wrath of God," as César Vallejo wrote. Blows like the one the six Supreme Court justices just dealt the country. Wounds like the one the highest court just inflicted upon itself when it declared that violations of Lydia Cacho's individual guarantees had either not taken place or else were not very serious. When it suggested that

the last recourse to which a citizen has access can do nothing for
him or her. When it transformed the suffering of the victims of
pedophilia into just another story. When it made of its verdict a
confabulary of corrupt governments, immoral businessmen, and
organized criminals. And just as a Federal Investigations Agency
(AFI) agent told Lydia Cacho when she was "lawfully kidnapped"
that "You don't have rights—you don't have shit," the Supreme
Court has just told the people of this country the same. You and I
have been left defenseless by those whose duty it is to protect our
rights but who nevertheless decided it wasn't their place to stand
up for them.

In voting as it did, the majority of justices drove a knife
through the heart of the Court, and it will be years before it
recovers from the wound, assuming it ever does. For this resolution will come to occupy a dishonorable place in the constitutional history of Mexico, similar to the place the Dred Scott
case[22] holds in the constitutional history of the United States. In
that 1856 case, the Court attempted to impose a judicial solution
on a political problem; in that case, it was declared—"in accordance with the law," just as in this case—that the institution
of slavery had legal legitimacy, that Dred Scott, being a slave,
had no rights, and that the Court therefore lacked jurisdiction
to intercede on his behalf. Today that case is still viewed as a
permanent blot, a source of collective shame, a self-inflicted
wound. Here, today, the members of the Court proved themselves to be contradictory and dishonest when they threw out the
case on the argument that the recorded telephone conversation
between Kamel Nacif and Mario Marín has no probative value
whatsoever, and when they ignored the 1,251 pages of exhaustive

---

22. In March of 1857, the Supreme Court of the United States, headed by Justice Roger
B. Taney, declared that all individuals of black race—both slaves and free persons—
were not and could never be citizens of the United States. The court also declared
the Missouri Compromise of 1820 to be unconstitutional, thereby allowing slavery to
continue in every territory of the country.

research that confirm the contents of that conversation. They proved themselves insensitive, or perhaps desensitized, when they chose to dismiss 377 files dealing with sexual crimes against minors. Proved themselves to be either unwilling or active accomplices when they claimed to be obeying a "higher interest" that just happens to coincide with the interests of the governor and his friends. Proved themselves to be representative of the worst kind of paternalism when they declared—in a press release that was nothing short of shameful—that their sophisticated decisions will not be "easily understood" by large portions of society.

Justice Mariano Azuela's downplaying of the importance of torture. Or, as Justice Aguirre asked him, "But thousands of people are tortured in this country—what is this woman complaining about? What makes her so different or so much more important that the Court should trouble itself with one individual case?"

Perhaps a violation of individual guarantees in Mexico will only ever be legally recognized once a Supreme Court justice's wife has been transported across state lines and held for twenty-three hours without due process. When some judge's mother is told that she will only be permitted to eat if she performs oral sex on the agents who have kidnapped her. When some magistrate's sister has a gun shoved in her mouth and the words "So pretty, but such a little bitch. Why'd you have to mess with the boss . . . the boss is gonna end you" whispered in her ear. When some lawyer's daughter is charged excessive bail to be released from prison, or threatened to be raped on the spot, or subjected to intimidating questioning, or a governor gives her a good "smacking." When some politician's daughter-in-law hears her torturers tell her, "I've got your medicine right here . . . a little cough syrup, you want some?" while they grope their genitals. When some state attorney general's granddaughter is raped by a pedophile protected by a "rule of law" that serves the powerful—who almost always win. When one of them is the unfortunate victim of a rotten judicial system. But not before. Only then.

So the Supreme Court is only hurting itself, but it allows the worst blow to fall on the nation, by demonstrating just how far it is from being an aggressive, independent guarantor of constitutional rights. How far it is from understanding the systematic abuse of millions of Mexicans harassed by the judicial system and crushed by the unspeakable alliances that have been forged within the political system. Just as Kamel Nacif calls Lydia Cacho a "goddamn fucking old lady," the majority of the members of the Supreme Court have just called you and me "goddamn fucking citizens." They've sent a message that we shouldn't bother them with such unimportant trifles as the defense of individual guarantees, because they're too busy shoring up the interests of powerful businessmen and their allies in other branches of government.

Perhaps that is why in her book *Memoir of a Scandal*, Lydia Cacho writes, "I pity my country. I weep for myself and for those who have the power to change it but instead choose to perpetuate the status quo." And we weep with you Lydia—our Lydia—but we refuse to surrender, even though six Supreme Court justices have done so. Because you're right—Mexico is more than a handful of corrupt rulers, immoral businessmen, organized criminals, and deaf judges. Mexico belongs to those who fight doggedly, tirelessly to return some small glimmer of dignity to the country. And though the Court may refuse to assume its rightful role in this common cause, there are many citizens who share Justice Juan Silva Meza's conviction "that there is no place for impunity in a constitutional, democratic state."

As for the media in the state of Puebla, the majority aligned itself with the governor, with such headlines as "Lydia Cacho Annihilated" or "Marín Is Innocent: No Ties to Pedophiles." The media were perfectly aware that such statements were lies, because the Supreme Court hadn't been trying the governor for his ties to child sexual abuse networks but for having violated my constitutional guarantees and ordered my torture. But none of that mattered, and that night, the governor threw a dinner party at his home to celebrate. Attending as guests were the directors of most of the different media outlets and many businessmen who just weeks earlier had demanded he step down.

Alfonso Bello, a federal deputy and member of the PAN, declared publicly that it was a disgrace that President Felipe Calderón, a member of his own party, had negotiated with Mario Marín to help the latter escape justice. Nothing but silence followed his statement. Not a single PAN member seconded him.

POLICE FOR TRUTH

One February morning in 2008, I arrived for an appointment with a doctor specialized in treating the physiological effects of torture. The PGR had already run tests looking into the psychological effects of the abuse I had undergone, but my activist friends had been urging me for months to see one of these specialists. I finally agreed to have an appointment with one, Dr. Velks. I came armed with all the various blood tests she required I have done before my first visit. When I walked in, she said it was an honor to meet me and that she had been following the news of my case closely.

Calmly seated opposite her at the desk, I observed how her face took on a look of circumspection. She picked up a pen and began taking notes. I told her that I felt good, that I'd woken up that morning with more energy than before and wasn't having headaches anymore. After a few minutes, she set her papers down on the desk and looked at me; she asked me to lie back on the table. She began her physical examination, continuing her questions as she did.

"How did you get here?" she asked, looking me in the eye with what appeared to me to be a flicker of compassion.

"I drove here, with my bodyguard—"

"No. What I mean is that it makes absolutely no sense that you look so well. Let me put it to you this way: If you were a car, you wouldn't be able to start your engine. Your whole system is out of whack; it's as if your body is short-circuiting, and yet you still haven't stopped to correct your health problems. Your blood pressure is extremely low. Your blood sugar is so high you're at risk for pre-diabetes. You have inflammation in your liver and bladder. Your blood work shows that you're suffering from anemia. And all your hepatic indicators are off."

The doctor, who specializes in gynecology, had spent years treating women who were victims of sexual abuse, and she had grown deeply knowledgeable of the effects of post-traumatic stress disorder (PTSD). I was familiar with the symptoms; after all, I myself had specialized in aiding victims of extreme violence at the women's shelter. The only response I could muster was that the Attorney General's Office had given me a PTSD test and it had come back positive. Our eyes met and we held each other's gaze for a moment— I, seated on the examination table, wearing my little hospital gown; she, standing in front of me, dressed in white.

"Listen, Lydia," she said seriously, "if you go on like this, you're going to end up in the hospital. If you want to protect the girls, you have to protect yourself first."

The doctor took my hand. This small physical contact was enough to break down the wall of emotional protection that had been working so well for me the past several years. I began to sob uncontrollably, like a lost little girl. She set a box of tissues at my side and continued her explanations while I let it all out.

"You know that when a person is tortured, the first thing that happens is that the suprarenal glands release large quantities of epinephrine or adrenaline. Epinephrine is the flight hormone—it sends a supercharge of energy to the muscles and increases the heart rate to keep the mind and body alert and able to flee when there's a dangerous situation. But if your brain realizes that you're *not* going to be able to flee, and if you're still being attacked or threatened, which is what's happening in your case, then your body says, 'We'd better stay alert so that we can continue to withstand all this stress, this stress that's not going to disappear because it's not being given any other outlet.' Once this message has been sent, your body begins to secrete mainly hydrocortisone, or cortisol.

"Cortisol is a hormone associated with stress, and its levels in the blood can become elevated—in your case, due to the aggressions you have experienced, as well as all the fear and pressure. Meanwhile, your immune system becomes depressed. Cortisol is an anti-stress hormone, but when it's present in excessive amounts, it favors the overproduction of insulin. If you don't take it seriously, you could very quickly find yourself developing hyperinsulinemia, a rise in the body's resistance to insulin. This leads to neuron death, it compromises your immune system, and it weakens your power of memory. And in your case, since you're starting out with just the one kidney, you could end up requiring intensive care."

She went on with her examinations, discovered several lumps that needed to be looked at, and arranged to call me once the results were in.

I fumbled around for my purse. That's where I keep the small Moleskine notebook I write everything down in. . . . It was true—in the last several months, I'd begun feeling more anxious about not being able to remember things.

My memory is starting to fail, I thought to myself. I felt a ripple of fear as it dawned on me that my body might fail me, that my mind might fail me, too. But the fight wouldn't stop; I couldn't stop.

I pulled out my notebook and set about writing down everything the doctor had just told me. At the same time, I appealed to her, saying that years and years spent following a regimen of meditation and yoga ought to have done *something* to help me. She said she was convinced that had I not been so conscientious about managing my stress, I would most surely have already been hospitalized by now. I pleaded with her to throw me a lifeline, something to keep me afloat, and she replied that only I could save myself. She wrote out a series of prescriptions, outlined some dietary changes, recommended various vitamin supplements, and admonished that I had to decide for myself if I was willing to place my health above my social battles; only I could make this determination.

I left the doctor's office and headed home. I was genuinely scared. I regretted not having asked my sister to come with me to the appointment. While I was picking up my prescriptions at the pharmacy, my phone rang. I could hear a deep voice, raspy now from years of chain-smoking, coming down the line. It was my lawyer.

"Lydia, congratulations. They've put out an arrest warrant."

"On who? The governor, Kamel . . .?"

"No. On Montaño and Pérez, the cops who tortured and tried to kill you. The Public Ministry ruled that they're responsible for the crime of torturing you. They just issued the warrant and they're sending the file to Cancun. It'll go to a federal judge, and we've got a good chance of beating them. We'll be asking for the maximum sentence."

"And if they're arrested, do you think they'll make a deal to get out of going to jail in exchange for telling the truth about how Kamel Nacif, the state attorney general, and the governor gave the order?"

"Maybe. So far everything is lining up in our favor."

I got home. Jorge was there, writing something up for the paper. He asked me how it had gone at the doctor's, and I, as I always do, put what was most immediate above what was most important. I told him about the ruling. He got up to hug me, and I broke down in tears. My sobs were a mixture of emotions—on the one hand, I was happy at having received this good news, and on the other, I was frightened by my diagnosis. But I didn't want to trouble him with more problems.

We sat down to run through all the scenarios and possible outcomes. Right then, a messenger arrived from my lawyer's office with a copy of the most recent updates to my case file. I signed for it and began to read aloud. We had managed to get the arrest warrants issued for the two agents thanks in large part to the voices of their colleagues—the honest policewomen and men who, unlikely though it may at times seem, really do exist.

One factor had been the fact that my federal-issue bodyguards, during questioning by the Attorney General's Office, stated that the police had in fact blocked off the street in order to arrest me and that they had believed, given the style of operation they were witnessing, that it might be a kidnapping; that while they were being held at the corner, they could hear that the police agents who hurt me with their guns had told everyone to freeze; that there were multiple cars securing the entrance and exit to the block; that there were several armed men in street clothes and unmarked vehicles; and that at no point was I shown an arrest warrant. But the declaration of a police officer from Cancun who participated in the operation was also key. He stated that my description of what had happened was accurate and truthful; that his superiors had instructed them to arrest me "extra-legally"; and that there had been additional armed men— "informers"—waiting in a white SUV. His declaration came on top of that made by Víctor Mendo Sánchez, an AFI agent in Puebla, who testified to the Attorney General's Office that he had received orders directly from the Puebla state attorney general to "fuck Lydia Cacho up, you know—beat her up or kill her." He explained that he was given these instructions a few days prior to my detention, although he did not number among those agents finally chosen for the operation.

The good mood brought on by this news didn't last. On May 6, nearly four months after the arrest warrant had been issued, the judge ruled that while there were indeed factors proving that a crime of torture had been committed, he was unable to sentence the two agents, who had not been arrested because the police had not managed to locate them (according to witnesses, they were still in Puebla). The judge stated that the law against police torture applied only to agents in the state of Quintana Roo and that these two agents must, therefore, be tried in Puebla itself. And so, availing himself of complicated, contradictory, and incomprehensible legal jargon, the judge washed his hands of the hottest case of the day.

Exhausted, I accompanied my lawyer, one of CIAM's legal representatives, to the courthouse in Cancun. There, we appealed the judge's decision and learned that everything had already been arranged—the federal judge was going to refer the case to a local judge (local judges are more easily manipulated, bought, and threatened). Later, as we were leaving, we were approached by a prosecutor, who asked us to meet with him, discreetly, on the corner of the street that runs outside the courthouse. Once we had all gathered there, the prosecutor informed us that the governor of Quintana Roo was moving to prevent the two Judicial Police agents from being sentenced.

"Don't let them transfer the case to Puebla," he told us, speaking under his breath. "They want to move it there to make the whole thing inadmissible and get it thrown out. They want to send you into the lion's den."

I asked him how he knew. He told me that he had been there when Kamel Nacif's lawyers and a high-ranking state official came to speak with the judge and enlighten him to the fact that the chief justice of the Superior Court of Justice of the state of Quintana Roo supported the governor's recommendation to shut down my case.

And that's precisely what happened. Despite eight months of effort—during which we presented additional evidence, investigated the different government officials involved, and publicly denounced the corruption in the court and the governor's hand in it all—on January 8, 2009, just as we had suspected, the state Superior Court threw out the torture case. Two days later, according to the information given to me by the assistant to the state Secretary of the Interior of my own state, the governor of Puebla called the governor of Quintana Roo to thank him for his help. The scandal had been hurting his party. After all, the PRI needed to maintain a united front—the elections were coming up, not to mention the reelection of the chief justice of the state Superior Court itself. Lizbeth Song, the chief justice of the Court at the time, was seeking reelection, and the governor had her in his pocket. Politics had trounced justice once again.

As it happens, by the time I learned the outcome of the case, my priorities were focused elsewhere. Back in December, I had paid visits to several doctors and one oncologist and had undergone surgery to remove my uterus and ovaries. The doctors all agreed that the dramatic hormonal changes I had experienced, together with other health problems resulting from the stress I had been subjected to, were factors that had contributed significantly to the growth of tumors in those organs. I had lost a great deal of weight and wasn't feeling capable of withstanding any new physical or emotional pain, but the surgery wasn't optional. I agreed to it, but not without first sitting down with my doctor, members of my family, and my personal security advisors. Over the course of the previous months, I had received threatening phone calls. We knew that they were from the Judicial Police agents who, anxious over the judge's impending sentence, wanted to see me dead rather than alive, or, at the very least, scared and upset.

My lawyer came to Cancun. An hour before I went in with my doctor to go over the details of the surgery, he told me in no uncertain terms that my life was in greater danger than ever.

"The governors, Nacif, and the judge are all maneuvering, but we filed an appeal to bring back the case against the two agents; if we win the appeal, they'll sing, and then we can really go after them all again."

My security advisor nodded. We met with the doctor, who'd brought in an anesthesiologist she knew and trusted, and we decided that I should be admitted under an alias. No one in the hospital would know my real name. I would receive no visitors outside my immediate family. And we followed the plan to the letter.

Then another wake-up call courtesy of my body: The removal of my ovaries had triggered a premature menopause. The endocrinologist who analyzed my test results cautioned me that I couldn't go on with business as usual if my stress indicators remained at such high levels. This sudden-onset menopause, a side effect of my surgery, was forcing my suprarenal glands to work twice as hard as usual to keep my hormone system in balance. If my body continued producing elevated levels of cortisol, anything might happen to me. I underwent the requisite medical treatments and followed all of my doctors' recommendations, save one—I was not willing to give up the case. Not until Jean Succar Kuri was convicted for child pornography. Otherwise, his vengeance against the girls who had spoken out against him would be brutal, merciless.

In May of 2009, Darío Ramírez, director of the Mexico chapter of ARTICLE 19, a London-headquartered organization dedicated to the protection of freedom of expression, approached me and offered to have his legal team take over my case. I accepted his proposal not only because they are specialists in human rights and freedom of expression, but because they are well versed in international litigation. They had studied the scope of the corruption surrounding my case and were prepared to do battle. Because they are a nongovernmental organization, their services would be offered free of charge. I would finally be able to stop struggling to put together the exorbitant sums required to mount a proper defense; the financial hardship had taken a brutal toll.

Mario, Cyntia, and Iván, three young experts, picked apart my case. Slowly but surely, from among thousands and thousands of sheets of paper all packed away in cardboard boxes, they were able to uncover information and piece together an increasingly clear picture of how files had been raided, evidence tossed out, and backroom judicial machinations concocted in an effort to prevent my case from succeeding, as well as who had been involved. I felt more confident than ever. This group of young women and men clearly belong to a new generation of trial attorneys who live and breathe human rights issues and have a deep understanding of the patterns of gender violence. They also took up the defense of a new civil suit brought against me by Kamel Nacif. He had managed to rope in a victim named Edith, who was among those to originally report him and who later accepted money in exchange for assisting him in his efforts to discredit me. There was a recording of Nacif saying, "We're going to sue her over and over again, until the bitch begs forgiveness." His lawyers used legal technicalities and loopholes to argue that because I do not hold a degree in journalism, I am not in fact a journalist. They also argued that my book *The Demons of Eden* exposed his personal, private affairs and that the publishers and I should therefore pay millions of pesos for the copyright and for having published a photo of Edith in Los Angeles with Succar's children (whose faces had been blacked out), in addition to either removing the book from the shelves or, alternately, putting out a new edition that would incorporate any changes they saw fit to include. In essence, this amounted to a claim that the rape of young girls and boys and the production of child pornography are "private issues." The absurdity of such an idea is beyond compare.

It was obvious that the goal of their strategy was to wear me down emotionally and financially. The trial was held in Mexico City, and I was living in Cancun; I would have to make frequent trips to the capital in order to participate in my defense. A group of the country's most renowned journalists had to testify before the Court to the effect that I am indeed a journalist. I submitted copies of more than two thousand articles of mine that had been published prior to my arrest, as well as countless journalism awards I have received over the length of my career.

On November 13, 2008, I got a telephone call from my dear friend, the lawyer and activist Chihuahua Lucha Castro. She greeted me warmly, asking how I was and if I had been taking care of myself, and after I told her that I had, her voice began to crack.

"Armando Rodríguez Carreón, the reporter at *El Diario*, has been shot to death," she told me.

My smile dissolved instantly and a hot flash overwhelmed me; I knew that Armando had received two death threats, sent via text message to his cell phone. He was a very well known journalist, somewhat shy with women, and thoughtful with his friends. I first met him when I was in Juarez covering a protest against the murders of several women there. And I had crossed paths with him on plenty of other occasions when traveling to Chihuahua to speak with fellow journalists. I was at a loss for words; I thought about his daughters and his newborn child, about his wife. About his colleagues, who, as I see it, are an outstandingly brave bunch. Every one of them. I imagined the grief they must be feeling. I couldn't sleep that night.

Some days later, my therapist explained to me, "It's survivor guilt, Lydia. It's very difficult, emotionally, to understand why other people have been killed and you haven't. It may seem like something silly, but it's not. You feel guilty for having survived, and you eat yourself up because you can't help them. It's not in your hands—there's nothing more you can do; you can barely manage with your own case."

I decided that same day that I would dedicate part of my time to sharing information about personal security tactics and strategies to combat stress—all the valuable experience I have picked up over the years—with my fellow journalists. For now, that's the only thing I can offer all these colleagues of mine who, like myself, are living in a state of constant uncertainty and doing everything they can to come to terms with danger, to find ways to live with it, in order to continue with their lives and work.

On May 31, 2010, a group of police agents carrying exclusive-military-use assault rifles attacked our women's shelter. A municipal police agent confronted our security guard over the intercom, demanding that we hand over his wife and son. He claimed that we had kidnapped the two of them and were holding them against their will. Our security team went on red alert and moved into action instantly. His wife was indeed at the shelter—he had tried to shoot her to death and had abused the baby boy. He had made use of police equipment to track the woman, with help from the State Attorney General's Office. As always, the CIAM team was up to the challenge. We made video recordings of everything: the unit members' badge numbers, the attack on the gate, and the arrival of additional armed, hooded officers to assist in the task of trying to kick down the doors.

Eventually, the abusive husband snarled at the guard on the other side of the door, "Tell that Lydia Cacho that I'm going to report her for kidnapping and that her days are numbered."

We were able to get the federal police to come to our aid. But to our surprise, the commander merely showed up, took a look around, and left, explaining to his superiors that the men had hoods and assault weapons and that although some of them were wearing police uniforms, he thought they might be members of the Zetas or some drug cartel. After the shelter had been under siege for several hours, the state attorney general finally ordered the police to fall back. We documented everything, and ARTICLE 19, the Committee for the Protection of Journalists (CPJ), Amnesty International, and other organizations put out a worldwide alert. The response from our governor was that the country was currently in a very difficult situation and the drug cartels had infiltrated the police. He recommended that we close down the shelter; he could not guarantee our safety or our lives, or those of the women and children in our shelter, who had already been victims of extreme violence.

Following several months of legal actions, the police agent who had attempted to break into the shelter was sanctioned to one week's unpaid suspension. Months later, Quintana Roo state attorney general Gaspar Armando García Torres admitted in the media that 70 percent of Cancun's municipal police force had been infiltrated by the drug cartels. We spoke out publicly, hoping to at least make the attacks that were likely to come more costly to them. The forty-three-woman, one-man CIAM team spent two months on red alert, day and night, implementing safety and security precautions at every step along the way. In addition to the usual assortment of aggressors, the strong arm of the police had now become our publicly sworn enemy.

We held a risk assessment meeting with a group of experts who had worked with threatened individuals in Colombia. President Calderón's false war on drugs had weakened the social fabric of Mexico's communities; victims of domestic abuse in a majority of areas in the country were no longer able to find help. What with all the kidnappings, death threats, and infiltrations, many non-governmental organizations were no longer willing to assist victims of organized crime, whose numbers were growing daily. So it was that our shelter, almost overnight, became one of the few safe places left in the country. We were giving refuge to victims of the big cartel bosses, victims of human trafficking, and even to the wife of a pilot who flew for the cartels. She gave the federal authorities all the information she had, but her narcotrafficking husband was never arrested, despite the fact that she had even provided aircraft registration numbers for the planes being used to transport drugs from Cancun to Monterrey and Durango. Additionally, SEIDO was provided with the addresses and telephone numbers of his accomplices. We discovered firsthand which cartels were being protected by Calderón's administration and which were under the protection of the state of Quintana Roo. Like the rest of the country, we found ourselves besieged, surrounded by unprecedented levels of violence whose only aim was to spread chaos and terror and to encourage a repressive police state and the curtailing of freedom and rights. It was a war against legality, not a struggle to impose the rule of law.

Likewise, the hypocrisy of the American government had left us exceedingly vulnerable. Hillary Clinton had just concluded a visit to Mexico in which she had promoted the opening of new shelters for victims of human trafficking. And yet no one—not the Obama administration, not the Zapatero administration in Spain, and not any of the other countries supporting and vaunting this ridiculous "war on crime"—were willing to grant humanitarian visas to the victims who had taken the witness stand to give their testimony in cases of atrocious crimes and who were consequently being hunted down by criminals, or at times even tracked down by the state, and killed. Not even human rights advocates or journalists whose family members had been murdered received humanitarian visas. These victims were not the only ones affected; the situation extended so far as to include journalists and human rights advocates from the northern part of the country, who were forced to flee for their lives and begin an existence of odious exile, treated as undocumented, immigrant outcasts by the same governments that were praising Calderón's war.

In the space of four years, there have been three hundred thousand forced disappearances—men, women, and children whose whereabouts and fates are unknown. More than twenty thousand people killed in gunfights with merciless assassins. Thousands of citizens kidnapped. We resisted this chaos; our desire was to continue defending life, to continue defending the right to build a real justice system for our country. We decided, amid the endless exhaustion and sweat, to try to find a way to counteract the violent, warlike clamor that had begun to work its way into the public discourse. We chose not to surrender in the face of the anger this useless war awakens. To educate in the ways of peace, that was the answer.

NOT WITH MY CHILD!

I had come to an important decision: If I had to spend my time constantly moving from one place to another, I might as well break my self-reinforcing cycle of anxiety and turn all those trips into something positive and useful. I got myself more organized and began giving conferences and workshops on the topics of journalism and aiding victims of violence. I visited some ten American universities—first New York University and Columbia, then Stanford, the University of Southern California, and the University of Utah, to name a few— and had the honor of receiving the Wallenberg Medal from the University of Michigan, where my adopted daughter studied. After speaking with fathers and mothers and receiving hundreds of letters from parents desperate for guidance on what to do in cases of abuse, I decided to write a manual for the prevention and treatment of child sexual abuse. I had interviewed plenty of experts over the years, as well as having been involved in legal proceedings for hundreds of different victims. I was more than prepared for the task. It would be the best response I could give the teachers, doctors, nurses, and parents who were constantly asking me, *What should I do if a girl or boy I know has been abused?* So I rolled up my sleeves and got down to work, and in late 2009, I published *Not with My Child: A Manual for the Prevention, Understanding, and Treatment of Child Sexual Abuse.* The book became a bestseller, and my publisher and I sat down and decided to put out a very cheap edition, almost at cost, so that teachers throughout Latin America could have easy access to it, ordering off my website. The book turned out to be a blessing for me; with the proceeds from the sales, I was able to pay my overdue legal fees to the lawyers who had worked on my case, and even to set aside an emergency fund. Because, despite what the skeptics may think, if I am alive today, it is because I've been making and following security strategies for years, because I take the threats against me seriously, and because I have on more than a few occasions left my home, my state, and even my country in order to avoid an imminent attack. If there's one thing I've learned from the deaths of my colleagues, it is that threats can give way to actual acts of violence in very specific, concrete moments and that what we must do is remove ourselves from those extremely precise moments when everything comes together to make an attack a reality.

In January 2010, the four brave Supreme Court justices who had voted to demand an investigation into child exploitation networks and Governor Marín's role in them surprised the nation. They announced the publication of a book, *The Ways of Power: The Lydia Cacho Case* (Porrúa). Everything about the book is symbolic; the cover even displays a photograph of a mural, located inside the courthouse itself, entitled "Rape," by the artist Rafael Cauduro. The painting shows a woman tied to a chair, at the mercy of four men who are torturing her.

Justices Genaro Góngora Pimentel, José Ramón Cossío, José de Jesús Gudiño Pelayo, and Juan Silva Meza are completely convinced that "the journalist's fundamental rights were seriously violated." But even more significant is the fact that, after laying out their juridical analyses of the case, they attest that "the authorities under indictment are protecting and promoting pedophilia and child pornography networks." The entire book is surprising, not only because of the clarity of each of the justice's arguments but because its mere existence is indicative of a paradox. Four members of the highest court in the land have been forced, in their own words, to write a book in order to defend freedom of expression, to give voice to the victims of crime, and to protect the Supreme Court's investigative power, outlined in Article 97 of the Constitution, which allows it to settle issues in cases where high-ranking government officials have abused their power to the detriment of the country's citizenry.

This is extremely significant because, as these justices themselves admit, the country's most powerful forces took my case as an opportunity to mobilize against the Supreme Court, to weaken it, and, according to them, some of these same forces attempted to avail themselves of legal technicalities and use "the Puebla/Cacho Case" as a way to shrink the Court's investigative power so that in the future, a normal citizen such as myself or anyone else would be unable to turn to the Supreme Court after all other bids for justice had operated in favor of the powers that be. I was jailed and persecuted for writing a book, and several years later, the most upstanding members of the Mexican Supreme Court had found themselves forced to publish another book in order to inform society about what the majority of the justices, in a politically motivated decision, wished to hide about the justice system's inner workings.

At the time when the book you are reading was published, the justices' tome had inspired sixteen law school theses and become all but required reading for the master's degree in human rights and jurisprudence in Mexico.

SLAVERY, INC.

On June 9, 2010, I presented the first edition of my book *Slavery, Inc.*, (*Esclavas del poder*) in Spain. I had spent five years researching it. I decided to use the time between different trials to follow the trail of the large-scale human-trafficking mafias known for dealing in women and children. I had enough evidence to prove that as a result of the inefficacy of the Mexican judicial system and the consequentially high level of impunity in the country, drug cartels were throwing themselves wholeheartedly into the business of sexual slavery, exploiting children, teenagers, and adults alike. The support I received from non-governmental organizations the world over, from central Asia to the United States and Argentina, was inspiring. I discovered thousands of people doing highly effective work against human trafficking and child pornography, as well as journalists from a variety of countries who were unwilling to stop at writing a mere press release or report—famous columnists like Nicholas Kristoff, who is normally known for covering wars but who, upon learning of the magnitude of these human-trafficking operations, decided to get involved, as a citizen of the world. As a result, there was increased promotion for campaigns such as *CNN Heroes* and organizations such as Free the Slaves, another called Not for Sale, created by American ex-banker Dave Batstone, and that headed by my dear friend Rushira Gupta, the coordinator of an immensely large project aimed at combating the sexual exploitation of girls in India. My investigative work made me feel stronger than ever, and the risk was worth the effort—the combined efforts of thousands were breaking down walls designed to encourage silence and obfuscation regarding the functioning of slavery in the 21st century.

Meanwhile, in August 2010, I returned to Spain at the invitation of Bibiana Aído, Minister of Equality, to be named as an international ambassador for the United Nations' Blue Heart Campaign against sex trafficking. I was sworn in by members of the Spanish government and Antonio María Costa, executive director of the United Nations Office on Drugs and Crime (UNDOC). We were joined by two other goodwill ambassadors, the actresses Mira Sorvino and Belén Rueda.

Following the formal swearing-in session, an expert in Spanish cyber-policing approached me and said that he had read *The Demons of Eden*, that it was his go-to book for understanding a large number of issues surrounding child abuse and how pedophiles operate. He pulled the book from his briefcase—it was absolutely covered in highlighting, underlining, and all manner of markings and notes. A sob choked my throat, and I felt a warm wave welling up behind my eyes. I signed his book and felt deeply honored.

I was completely worn out but glad to see the large number of countries that were bringing the issue of human trafficking to light, and at the same time, I was able to witness how the media is slowly changing its discourse regarding prostitution and sexual violence. Many journalists have learned to differentiate between human trafficking and prostitution, and to not discriminate against women working in the sex industry. There's a long way to go yet, but achievements *have* been made.

It became clear almost overnight that the many steps being taken were finally leading forward, and several of the more-developed countries were beginning to admit that they, too, bore a share of the responsibility for the global exploitation of slaves.

Flying back from Spain, I felt unequivocally privileged to be living in this of all centuries, and privileged to have the strength required to face the challenges that my profession and my convictions bring me into contact with. *What I do is of service, and taken together with the work of thousands of people throughout the world, its transformative power is even greater*, I thought to myself. I leaned back in my seat, smiled, and sipped my water. I was happy, simply and completely happy.

A few months afterward, on December 6, 2010, our daughter, Clara, gave birth to a baby. When I finally got the chance to hold this beautiful, smiling boy in my arms, I felt something happen inside me. Four months later, while I was playing with him on the beach in Cancun, he turned to me with a peal of laughter that lit up his small, blue eyes, he rocked back and forth and bounced in my arms, then he placed his two tiny hands on my face. My breast swelled with an inner strength I had never known, and I made a silent vow that if I ever had to, I would give my life to protect this child from anyone who might do him harm. Babies are born every single day in this world, but when these newly arrived creatures look at us and smile, we are struck by the thought that there is something miraculous about their existence—an entire world's worth of hope dwells in their eyes. The birth of this little one filled me with strength, with happiness. After all these years, I had an epiphany—the strength that I have developed over time as a result of effort, circumstance, and the decisions of the powerful and corrupt has not reached its limit, it can grow greater still. Press on, every day, until there is not a single person on the face of this planet who thinks that abusing young girls and boy is normal or acceptable. Because to rape, harm, and abuse them is to rape, harm, and abuse the whole of humanity; it is a never-ending cycle of dehumanization. It has been said countless times before—to protect a young girl, a young boy, to give them a loving, wholesome childhood, is nothing less than to take a step toward changing the world.

POETIC JUSTICE

The sun was setting on Wednesday, August 31, 2011. I was in my car when I got an unexpected call. Araceli Andrade, one of the lawyers on the legal team working against Succar Kuri, told me that my presence was required at the federal courthouse in Cancun. The judge in charge of the Succar case, José Mata Oliva, wished to speak with me personally. I hung up and immediately called Lety, the head of security for CIAM Cancun. Then I alerted my lawyers at ARTICLE 19 and organized the trip to the courts, making sure I had my judicial injunction with me. (Every so often, my lawyers take out an injunction for me, so that I cannot be arrested by the Cancun police.) "The whole thing could be a trap, and we don't want any surprises," my lawyer cautioned me.

I identified myself at the entrance to the building, and several minutes went by before the judge's assistant arrived to show me in. I walked into his office, he greeted me with scrupulous formality, and I took a seat across from him at his desk, next to Araceli. I had never seen him in person. Until then, the only thing I knew about him was that he had been charged with reviewing the case after Quintana Roo judge Gabriel García Lanz, in a blatant act of corruption, had the audacity to sentence Succar to a mere thirteen years in prison for his crimes of child pornography and corruption of minors. García Lanz had imposed a fine of just 85,837 pesos on this multimillionaire. Emboldened, Succar appealed the sentence, demanding that he be set free. At the same time, the defense— which was being handled by the Attorney General's Office on behalf of the girls Succar had abused—made its own appeal, and it was at that point that the case fell into the lap of this judge before whom I now found myself sitting, a judge who had a solid reputation for incorruptibility. I scarcely breathed as I listened to what he had to say.

"I can tell you this now, because Jean Succar Kuri and his lawyers heard the sentence a few hours ago and they know all about it."

"Tell me, your honor," I asked in a barely audible voice, fearing the worst—an exoneration.

"I should tell you that have I reviewed each and every piece of evidence carefully. You are familiar with the evidence, are you not?"

I nodded silently.

"Not once in my career as a judge have I ever seen anything as horrifying as the videos Succar and his wife made of themselves preparing those little girls, girls less than eight years old, to be raped. It's inhuman."

"Yes, I know," I said, glancing at Araceli.

"The sentence, which the victims as well as the perpetrators will have formal access to as of now, is 112 years in prison and a fine of 527,174 pesos, and he will also be required to pay 320,000 pesos in damages per victim, a figure designed to allow them to cover the costs of their therapy, future studies, and any health problems resulting from their trauma. In other words, he will be required to pay 2.5 million pesos."

Araceli and I clasped each other's hands. We wanted to cry but couldn't help smiling. A smile accompanied by feelings of incredulity and relief.

"I made the decision to sentence him for each individual case," the judge went on, "because the law allows me to do so, and because of the seriousness of the crimes. I based my decision on the law against child pornography and human trafficking. And while Article 25 of the Federal Penal Code only allows for a maximum sentence of sixty years in prison, I wanted these girls and boys to understand that this court recognizes their bravery and that these crimes have been substantiated beyond all doubt."

"But he can appeal this sentence, can't he?" I asked, fearful of becoming caught up in yet another judicial imbroglio. "He's sixty-eight years old and he has health problems . . ."

"Yes, he can and he will, but the sentence is firm and the evidence is solid. This man's powerful position is what's allowed his defense team to secure him his due process all these years. Would you like to call the girls?" he asked, noticing that I'd been fidgeting with my cell phone.

I looked down at the phone and found that I couldn't shake the voice of Carmen, the girl who called me the morning we lost our case before the Supreme Court, from my mind. I dialed, and she picked up almost immediately. I told her the good news. Contrary to what I had expected, she remained silent at first, and then spoke calmly.

"Now we can move on with our lives—he won't abuse any more girls."

"That's right," I replied, impressed by the maturity this girl had developed over the course of seven years of judicial nightmares. I recalled that she was just nine years old when she was freed from the pornography ring, barely capable of speaking, and suffering from severe depression.

"Thank you, Lydia," she told me. "I'm overwhelmed. I'm going to hang up so that I can call the others."

"All right," I said happily.

The courthouse was abuzz with collective excitement. I looked at the young women and men who worked side by side with this exemplary judge, this judge who had never given in to the offers of money or the threats.

One of the young men working at the courthouse had a copy of *The Demons of Eden*. He held out a pen to me and asked with a smile, "Would you dedicate this? I was in Puebla studying law when you were arrested, and ever since that day, I've been working to specialize in these areas; things have to change in Mexico."

When we left the building, the press was already waiting for us. Araceli and I stuck to what was most important: *The sentence is a historic one for Latin America, for Mexico; it establishes a precedent against child pornography and human trafficking; there are still three active cases involving young girls and boys abused at the hands of the same network Succar Kuri headed; we mustn't forget about them.*

We said our good-byes, and I drove home. I called my family to tell them about the good news.

So this is what it feels like to win, I thought as I sat next to Jorge at our home in Cancun. *This is what peace of mind is, this is the peace that justice brings. It's so different from the dissatisfaction of vengeance.*

One week later, I received a telephone call from an unknown number. This time, when I picked up, I felt distracted and carefree. But then a colleague of mine spoke abruptly on the other end of the phone.

"Lydia," she said in an anxious tone, "I understand that you're happy, but you mustn't forget that when the judge called you to testify against Succar, Succar swore right there in the middle of that high-security prison, in front of your lawyers and the judge himself, that if he was sentenced, he would see to it that you were killed, even if it was the last thing he did in his life."

"I know, I remember," I replied, weary at noting the bitter taste of worry in my mouth once more. I hung up, but not without first promising her that I would get together with my lawyers and security advisor to assess the seriousness of the threat.

While preparing my security strategy, a source working at the United States Immigration and Customs Enforcement agency (ICE) in Mexico City contacted me to request a meeting. I imagined he wanted to speak to me about my investigations into human trafficking, or perhaps about my book *Slavery, Inc.* Many American and Canadian citizens travel to the Playa del Carmen to have sex with minors, and I thought he might have some questions for me on the subject.

I met with him in Mexico City. To my surprise, the topic of conversation was neither the white slave trade nor the trafficking of undocumented immigrants, issues that he and I had discussed during an interview a year earlier. What he wanted was to alert me to the fact that intelligence sources had learned that Succar's wife and children were back in Cancun, staying at the Solymar Villas.

Although Gloria Pita, wife and accomplice of the recently sentenced pedophile, was still living in her Los Angeles mansion, she had accompanied her children to Cancun, and the ICE had received a tip from a Mexican source that the Succars had been putting out feelers among corrupt police agents to find a hit man for a "little job" that needed doing. This American ICE agent thought the "little job" might be a hit on me, and he wanted to warn me. Although his information was of little use to me without proof, I thanked him for thinking of me and taking the trouble to warn me. And even if I did have proof, I explained to him, the authorities have told me in no uncertain terms that making death threats is not a crime, and neither is hiring someone. If there's no weapon and no crime has been committed, no charges can be brought, as the special prosecutor for crimes against journalists informed me.

"Perhaps, Ms. Cacho," the agent suggested, "you could ask my government to reopen the case against Mrs. Pita; after all, the evidence is there, and we don't really know for sure—it could be that the network is still operating inside the United States with American girls. Don't forget, Succar's capture in 2004 was made possible because the U.S. Marshals Service in Los Angeles was acting on a provisional arrest warrant issued as part of an extradition process. Why don't your lawyers check with the Mexican embassy? This is a case of binational jurisdiction; it's not just a Mexican problem. We've got hundreds of Mexican girls being trafficked into my country to be exploited in illegal brothels. You know this."

I did know it, but the problem was unmanageably big. There was no money left to keep paying lawyers who might take the case to Los Angeles. Moreover, we would need the support of the Calderón administration, and as we were already well aware, his administration was in fact protecting the political heads who were running the network. We would have to get the United States Justice Department involved and confirm whether Succar had set up his bank accounts in his wife's and children's names. And then, if we managed to prove the wife's guilt (theoretically, the same videos the American judge had seen and upon the strength of whose content he had decided to extradite Succar should provide evidence enough), we could demand an investigation and demonstrate the ties existing between these child pornography, human trafficking, and money laundering mafias, whose ranks include Mexican politicians and businessmen. Kamel Nacif, Succar's protector, already had a criminal record in the American state of Nevada and he had been denied an American entry visa under the Obama administration. All the cards were on the table.

One week after this meeting, I was forced to leave my home suddenly, escorted by the organized crime unit of the police, because of information from a Mexican police report that a contract killer was on my tail and that he had orders to murder me. I have since returned home, but only after spending several weeks in Europe waiting for everything to blow over. I did what I have done on countless other occasions and what I will no doubt have to do again on countless more—I publicly condemned the threats made against me, and I fled to save my life and to give my colleagues and the ranks of honest police officers time to investigate those seeking to harm me, while my lawyers reported the threats for the umpteenth time. The key is to let these hit men know that *we* know where they are, that we have video cameras, alarm systems, and, in some cases, even their telephone numbers. It's a pitched battle in which admitting defeat can mean losing your life. I have witnessed the deaths of several of my fellow journalists. I have spoken to young reporters who didn't believe the threats would amount to anything and who ended up murdered mere weeks later because they refused to report anything, to get out of town, to search for clues, names, emails, and likely suspects. We are at war, a war against freedom of expression, against human rights, and it is far better to err on the side of caution than to lose one's life.

ARTICLE 19 published an investigative report focusing on the situation of aggression against journalists in Mexico. The report proves that during the 2009–2011 period, the main perpetrators of acts of aggression against journalists were overwhelmingly state actors. Seventy-seven journalists were attacked by members of state police forces; federal police agents assaulted six journalists; municipal police agents, seven; and members of the armed forces, forty-one. To put it another way, state security forces, the very same forces that are charged with maintaining law and order, were responsible not only for a third of all assaults occurring from 2009 to 2011 but for half of the assaults committed specifically against members of the press in that same two-year period. In other words, the police state operates as an oppressor of freedom of expression.

Similarly, twenty-four assaults with a firearm or explosives against the offices of media outlets were linked to organized crime, as were twelve of the total twenty-seven murders involving journalists and other media collaborators, and two out of four cases of forced disappearance. In short, seven out of ten serious assaults are related to organized crime.

We journalists are endeavoring to document the reality of the situation on the ground in Mexico, and we have been caught between two sets of crosshairs. The trouble is that when we report on the state's complicity with mafia activity, *both* sides end up turning their sights on us. We can trust no one but ourselves.

The ARTICLE 19 report reminds us that stepping out of line and daring to finger a criminal boss are acts that will be punished and that more often than not, retribution will be marked by extreme brutality.

Lucía Lagunes, director of the women's-rights-focused news agency CIMAC Noticias—the first agency I ever worked at, more than fifteen years ago—reminds me that being a reporter who happens to be female is doubly dangerous. Femicides have increased 68 percent in the year from 2010 to 2011. In the space of fifteen months, 3,140 women and girls have disappeared from nine states across the country, while the corresponding state attorneys general's offices do nothing to enforce their search-and-rescue protocols, alleging that these women and girls have simply run away of their own volition.

Colombia experienced a similar phenomenon with the strengthening of their drug cartels and the weakening of their state. During that country's own war on drugs, Colombian women came to be treated as objects of lust, and their disappearance was viewed as utterly inconsequential in a context of war and exacerbated violence. In Mexico today, just like in Colombia, we are seeing how cartels are involved in the sexual exploitation of women, in kidnapping for the purposes of rape and murder. When the cat's away, the mice will have their field day.

Not even a small portion of the weight of the law has been brought to bear in Mexico on those who ended the lives of thirteen female journalists, or on those who made death threats against another hundred more and jailed and persecuted them. Nor has any light been shed on the deaths of eleven human rights advocates—four of whom were colleagues and personal friends of mine—who dedicated themselves body and soul to protecting the lives and integrity of the people in their communities. Our fears are well founded, which is why when I know that a particular threat creates a window of opportunity to kill me, I protect myself and leave the country. But I always come back, because I refuse to be forcibly pushed out or silenced by corrupt powers. Because I have the inalienable right to live in my own home, in my own land.

THE SLAVES SPEAK OUT

In January 2009, my publishing house gave me an advance to cover expenses for the second part of the travels I was making to investigate human trafficking networks operating in different areas of the world. I had previously put together a detailed layout of the routes the cartels and mafias use to transport women and girls around the globe. I packed a large canvas duffel bag with cold-weather clothing and set out on a journey that would last several months.

Alone, with my camera, my tape recorder, a notebook, and my list of NGO contacts as my only provisions, I traveled to London, Turkey, Kyrgyzstan, Uzbekistan, Tajikistan, Afghanistan, and the Afghan border with China. From there I flew to Thailand, where I traced the routes along which young girls are traded, venturing through the interior of the country to Burma (Myanmar). I then traveled through the villages of Vietnam, which I found reminded me a great deal of Mexico. After concluding this portion of my investigation, I headed to Japan to investigate the Yakuza in Tokyo and Osaka. And from there I flew to Los Angeles in order to document the Tokyo-Hawai'i-California route for the transportation of drugs and Asian women to the United States. I had investigated human trafficking in India, Nepal, and Sri Lanka, as well as in Latin America, on earlier trips. I was making progress on my documentation for *Slavery, Inc.*, and I felt sure that my work would be a positive contribution—demonstrating how ties between different cartels and human trafficking mafias are formed at the global level, investigating the origins of the problem, and documenting who the clients of these networks were in all the different parts of the world, as well as who their protectors were.

LOOKING AT MY HEALTH AND THE FUTURE

In the latter part of 2010, I began a new battle for my health. I had started falling ill constantly, despite following a slew of preventative medical measures and sticking to a healthy diet. I had just launched *Slavery, Inc.*, and while the subsequent tour was no doubt responsible for my exhaustion, it could not be the sole cause of the imbalances that were showing up on every one of my laboratory tests. Nobody, not even I myself, could understand it; I didn't look—and I don't look—like a sick person; all my friends reminded me of this fact constantly. Nevertheless, during the landing on a flight to the capital one afternoon, I collapsed in the airplane, and when I came to, I found myself in an ambulance at the Mexico City airport. I called my brother José, and he took me to a hospital emergency room. I eventually found an excellent doctor. Under the care of Dr. Valpuesta and an expert hepatologist, I underwent a biopsy, only to discover that I suffer from the same autoimmune disease that had killed my mother. After repeating the tests to confirm the results and then seeking out additional opinions, the doctors agreed that my disease was genetic in origin, and that extreme precautions had to be taken. My liver and remaining kidney were severely damaged.

Although stress may well have weakened my immune system, all the tests indicated that my body wasn't going to hold out much longer, as a hepatologist in Barcelona, Spain, informed me. Ghostly visions of the suffering my mother had endured for three agonizing years before passing away haunted my dreams and my waking thoughts. I made the decision to isolate myself from other people. I had a tour planned for France, Italy, Sweden, and other countries where translations of my book had been published. But what I needed was to be alone, in my home near the ocean. Only there, surrounded by the tranquility of that special place, near my flower and vegetable gardens, would I be able to recover the calm I needed to be able to make decisions. Several months went by, during which I worked radically less than usual. I handed over my post at CIAM entirely, leaving it in the expert hands of my dedicated colleagues. For whole wretched weeks at a time, I lay in bed, unable to move as the days went by and the doctors went after my disease with experimental treatments that left me completely spent. I felt a fear that was unfamiliar to me, fear at waking up one day to find my body paralyzed, unresponsive to my strength of will. Fear at the weakness of cloudy eyes no longer able to read. Fear at discovering my memory reduced to a feeling of having already written everything there is to say and being confronted now with a blank page and nothing but questions. I cried myself to sleep on many of those nights, curled up with a pain that was tearing at my veins, focused on the murmuring sound of my heart, beating slowly, like the heart of a wounded soldier gradually slipping away, giving himself over to the dark, cold night.

No more of this! I thought during these months of voluntary isolation. I've never had the heart of a nun or any such self-sacrificing woman; I refuse to become a perennial victim. Nobody, myself included, deserves suffering, uncertainty, the torment of death, or the never-ending howl of violence. This is a battle for dignity, not for martyrdom or sacrifice. At my side, my family, my dear friends, my therapists—all of them repeating fervently, *If you give up, you accept that the disease is going to take you.* One evening when I was feverish and exhausted, a kind friend placed a piece of paper in my hand. It was a fragment of a poem by Mario Benedetti, the poet of my teenage years:

> Don't give up, please, don't give in,
> Though the cold may scorch,
> Though fear may gnaw,
> Though the sun may set and the wind fall silent
> There is still fire in your soul,
> There is still life in your dreams,
> Because each day is a new beginning,
> Because the time and the best moment are now.
> Because you are not alone, because I love you.

My assistant Karla began the task of sorting through the overwhelming number of emails I was receiving, sometimes over a hundred a day. There were invitations to give talks on the prevention of violence, requests to file claims on behalf of many dozens of victims seeking my moral support. It was only then, knowing that I couldn't even make it down the stairs in my own home, that I became fully aware of the need for more heroes and heroines in this country. There are victims who require proper refuge, and it is not enough for them to be seen and heard—they need a working justice system and for their communities to have the capacity to protect them and help them overcome their pain. Marches and protests can make it easier for people to visualize and comprehend the magnitude of a tragedy, but at times they can generate an even greater sense of frustration and the whole thing can become something like moving through the Stations of the Cross—shouldering causes back and forth, shouldering sadness back and forth, feeding feelings of desperation and anger. It's strange: So many people seek me out to ask for help or guidance or inspiration, despite the fact that I've lost the majority of my legal battles; they want to know the secret of my fortitude, to drink it in, to go on believing that change is something they can hope for.

The mother of a girl who had been kidnapped by the Zetas to be used as a sex slave in a bar wrote to me one day as follows: "Lydia, for the love of God, help us, only you can stand up to the people who took my little girl. I pray to the glorious Virgin and to you, protect my daughter." I read these words of hers and I wept, right there in my bedroom. I am no one special, I'm a normal, middle-class Mexican woman; I've simply learned to use my strength for something I consider to be of vital importance—the eradication of violence and inequality.

Karla set energetically about referring all these victims who were contacting me to other activists, some to Javier Sicilia and others to the Child Rights Network, an organization offering protection and assistance to girls and boys.

I was forced to cancel the presentation of my book in Germany, where I would have sat side by side with my revered masters Günter Wallraff and Carolin Emcke. I did manage to attend one awards ceremony, spending the entire day in the hotel beforehand in order to recover from the journey there and to keep up my strength for the event itself.

This is the first time I have ever discussed my illness publicly. When your public persona comes to acquire a certain degree of fame, that life can intrude on and interfere with your private life, too; we lose those essential spaces that allow what my mother called our secret lives—the part of our lives that feeds our souls, a *dear little life* that no one can touch or spoil—to take place. Fame can be a difficult thing to live with in such a context, because society's conception of power is plagued with false expectations; it requires masks and a simplistic view of who leaders are and what leadership is. To journey down the path of notoriety is to venture into a minefield where arrogance and an outsize attention to one's own ego can become overwhelming. To understand fame as the objective of a journalist's career is to turn experts into boors, individuals of courage into cynics, and accidental victims into professional ones. The truth is that we are *all* survivors of human tragedy, of a dehumanizing, reductionist system that downplays the importance of everything that compels us to polish, care for, and shore up that immense mirror that allows us a clear view into that which is human and good, as well as all that which destroys good. The freedom of expression that we defend, sometimes at the expense of our lives, our health, or our solitude, is no less than a life-giving draught, because where there is communication among people, there is understanding. People who understand each other can feel compassion for one another despite the differences that may exist between them, and those who recognize those differences and acknowledge the humanity of others are the ones who come together to take water where there is drought, to bring justice to those who have been aggressed, or to help plant food for those who are hungry. When communication is manipulated by the powers that be, it tears apart the most human facets of our lives and our society, it crushes hope, it divides us and forces us to retreat, because it makes us believe that it is all but impossible for any of us to be heroes or heroines.

Good journalism, together with social activism, is an essential tool that serves to humanize; it helps us to see ourselves more clearly. To remember that the lives of others are valuable, to remember the importance of our own lives, not as heroic figures but simply as people who experience love and happiness, who strive for freedom, and who create a framework of leadership to promote those ideas.

I am distrustful of that brand of fame and all those who seek to label us as "special." For that reason, I avoid the cliques of movers and shakers, the in-groups of power that are perpetuated in the world of the media just as they are in any other world. I almost never discuss my fragile health. I prefer to focus on everything positive that has happened over the years, on the many achievements and demonstrations of solidarity I have witnessed. On that pristine drop of water that falls over and over, second after second, and that is slowly transforming the landscape of humanity. The scale of our combined efforts to build peace is astounding. I am filled with the spirit of these efforts every time sickness confines me to my bed, and then I breathe easy. It's worth being a part of that wellspring of life, of course it's worth it—just look around you.

On Saturday, November 12, 2011, I got myself out of bed in order to accompany two thousand high school and university students on a march organized by I Am Not for Sale, a campaign I thought up while seated alone at my computer and later brought to fruition with the help of the team at CIAM. While on bed rest, I developed a tool kit of educational materials that would be distributed to students between the ages of thirteen and twenty-one. I led an initial workshop to train five hundred young people and their teachers. The idea is very simple: To educate is to bring out and share something you have within yourself, and so in order to educate these girls and boys about human trafficking, we put together a model that allowed them to see how human trafficking networks operate, how they snare their victims. Rather than scaring these potential victims, we would have to offer them empowerment, knowledge, and tools.

And that is precisely what we did—after a year of work, nearly ten thousand young people were now qualified to train other students, specifically, to teach them to detect traffickers who might be hanging around outside schools and to understand the effects of forced prostitution. We need thousands of young activists, and we need them to avoid becoming victims themselves, so that they can uncover the strength and bravery that will allow them to protect themselves and others.

And the campaign worked. The march the students organized was an inspiring display. As they each took their turn at the podium, they spoke about their experiences educating elementary school children, both girls and boys, about human trafficking. One young man brought tears to my eyes when he took the microphone and told those listening how he had been stopped and offered money to get into a luxury-model car and have sex with a man inside. The boy was in need of money for books, but now that he understood the dangers of sexual exploitation, he ran away. When I returned home after the event, I was both exhausted and moved. *This is what we have to do*, I thought to myself: to beg children's forgiveness for the world we are leaving them and equip them with the tools they need to change the course of things, with peaceful, compassionate leaders, not warriors or conquerors, but transformers, because their bravery lies not in weapons or a will to control but in their convictions and their ability to live together peaceably.

Now that I was back home, my sickness and the intense treatment I was undergoing left me no other choice than to go back to reading poetry, meditating, and taking sunset walks on the beach. I fell off the map, and except for the columns I was writing, I did very little apart from resting and trying to stay on top of a combined course of alternative and allopathic treatments in order to keep my body in some approximation of a balanced state. I began to take a turn for the worse in December of 2011, when my health collapsed to the point that my life was in danger. As always, my friends Alicia, Lía, and Dr. María were there to take care of me, as were my family and other close friends. At the end of that same month, my relationship with Jorge, which had recently begun to break down, came to a definitive end. He was unable to take on my illness—he was experiencing his own difficulties—and we bid each other a sorrowful good-bye.

True to form, my family—my tribe—rushed to the rescue. They took turns caring for me, and they made sure I always had all the medicine and treatments I needed. As 2012 dawned, I felt a new, different strength stirring within me. In a meeting I had with her in Mexico City, Jean Shinoda Bolen, Jungian analyst and author of the book *Goddesses in Everywoman*, insisted that what I noticed within myself, that novel strength, is what is known as wisdom. I'm not entirely convinced that this is the case, but I acknowledge, as she requested I do, that at forty-nine years of age, I have lived a life full of marvelous adventures and challenges that have made me an example for others. I accept this role with the utmost humility possible.

January 2012 came around after a month of great changes. Following a lengthy, thorough process of reflection, the team and I determined that it was no longer feasible for the women and children's shelter to continue to operate. I had previously handed over the day-to-day management to my colleagues, but I was still the president of the board. Some adjustments had been made to accommodate everyone in the new situation, but the wear and tear on the rest of the team was simply too great, and for some time I had already been considering shifting the focus of my work to comprehensive education for peace. The team was ready; they had enough experience to allow them to train thousands of people in victim assistance and to work with children and young people against the resurgence of sexism and the culture of violence and murder for hire that this disgraceful war against drugs had unleashed.

While I was in the hospital, several members of the team made a public announcement to the effect that the Comprehensive Women's Care Center (CIAM Cancun, NPC), our shelter for women and their children, would slowly be converted into a training and education center for peace and the prevention of gender and social violence. I wrote the following letter, which was circulated publicly:

As of January 2012, CIAM will cease to offer assistance, rescue, and shelter services to women and children, in order to focus on the education and orientation of social and educational institutions directly or closely involved in assisting victims of gender violence, be they women, young people, or children. We are not shutting down, we are transforming.

On the one hand, ten years of experience in the field of victim assistance has allowed us to develop a model that has garnered multiple international recognitions and is capable of being reproduced in communities in practically every corner of the globe, and in Latin America in particular. The work carried out by our team of women and men has produced some invaluable results, including the specialization of experts in the areas of prevention, rescue, attention, and social reintegration of victims of all manner of gender violence. Additionally, we have generated a database detailing the characteristics of victims, their aggressors, and their children, their sociocultural backgrounds, their origins, educational levels, and so on. This has allowed us to dispel some of the myths surrounding the topic of violence against women, young people, and children. Every life saved, every family that has been able to develop the tools they need to reconstruct their lives in a context free from violence was worth all the effort, all the threats, all the government and mafia pressure.

Every institution goes through a life cycle; those that remain stuck in the past tend to become fragmented, worn out, and their missions eventually become bereft of meaning. Over the course of the last decade, we have trained hundreds of people and opened new shelters for women and children in Quintana Roo; these shelters will see to it that victims there are not left unprotected.

The number of women, young people, and children affected by this phenomenon all over the world, and in Mexico in particular, continues to increase rather than decrease. Gender violence is not only on the rise, it is becoming markedly crueler—femicides, sexual violence, and human trafficking have all experienced upsurges. The direct and indirect activities of organized crime networks, taken together with negligence on the part of the state and the proven links between organized crime and law enforcement, make it impossible to safeguard the defense and protection of human rights, not only the rights of victims and their families but also of skilled human rights advocates who lay their lives and honor on the line every day.

We understand that within Mexico's current context of violence, progress will not be possible as long as the source of the violence remains unaddressed. It is clear to us that our experience in this field allows us to participate more directly and assertively in these matters and to have a greater impact on the creation of a peaceful society that will apply an appropriate gender perspective not only to women and girls but also to boys, who can fall victim to nascent conceptions of masculinity that push them toward violence and social exclusion.

Our extraordinary success these past ten years, together with the more recent I Am Not for Sale campaign—which was initiated by CIAM Cancun, NPO, and for the last several months has been headed and run by nearly eight thousand students between the ages of ten and twenty-one—demonstrates that a strategy of working together with new generations, of promoting prevention, and of educating in positive values aimed at peaceful, egalitarian coexistence is the best strategy in both the medium and the long term.

On the other hand, the funding crisis that nonprofit organizations have been experiencing has deepened in recent years, making the financing of our activities impossible. The economic downturn has hardened public policy and cut the federal, state, and municipal budgets that allow our nurses, psychologists, social workers, peace educators, and lawyers to draw anything resembling a reasonable salary in exchange for their work assisting thousands of women and children. Philanthropic organizations from the private sector at both the national and international level have likewise made significant reductions in their support of efforts against gender violence, and particularly in the areas of human trafficking and violence against women. There are sufficient resources to fund victims' rescues, but not enough for them to rebuild independent lives for themselves. The tendency on the part of governments to hold up tallies of rescued trafficking victims as evidence that they are complying with international policies has given rise to a perverse perspective in which it is only victims' pasts that hold any importance, and not their futures as survivors able to live in conditions of freedom and safety.

We are deeply grateful to all those who have been able to join with us over the years and aid more than ten thousand people annually through special donations and moral and financial support. Every life that we were able to help was worth all the effort, every rekindled sense of optimism reawakened our own hope that Mexico will one day be a country free from violence, where equality is an absolute right rather than an occasional, unexpected boon.

We are still here, and we will continue do what we can with what we have.

Here we stand, for equality and peace, and we will never take a single step backward.

When I founded CIAM, I decided that I would never draw a salary from it—I always lived off my work as a journalist and from giving conferences and workshops—but I worried now about what might happen to the other team members if they ended up out of work. Fortunately, with the training and experience they had gained at CIAM, they all found positions in other organizations. It was a moment of great sadness for all of us; we felt a distinct sense of loss, but we knew that we had to adapt and move forward. We would not give up—we simply needed to find different strategies to continue working without making outrageous sacrifices, to continue working from a position of greater strength and security. Logical coherence dictates that human rights advocates must protect and defend themselves in the same manner and to the same degree as they protect the victims they aid; in this, too, there must be equality.

CIAM remained in operation with a small working group of thirteen individuals who are currently developing an educational model for the *prevention* of gender and social violence, as well as continuing work on the I Am Not for Sale campaign. I assisted these colleagues of mine in the development of a master plan for peace education that incorporates a gender perspective and then left the institution in their hands. It was an institution that had begun as a dream of mine more than fourteen years ago, when I came to the realization that it was not enough to condemn violence, but that instruments would have to be created to break the cycle of that violence and ensure that those who have suffered as a result of it know that society stands with them and is protecting them, so that they, in turn, can educate society about other forms of coexistence. Now I left this institution behind, and I cofounded the Red Nacional de Refugios para Mujeres [National Network of Women's Shelters], which currently operates forty nonprofit women's aid shelters across the country. When we started out, thirteen years ago, there were four. The numbers are encouraging, and our achievements are tangible.

FOLLOW THE MONEY TO FIND THE CRIME

There is a maxim in the world of journalism: If you want to find the crime, you have to follow the money. This strategy can sometimes work, and on this occasion—to the dismay of Mario Marín, the famous "Precious Guv'"—it did. With the arrival of a new governor in the state of Puebla, public records came to light revealing that embezzlement and indebtedness incurred during Marín's six-year term in office. SEIDO opened an investigation, looking to confirm possible illicit gains made by the former governor. In February 2012, while Governor Marín was busy leaving his state with a public debt of nine billion pesos, his son, Mario Marín García, having recently married the young Austrian woman Nadja Ludmer, was sharing photographs on Facebook of his luxurious lifestyle in Europe. The new couple was showing off their chalet in Wels, an Alpine region in Austria, to their friends from Puebla.

The reporter Roberto Soriano followed the lead and discovered that this home, owned by the governor's son, is "located in one of the most exclusive regions in the world, renowned as a refuge for princes, kings, magnates, and the Hollywood elite." The property is valued at US$5 million. Investigations were also able to uncover the existence of a mansion in Converse, Texas, at 8415 Whitebrush Street, worth over US$1.5 million. Additionally, official registries in Hialeah, Florida, list Marín García as the owner of a Lago Grande residence, Condo Three, valued at more than US$1 million. In conjunction with the investigations carried out by journalists and the federal authorities, it was documented that Marín's children, nieces, and nephews, as well as the former governor himself, were driving Porsche, BMW, and Cadillac sports cars in both Mexico and the United States.

Mario Marín's son acted as a straw owner of his father's fortune. It is impossible, according to SEIDO authorities, for a person of his age to have acquired such wealth. The authorities are investigating the methods used to triangulate monetary resources that may have come from a combination of public funds misappropriated by the governor directly and kickbacks received in exchange for political favors, as it is plain that the income generated from the legal businesses in his name does not match up with either the total amount of wealth he has accumulated to date or the lifestyle he, his children, and his wife enjoy.

During those same first few months of 2012, the authorities detained several members of Marín's inner circle. Alfredo Arango García, Secretary of Health during Marín's term, was arrested for illicit gain. As of the present moment in 2013, SEIDO continues to pursue Marín and, as part of Criminal Case Number 6/2012, has already submitted evidence attesting to illicit gains on the part of the former governor and eight others to the judge at the Twelfth District Court for Federal Criminal Cases of Mexico City.

Writing in the weekly *Acento Veintiuno* about how Marín had absconded from justice, Roberto Soriano wrote, "Intelligence agencies report that he has already left the country in order to avoid his imminent detention; the country he has chosen to make his escape to: Holland." I tasked myself with trying to confirm whether there were any indications of Marín's having entered that particular country. Immigration services did indeed register him as having made an arrival in Amsterdam, but he then returned to Puebla and has held meetings with high-ranking members of the PRI there on five occasions since. On February 22, 2013, the Puebla edition of the daily *Acento Veintiuno* published the following information on Mario Marín's reappearance in Mexico:

Last Friday, February 15, 2013, Julieta Octavia Marín Torres— former federal deputy for the 16th District, headquartered in Ajalpan, and sister of the "Precious Guv'"—attended the meeting held by the PRI in Puebla, a meeting at which the party's national leadership, headed by César Camacho and Ivonne Ortega, was also present.

When interviewed, Ms. Marín confirmed the former governor's intention to return to politics, a move that would allow him to emerge from the state of ostracism in which he has been mired since 2010, when he left his post amid serious suspicions of corruption. The accusations even led to the jailing of his former health secretary, while his colleague and friend Javier García Ramírez still has an active arrest warrant out against him.

"We aren't going to count ourselves out, we're waiting for the party primary to be called and then, if we can, why not? We're not dead, we're alive."

"It's payback time," he told many of his former colleagues and accomplices after gathering them together at the close of the previous year at a resort spa owned by Rodolfo Chávez Carretero, where they were discovered plotting and scheming.

The photographic evidence is irrefutable. There can be no doubt—the conspiracy to regain power in Puebla is under way. The words of the "Precious Guv'" leave no room for doubt, either: "We are going to take back Puebla for the PRI and for ourselves."

I took up my notes from the Succar-Nacif-Marín case and began to go over them again. One of the young Mexican girls who had fallen victim to the Cancun sex trafficking network affirmed in a statement in 2004 that three American girls from Florida were brought over on a private plane, which they said belonged to a governor. That line of investigation was never followed up on, but now, in 2012, the American Drug Enforcement Agency (DEA) has uncovered the existence of a company called Servicios Aéreos Mileneo [S.A. de C.V.; a variable capital society whose name translates as Millennium Air Services], whose main clients are the Puebla state government and the PRI administrations in nine other Mexican states. Former governor Marín is known to have made an illegal allocation of US$66.4 million of public funds for the purchase of a fleet of helicopters and airplanes through his son Mario Marín García and other straw men, who have already given statements to the authorities.

I verified with official sources at the DEA that their investigation is in fact the fruit of a joint effort undertaken with SEIDO. The weekly *Acento Veintiuno* published a conversation in which the Puebla state deputy Ricardo Urzúa (PRI) explains how the then governor of Quintana Roo, Joaquín Hendricks, gave the "Precious Guv'" US$3 million for the fleet. The company was created with public funds but is owned by Marín's son, who is now under investigation because, according to both the DEA and SEIDO, drug boss Arturo Beltrán Leyva is known to have traveled on one of its airplanes several times in 2010. This all came to light because Mexican businessman Darío López Fernández was arrested at Miami International Airport in July 2010 for bulk cash smuggling. The DEA and SEIDO confirmed that López Fernández had purchased a Bell helicopter, registration number XA-IMS, from Maclovio Hernández, who has been tied to narcotrafficking operations. López Fernández and Hernández owned a business that used a Beechcraft King Air, registration number XB-DLS, and a Cessna 182, registration number XB-KWE, which is how the Mexican Attorney General's Office identified that the aircraft had also been used by Beltrán Leyva in order to escape a police raid in Puebla. It is the very same aircraft that was used to transport Marín's chosen successor to the governorship, Javier López Zavala, during the latter's electoral campaign. Marín was under close scrutiny at this point, with serious accusations having already been made against him to the effect that he was protecting a criminal network involved in the sex trafficking of minors, and yet his businesses and his ties to dangerous friends were allowed to continue without ever missing a beat.

On November 15, 2010, I published this information in my column in the national newspaper *El Universal*; I included all the same aircraft information that you, the reader, will find below. A few days later, during a layover at the Mexico City airport while returning to Cancun from Spain, where I had been doing some investigative work, a man approached me.

"Ms. Cacho," he addressed me amiably in front of ten or so other people who, like me, were all waiting in line to board the airplane. "I read your column about Mario Marín and his airplanes. It was very good, but it's very dangerous, isn't it? I bet you're scared to be flying back to Cancun."

Still smiling, the individual made a smooth about-face and sauntered away toward the international departure gates without even waiting for my reply. A businessman from Cancun who was a longtime acquaintance of mine had been standing next to me the entire time, and now he leaned in toward me, his face pale.

"Did I hear that right? I think he just threatened you—we have to do something."

Ex-governor Mario Marín is the owner of seven 407-model Bell helicopters worth a total of US$21 million, two 206 Bells, and two Augusta helicopters valued at US$16 million. Additionally, he paid US$600,000 for two Cessna 2008 XA-TWT aircraft. He also has a Sabre Cinergo, registration number XA-GUR, worth US$300,000, a Dassault Falcon 20 priced at US$350,000, and four Learjet 45s. An INTERPOL agent assures me that the evidence to back all this up is rock solid. I followed the trail of several of these aircraft personally, through a variety of different civilian airports. Flying on them at one time or another, among others, were the following men, all governors at the time: Mario Marín (Puebla), Joaquín Hendricks (Quintana Roo), Pablo Salazar (Chiapas), Fidel Herrera (Veracruz), Ulises Ruiz (Oaxaca), Ismael Hernández (candidate and governor of Durango), Enrique Peña Nieto (then governor of the State of Mexico), and Tomás Yarrington (Tamaulipas). The governors of the states of Nuevo León, Nayarit, Querétaro, and Tabasco also chartered these aircraft at different points. All of them were aware that the company belongs to Marín, and all of them contributed public funds to it, in a business model that could be likened to a timeshare. A variety of senators and congressional deputies are also known to have hired the company's aircraft when they wished to give third parties the impression they owned a private airplane. But lies are no match for official record books.

Both President Felipe Calderón and the attorney general of Mexico, Marisela Morales, had access to this information. Intelligence personnel from the American embassy in Mexico informed me that their country's ICE had used diplomatic channels to petition for special attention to be paid to any and all aircraft and properties registered in Mario Marín's name. There was sufficient formal evidence to prove collusion on the part of public servants, illicit transportation of undeclared cash, and probable links to organized crime. The president was in a position to make a high-profile arrest in order to demonstrate that his government was truly willing to take a stand against the ever-strengthening ties between mafias and state governors. Personnel from the Mexican Army Air Force who collaborated with the DEA and ICE to catch Darío López Fernández smuggling cash into Florida insisted there was evidence against Marín. A general who was a member of the intelligence team for the Mérida Initiative[23] revealed the following information to me in an interview: "We told the president that Mario Marín was an exemplary case, given his history of protecting pedophiles, and now all of this on top of it . . . but he didn't want anything to do with the case; nobody understands why the president simply didn't want anything to do with it."

The case provided clear documentation of the shameful squandering of millions of dollars of public money on Mario Marín's aircraft company. Mayors, governors, and senators flitting around in private jets and helicopters, not for emergency reasons but to improve their own political images. A company that was used, according to binational investigations, to export large sums of cash from Mexico to Texas and Florida. A company operating under the opacity of straw men, whose identities have since been revealed; a company used to transport minors, dirty money,

---

23. Translator's Note: The Mérida Initiative is a security cooperation agreement between the governments of the United States, Mexico, and the Central American countries. Its purpose is to combat the interrelated problems of organized crime, money laundering, and drug trafficking.

criminals, and politicians. All the evidence was handed over to the authorities. Now, from 2013 to 2017, the case will be in the hands of the current Mexican attorney general, Jesús Murillo Karam, a member of the PRI and personal friend of over half the governors who made use of the aircraft in question. Despite all of this, the case may still move forward; only time will tell. The well-wishing of some of Marín's colleagues notwithstanding, the truth of the matter is that both SEIDO and INTERPOL have files open on the former governor—files that include my own formal complaints and now others, as well—for acts of corruption, misappropriation of public funds, and a whole range of violations of citizens' individual guarantees committed during his term in office. At the end of 2012, the online newspaper *sinembargo.mx* published the following article about Marín's return:

> Fernando Moreno Peña, the National Executive Committee (CEN) delegate for the Institutional Revolutionary Party (PRI), has declared that he met with former governor Mario Marín Torres, a personal friend of his, a few days before the party's candidates were to be nominated.
>
> He stressed that the former Puebla governor—in contrast to Elba Esther Gordillo Morales, the erstwhile longtime leader of the National Education Workers Union (SNTE)—has not been charged with anything and is not in jail.
>
> "I have seen Mario Marín in private conversations and he is an active member of the PRI; his presence will not affect the party, but this whole Elba Ester thing will, because she's in jail for being involved in organized crime, while Mario Marín is free," he explained.
>
> Moreno Peña went on to mention that Marín's outfit would be working with the PRI on the current electoral campaign, and that party activists—Marín included—were eager to make up the seats they lost in 2010.

He denied that Marín Torres's image would have an effect on his party, given that the former governor's name would not be appearing on any election ballots, his participation would be limited to supporting the party through his membership, and he had not, moreover, been charged with any crime.

"According to the international ratings agency Standard and Poor's, Marín Torres negotiated a skillful capital repayment on the entirety of the state's debt, using the revenue shares the state of Puebla would receive from the federal government—the transfer of said shares having begun to be paid out in this case in August 2011—as collateral."

"At the beginning of Marín Torres's term, the state of Puebla owed almost zero liabilities. But by 2008, Marín Torres was facing a legal case against him for the scandal surrounding the recorded conversations of his, a scandal that led to the illegal, arbitrary detention of the journalist Lydia Cacho," the website puebl@ media.com explains.

"This led in turn to an initial public debt of 3.5 billion pesos, which he spent on his legal defense before the Supreme Court of Justice of the Nation. He then chartered more than 500 hours of helicopter flights for himself and his defense team, led by attorney Juan Velázquez. The 'Precious Guv" spent more than 32 million pesos of state money on this transaction. The numbers are overwhelming if one considers that every hour of flight costs US$5,000, according to the airplane and helicopter rental agency Flyjets, whose calculations took into account the aircraft models and Mario Marín's flight distances and times," the puebl@media. com article says.

According to puebl@media.com, "the travel stipends for his defense team allowed, among other things, for luxury hotels on Campos Elíseos Avenue in Mexico City, at upwards of ten thousand pesos per night per room. By July of 2010, Mario Marín had paid out 500 million from the Puebla treasury for a marketing and advertising campaign aimed at restoring his public image, which had deteriorated not only at the state level but across the entire country."

Despite the fact that Marín claimed publicly to still be working at his public notary office, those offices are in fact semi-deserted, and Marín's substitute, Vicente Gil Luna, who oversees some of the office's operations, has not been officially designated as a deputy notary. The logs for the INTERPOL special investigation unit and a similar unit at the Mexican Bureau of Investigation and National Security (CISEN) report the following:

Mario Marín Torres is known to be in the habit of hiring escorts for private functions. There is evidence confirming his various romantic interests as well as his relationship with a minor. Marín has met with Kamel Nacif on two occasions in the city of London, England, where he is being monitored by the authorities. Possible ties to businessmen involved in acts of fraud. Of the several straw owners he makes use of, three are individuals who are under investigation. He is known to have a penchant for underage women. His right-hand man, Javier García Ramírez, has an active arrest warrant against him for illicit gain. Mario Marín and Valentín Meneses made a transaction with the Spanish company OHL for nearly 5.66 billion euros; fraud was detected. Valentín Meneses was sworn in as Secretary of Transportation while simultaneously drawing a salary as an advisor to OHL. The organization Pueblos En Defensa De La Tierra Y El Agua [Towns for the Protection of the Earth and Water] has initiated a lawsuit and will seek damages from Mario Plutarco Marín Torres and Valentín Meneses. The portion of Mario Marín's personal wealth held in his son's name is 15 billion pesos.

There is an information sheet attached to the file for the case that SEIDO currently has open on Mario Marín Torres and Mario Marín García, which reads:

During the period when Mario Plutarco Marín Torres (MPMT) was in office, fraudulent public works projects proliferated throughout the state. The Tetela de Ocampo, Izúcar de Matamoros, and Cuetzalan public hospitals were inaugurated but unusable, because they had been built without plumbing, potable water, electricity, or equipment. The Pahuatlán and Ahuacatlán hospitals were built on top of PEMEX[24] pipes and below high-tension wires. The federal government, through the Special Unit for the Investigation of Operations Involving Illicitly Acquired Funds (UEIORPI) joined together all its separate files, and the Federal Public Ministry agent assigned to the Assistant Attorney General's Office for Special Investigations on Organized Crime (SEIDO) submitted evidence at the beginning of the year that attests to illicit gains on the part of Mario Marín Torres and eight other individuals to the judge at the Twelfth District Court for Federal Criminal Cases of Mexico City, as part of Criminal Case Number 6/2012. Currently (March 2013), the Comptroller General's Office reports having initiated 187 legal proceedings against public servants operating under the direction of MPMT in the state of Puebla.

THE DEVIL IN DANGER

On July 18, 2012, rumors began to circulate that Succar, whom the other prisoners had nicknamed "The Devil," had died in Altiplano, the high-security prison in Toluca. That same day, the press published a note by the news agency APRO.

> CANCUN, Q. Roo (APRO)—The Lebanese businessman Jean Succar Kuri, who is currently serving a 112-year prison sentence for pedophilia and trafficking of minors, left the Altiplano maximum security prison facility last Sunday and was admitted to Adolfo López Mateos regional hospital in Toluca, in the State

---

24. Translator's Note: Petroleos México, Mexico's state-owned oil company.

of Mexico, for reasons of renal insufficiency. 68-year-old Jean
Thouma Hanna Succar Kuri, alias "El Johnny," was released
today; his return to prison was scheduled for later in the day.

Prison authorities confirmed that Succar was suffering from
serious prostate trouble but noted that he was receiving medical
attention and had full access to his medications. Despite having
proven himself to be a dangerous prisoner, his lawyers were attempting to remove him from the high-security prison where he was being
held under strict watch, insisting that for reasons of age and health,
he should be allowed to serve out the remainder of his sentence at
his beachside villa development in Cancun. My sources inside the
prison told me that "El Johnny" was afraid of the other prisoners,
who tormented him constantly, that his family no longer came to
visit him, and that he was deeply depressed.

FLEE TOWARD LIFE

The end of 2012 found me meeting with specialists to work out how
I might be able to return home after having fled suddenly in the
face of a death threat that crackled down the line to me through
a voice scrambler attached to a type of radiotelephone only drug
cartel bosses have access to. I had learned some time ago that death
threats serve two purposes. The first is to allow criminals the opportunity to revel in the thought of their murderous act. The antici-
patory pleasure that contract killers experience is something like
what a hungry hyena feels when it catches the scent of fear on the
air. The second is to make victims emotionally unstable, to prompt
individual self-censorship as well as censorship on a collective scale.
I can't remember how many times I've heard press directors tell me
that when they send reporters into the field to cover certain stories,
the latter retort, "And what if the same thing happens to me as happened to Lydia Cacho?" What they are really asking is if they are
persecuted or jailed, who will protect them.

I was in Veracruz, working on tracking down information about a pedophiliac priest involved in a child pornography network; that trip was the last time I ever saw Veracruz journalist Miguel Ángel López, whom everyone called Milo. He had told me that he'd received new threats but that he felt he could no longer continue obeying his fear and leaving the state at the drop of a hat every time someone warned him he was going to die. He and I had spoken precisely about how expensive it is to be moving constantly from place to place. On June 20, 2011, a colleague of mine telephoned me, crying. Hired gunmen had just murdered Milo, along with his wife and his youngest child, a professional photographer who, like his father, worked at the Veracruz newspaper *Notiver*. Two other colleagues of mine, Gabriel Huge and Guillermo Luna, who had also received threats and with whom I'd previously compared notes on security strategies, fled Veracruz immediately. Milo's murder reminded them that threats are part of a deadly game and must not be ignored. The ARTICLE 19 lawyers, who were Gabriel and Guillermo's legal representatives as well as my own, helped the two men get to a safe location outside Veracruz.

Almost nobody stops to think about the enormous emotional and financial costs involved in working as a journalist under these conditions. Emotional instability prompts health problems; some turn to alcohol in order to be able to sleep at night, others take drugs, and still others use tranquilizers to help them withstand their depression and anxiety. Leaving your home and relocating, sometimes with nothing more than the clothes on your back or one small suitcase, leaving behind your family, small children, and pets—it all adds a little more to your overall state of fatigue. In fact, those who threaten us manage to make us feel what a fugitive on the lam must experience—the sensation of having one's world turned upside down. A dear colleague of mine asked me to go to Milo's burial in Veracruz, to help buck up all our fellow journalists there who were now feeling so vulnerable. But my health once again prevented me from traveling. I went up to my study and lit a candle, and I thought about all the work still left to be done, about my colleagues throughout the country who continue to work with great diligence and astuteness for meager pay. *We need strength*, I repeated to myself like a mantra. I looked at several photos of Gabriel and "Memo," two young men chock full of convictions, and I hoped with all my heart that they would be safe, that what had happened to Milo and his son would not happen to them.

It was April 28, 2012, and I had finally found the time to celebrate my forty-ninth birthday, at a restful getaway at Bacalar Lagoon with some friends. My telephone rang. The voice on the other end stammered, barely able to get the words out.

"They killed her, they killed Regina, right in her very own home."

Regina Martínez was an indigenous Totonac,[25] a rather shy woman who was never without her tape recorder, her notebook, and a black pen and who had the habit of adjusting her glasses periodically, almost like a nervous tic, whenever she was especially focused during an interview. For years, she had been *La Jornada*'s correspondent in Veracruz, and like all good reporters in Mexico, she moonlighted in the local press to make ends meet; at the time of her death, she was working as a correspondent for *Proceso*. She was found murdered in her home, severely beaten.

From 2000 to 2011, seventy-seven journalists were violently assassinated by criminal organizations.

In more recent months, these same groups have killed fifteen reporters, "disappeared" three others, and used firearms or explosives to attack nineteen radio and newspaper offices. We know that a large portion of these attacks against journalists were perpetrated by agents of the state—governors, mayors, police officers, and members of the military who start to squirm whenever they are confronted with truthful reporting. None of us could forget the fact

---

25. Translator's Note: The Totonacs are an indigenous people now residing mainly in the Mexican states of Puebla and Veracruz.

that Regina's was the fifth murder of a journalist in Veracruz during Javier Duarte's[26] tenure in office, or that thirteen other journalists had fled the state as a consequence of death threats or censorship. Regina's final piece for *Proceso* read: "9 Police Officers with Ties to Narcotrafficking Arrested in Veracruz" and "Alleged Top Hit Man 'Comandante Tere' Captured in Veracruz."

Then on May 3, 2012, having since returned home following what they thought was an appropriate absence after reporting the threats made against them, Gabriel and Guillermo were found dead. Their lifeless bodies, displaying signs of torture, had been dismembered, just as the individuals who'd threatened them said they would be. I didn't have the strength to attend the funeral. It was months earlier that the ARTICLE 19 lawyers helped them flee after the two were jailed and tortured for five hours by a group of militarized individuals within the Federal Police force seeking to dissuade them from sticking their noses into the so-called War on Narcotrafficking with their investigations.

The Organization of American States (OAS) had been alerted to the threats, having received reports from ARTICLE 19 as well as from Carlos Lauría of the Center for the Protection of Journalists, in New York, highlighting the oft-overlooked phenomenon of journalists being forcibly displaced in Mexico. Neither the two Veracruz journalists nor I had much trust in our own country's authorities.

In recent years, I have met with some twenty newspaper directors throughout Mexico. The majority of them have stressed that they are proud to head offices where women make up more than 50 percent of their reporting and editing staff. They emphasize the importance of these women's work, their sense of responsibility and strong work ethic, their sensitivity, and how they bring a unique perspective to the news. Perhaps, they say, they are more empathetic because they are mothers, or because they are women. I believe that the ability to practice ethical journalism is not a

---

26. Translator's Note: Javier Duarte has served as governor of the state of Veracruz since 2010.

question of gender—there are just as many good or bad journalists among the ranks of each of the sexes. But the reality is that in a sexist country, women who become involved in serious investigative journalism lay their lives and freedom on the line in different ways than men. Violence against female journalists invariably takes on an added layer of misogynistic spite. It is likewise true that many women who rebel against sexism and machismo do write from a distinct perspective than men; there is a sort of understanding of differences that filters down to their investigations and the ways they report on and connect with the female victims they are interviewing.

In Felipe Calderon's 2006–2012 term alone, forty-five members of the press were murdered. In my mind's eye, every one of them has a face, a name. I knew many of their voices, I had laughed with some of them, admired their written, radio, or photojournalism work; we'd done tequila shots and drunk beer together, we'd buoyed each other's spirits in times of hardship, we'd shared information and tips. We'd exchanged our knowing, local-reporter glances during forums on freedom of expression; we'd read each other's work voraciously, because we'd all come to realize that we belong to a tribe of like-minded individuals working in search of truth and freedom of speech. Being a local reporter is nothing at all like being a high-profile journalist in the capital city.

The day Regina died, I went up to my room; I needed to be alone. My thoughts wandered to a Luis Eduardo Auté song, and before I knew it, I was looking it up on my iPod. *What can we do?* my colleagues and I kept asking ourselves. And I was at a loss to make any sort of reply. Listening to the song helped me to cry; then I sat down to write my column dedicated to Regina. *What can we do when being ourselves is like being in a horror film . . . what can we do when success means killing the underdog, what can we do when imposters don't even need to wear masks. Flee, perhaps—flee toward life. Live, perhaps—live in flight.*

No, we are not going to our deaths, as some people believe. We are fleeing toward life, because we defend our right to live in a free country. We live in flight, as the poet says, because one's own individual freedom cannot truly and realistically be defended if the freedom of others is not protected as well, and we defend all people's right to know and understand the realities that surround them, and to denounce them when necessary. It's our job, but it is also our professional mission, our calling. And somewhere along the way, in the face of such extreme levels of violence, journalism became a part of our lives—it *is* our life today—because our profession conditions our way of being in the world, and surviving in it.

A STEP FORWARD

At seven in the evening on January 30, 2013, while I was up in my study, hard at work on a new book, I got the news that the Supreme Court of Justice of the Nation had ruled in my favor in the most recent case brought against me by the child trafficking mafias, a case that had begun as a civil suit back in 2008. Sitting next to me at the time was my dog Luna, a Rottweiler with an uncanny ability to sense shifts in my emotions. When she heard my voice, she immediately pricked up and began licking my hand, searching out my eyes with hers.

Supreme Court justice Arturo Zaldívar stated in his ruling that "in this case, the author Lydia Cacho Ribeiro and the publishing house Random House Mondadori are absolved of all responsibility for damages," for the plain reason that the contents of my book *The Demons of Eden* place the general public interest above the private interests of businessmen. I started jumping up and down in my study like a schoolgirl, weeping tears of joy and babbling a mile a minute to my dog, who couldn't tell whether I was extremely happy or had simply gone crazy. I lost count of how many times I exclaimed out loud, "A precedent for freedom of the press in Mexico, we've set a precedent for freedom of the press in Mexico!" I called my father, my sister, and my friend Joe, who had been taking care of me and keeping me company in my worst moments of sickness for the past several months. I spoke to the director at my publisher, Random House, and my lawyers at ARTICLE 19. We all agreed—this called for tequila.

Justice Zaldívar wrote the following in his final sentence:

> On the one hand, the matter of a crime having been committed by a criminal organization is a matter of maximum public interest (recall, as regards this, that the information revealed in the aforementioned book [*The Demons of Eden*] made it possible to form a clear picture of the consequences that pedophilia and child prostitution have on their victims, as well as of the collusion of the economic and political actors that allow these acts to be committed with impunity); on the other hand, this specific instance of invasion of privacy was not particularly extreme, given the measures taken by the journalist to avoid revealing the identity of the individual in question, who is widely known among the general public, having come to occupy a position of notoriety in large part as a consequence of his own conduct.

The Supreme Court was acknowledging, for the second time in two years, that the crimes I denounced in *The Demons of Eden* are real, that in keeping with my responsibilities as a journalist, I made proper use of pseudonyms to avoid revealing victims' identities as well as including black bars in photographs to cover the faces of the innocent people who had provided evidence regarding the facts in the case, that is, evidence of the transportation of the victim from Cancun to Los Angeles. It was never my intention to write a book about human trafficking or child pornography without fingering the culprits; they are and indeed ought to be the focus of the story. Many powerful criminals use the justice system to silence the press, and every successful case against such crooked individuals represents a collective achievement.

And this is true the world over. From Mexico to Guatemala, the United States, Turkey, and the United Kingdom, hundreds of journalists are currently facing civil suits brought against them by individuals who first commit crimes and then, upon discovering that good reporting has begun to shed unwanted light on their activities, turn to the courts to accuse those journalists of unlawfully exposing their private lives. The judge must then weigh all the different factors in the case and make a final assessment, but above all, she or he must determine if the journalist's work sought to inform society about some real danger or violation of human rights. I am not the first journalist—nor will I be the last—to be jailed and persecuted for bringing to light a truth that ought to be publicly known. In fact, many have had even worse experiences than I, but it is important to make clear that every time a precedent is set in these cases, we all take a step forward—we reinforce the notion that those who are in positions of power and are discovered to be breaking the law must not be permitted to use the justice system as a tool of retaliation to punish those of us who point the finger at them.

In December 2012, Enrique Peña Nieto was sworn in as president of Mexico. With him, some of the country's most recalcitrant politicians—former participants in the seventy-year-long government monopoly that appeared to have ended when the PAN's Vicente Fox acceded to the presidency in 2000—returned to power. At the end of that brief, proto-democratic period, Fox was succeeded by Felipe Calderón, an ambitious economist who quickly discovered his Napoleonic side and a passion for war and authoritarianism. With the help of Barack Obama, who supplied him with the necessary cash and weapons, he plunged Mexico into a bloodbath, an unjustified war that has exacted a toll of more than fifty thousand deaths and several thousands of forced disappearances of people young and old. And all without putting the slightest dent in the operations of the drug cartels, the volume of their output, or the movement of drugs to end consumers in the United States. All wars create conditions that make human rights violations more likely to occur, but it is those wars that aim to supplant the very justice system that are the most brutal of all, because they weaken society and the state itself. This drug war, dreamed up in Washington and given an obedient stamp of approval by President Calderón, has strengthened the mafias, and it has created a wartime discourse of hatred and anger, of revelry in death. *Whoever kills the most has the most power*, media outlets loyal to Calderón seemed to be telling the country. This active promotion of war inspired thousands of young people to turn to contract killing and drug trafficking as a way of life, as an act of rebellion against a violent state and a violent society that, from their perspective, consign them to a life spent wasting away in ghettos of poverty. Their newly chosen governing elite, the drug bosses, take on the role of the state—they offer them jobs, wellbeing, protection, and power. There is no justice in war, only revenge and the colonization of both territory and minds; thousands of young people found a calling, found direction for their lives in this warlike discourse, in rebelling against a weak, inoperative state that so often ignores them.

A fierce contest ensued among the cartels, which now began vying with each other to co-opt public servants in an effort to infiltrate every police force and government department in the country. Women and children became the main spoils of war. There were no winners in this conflict, we all lost, but the biggest losers of all were the children—unprotected, fearful, and abused. As this book was being completed in 2013, the renowned and valiant journalist Adela Navarro, director of the weekly newspaper *Zeta* [which translates as "Zee"], declared that the issue of greatest importance, the issue most deserving of scrutiny during the first one hundred days of Peña Nieto's presidency, was the PRI's shutting down of access to information. In some cases, there is no access to information, and in others, information is being falsified. Adela explains,

As we were preparing this information, for instance, in the case of Baja California, where *Zeta* has its head office, the National Secretary General's Office quotes 15 homicides, while a sum of daily police counts in these first 100 days yields 59. Seeing the disparity in these numbers—between what the government is telling us and what the reality on the ground is—we decided to consult with other papers in other states. Research and collaboration with various government institutions and journalism organizations in different states around the country allowed us to compile the following statistics: 4,549 murders were committed in Peña Nieto's first 100 days, and high-intensity violence is most prevalent in the states of Guerrero, with 463 murders, Chihuahua, with 417, Mexico State, with 407, Jalisco, with 372, and Sinaloa, with 324.

The PRI is back and will govern until 2018, and its old ways and wiles are back, too. PRI governors control 90 percent of the thirty-two states that make up the Mexican Republic. You can already catch a whiff of that old, familiar pro-presidential connivance in the country's main newspapers. Large sums of money go to perpetuating the soap-opera-heartthrob image President Peña Nieto has cultivated since the outset of his campaign. Human rights, especially the rights of women and children, are not and have never been an important part of Peña Nieto's political agenda; prior to becoming president, he served as governor of Mexico State, where femicide rates rose while the justice system's responsiveness to women and children's went by the wayside.

Some of the men I have exposed in my investigations, men who continue to take part in the tangled webs of human trafficking mafias, drug cartels, and money laundering outfits, are now proudly ensconced at the new president's side, secure in their political immunity. We may never manage to bring them to justice, but by keeping close tabs on them, we can prevent them from strengthening their protection of these networks that bring such harm upon the women and children of Mexico.

I have identified and reported the complete, true names of a hundred human traffickers, narcotraffickers, and corrupt politicians. I have published their stories and given voice to their victims. The most recent threats I received were from Raúl Martins, a former Argentinian Secret Service agent whose story I laid out in *Slaves of Power*. Martins has been named by the teenagers who were bought and sexually exploited in his brothels in Argentina, Cancun, and Playa del Carmen. His case has now reached the courts. A colleague came to me recently to tell me that she had been at one of Martins's table dance clubs. He warned her there, "If you know that Lydia Cacho, tell her to shut her mouth. Her days are numbered, and when she least expects it, she's gonna turn up dead."

I understand that sometimes an enemy made is an enemy for life. The truth is that when our work succeeds, theirs becomes more difficult, if not impossible. Our journalistic success is their disgrace, and that fact, as my lawyers have explained to me, could spell my death sentence. I hope that I can continue to dodge any and all of the bullets meant for me, but should that prove not to be the case, at least I know with certainty that I am proud of my life and my professionalism. I have loved and I have been loved, I have danced and laughed until sunup. I have had whole days and nights filled with a happiness I hope all human beings can one day experience. I had a dysfunctional childhood but a loving one, with a roof over my head, education, food, and play. A childhood like that is the minimum standard I hope will be secured for every child the world over. Because the little girl who still resides within me knows that all girls deserve loving protection, a bright light to lead the way, education, and the right to dream and be free. It is only in a life steeped in freedom and love that such rights can be defended past childhood, into adulthood, and until the day we die.

BY WAY OF GOOD-BYE

The calendar on my desk is flipped open to 2013, and as I pen the final lines to this book, I gaze at the photographs of the children who have finally, after so many years, been able to put that fateful year of 2004 behind them, a year we all felt sure we would never be able to move past.

One of them has just completed her pre-university program and is studying to become a psychologist. She would like to open a free psychology clinic for girls.

One young man, one of the two male victims who still keep in touch with me, is halfway through a technical degree, still deciding whether he wants to work as a hotelier or at an airline. He has a girlfriend, and he speaks to her often about children's rights and the importance of taking good care of society's youngest.

Another young woman lives in Mérida. She has completed her counseling and now, nine years later, is convinced she has overcome the worst of the trauma she experienced as a result of having been sexually exploited for four years, beginning at the age of six. She has overcome her phobias and is romantically involved with someone. She wants to be a chef and says that she is truly a full-time survivor at last, a victim never more.

Another is studying social work in Monterrey. She hopes to use her experience as a survivor to help other women, although she desires never to speak of the past again. She explains how she buried her past one day, in a little wooden box containing burned papers and a photograph of Succar, her tormentor, taken the day he was sentenced to 113 years in prison.

One woman has returned to the same networks she escaped as a child. Now an adult, she works for a Tijuana madam who runs a VIP escort service. That's the last I heard of her, a few years back now. "I hate men, they used me, so now I'm going to use them," she said in the painful final letter she wrote to tell me that it meant nothing to her that Succar had been sentenced.

Another young girl who had been progressing very well in her therapy sessions was taken to Mérida by her uncle, a move that went against the warnings in the girl's list of special care requirements. These guidelines are vital to her wellbeing because of the depth of the trauma she suffered, since she was extremely young when she was exploited and forced to take part in the creation of pornographic films. The last I heard, her uncle had been looking for help and was offered the chance for her to continue her therapy in another state in the country; the girl says her uncle moved her because Succar gave him 600,000 pesos to get her out of Cancun so that she couldn't testify against him.

I could fill a hundred pages with the success stories of the girls and boys who have changed their lives with the help of social, therapeutic, educational, emotional, and legal support, and not just in Mexico but all over the world—in the United States, for instance, where the organization GEMS (Girls' Educational and Mentoring Services) rescues women and girls and helps them to heal and to transform their lives.

It must be acknowledged that some girls and boys do end up getting left behind. They may develop severe personality disorders as a result of the abuses suffered in their childhoods. They learn to hate and distrust everyone; they don't understand the meaning of unconditional love. Sadly, some of these young people lack the wherewithal to switch on that inner resilience that others are able to rely on. There is still much to be learned in terms of how forced participation in child pornography and other forms of violent and degrading treatment affect the psycho-emotional and psycho-sexual health of their victims. But I have seen with my own eyes, from Kyrgyzstan to Cambodia, from Mexico to the United States, from Argentina to Sweden, Russia, and the United Kingdom, that there are growing numbers of groups developing ever better methods for the rescue and proper recovery of these victims, and that men are increasingly becoming involved in the prevention of these sorts of crimes. I have seen how giving a name to the pain an individual is experiencing can give that person a renewed sense of self and self-worth.

Traditionally, charitable organizations have tended to pressure victims into taking steps the latter are not yet prepared for, but these old models are now becoming obsolete. And a great deal of work remains to be done in order to demonstrate to society how pushes by the commercial sex industry and certain prostitution advocacy groups can in fact jeopardize the rights of girls and young women through the use of campaigns aimed at normalizing the practices of teenage prostitution and pornography.

Just as in the Wachowskis' film, we must take our daughters and sons by the hand and help them to discover the Matrix, or, in other words, the value system that prizes mistreatment and abuse. This real-life Matrix is not an unshakable reality. Like the character Neo, whom I discussed at the beginning of this book, we can learn to see with new eyes and build a new freedom, one far removed from any type of ideological, sexual, or political slavery.

The challenges are enormous, but they are commensurate with the achievements to be made. One of the greatest tasks is to ensure that governments across the globe, the Mexican government included, understand that they are duty-bound to be on the side of society, on the side of children, and not the mafias. It is for this reason that it is so vital for us to continue to investigate these individuals, to continue to identify all those who contrive to commit acts of sexual violence against girls, boys, and young adults, either directly or through political alliances, because it is they who are perpetuating the "manufacturing" of new aggressors and exploiters.

At some point before the close of 2013, my case will be brought before the Inter-American Court of Human Rights in Washington, and we will await the sentence.

Perhaps, as is the case for millions of others, justice will not come in time for me, Lydia Cacho. But it is worth the effort to try; it is worth the effort to shed light on the wreckage of this country, this world we seek to transform. Because if we have learned any-thing over the course of these past ten years of persecutions, threats, and trials, it is that true triumph does not consist of seeing the fruits of our own personal efforts but rather of ensuring that our time spent on this earth will allow others to reap the seeds sown by our perseverance.

Democracy and human rights are not unmoving goals but instead constitute a living process, a life-form that requires consis-tency, access to information, passion, and patience if it is to survive and thrive.

Journalism, as a Spanish friend once explained, is not the fourth estate. Good journalism is in fact a counterweight. A stalwart presence, it does not shrink in the face of the crushing resilience of the patriarchy, it does not submit to official discourses, it does not bend to corruption. But above all, the variety of journalism that best serves society is that which does not churn its profits from flattery and scandal but works to analyze and clarify a multiplicity of truths and acknowledge every person's humanity. Good journalism creates democratic balance by giving real weight to voices that would oth-erwise be silenced by the overwhelming power of those who control politics, the economy, and all that is born of them. I believe that as Carol Gilligan said, "the opposite of patriarchy is democracy rooted in voice, not violence."

We must continue to ask questions, to search for answers, and to join forces against corruption, impunity, slavery, and injustice in every corner of the planet, until not one single girl or boy remains lost in the shadows of a society that looks silently on rapists, that looks silently on the blindness of a judicial system that is incapable of understanding for once and for all that every abused girl is at risk of turning into an abusive adult or a perennial victim, that every abused boy could in turn grow up to become an abuser, or a Supreme Court justice with a heart full of hate, or a fearful, unhappy man.

We do not yet know whether we will win our case at the United Nations High Commission on Human Rights; in the meantime, there are two important achievements that nobody can take away from me. The first is having survived in the face of so many forms of violence with my sense of hope intact and my sense of dignity redoubled, for I give no credence to the notion of penitence through suffering. Rather, I believe in standing up for freedom and my right to live happily in the company of my loved ones. The other is knowing that I have fulfilled my promise to the girls and boys who were abused by this loathsome network. Their captor is in prison and will never be let out. Now they can sleep soundly; the reign of terror has ended, just as it must end for all the girls and boys in this world. Because arresting one pedophile is all well and good, but preventing our societies from continuing to create them is the real cultural battle of our century.

APPENDIX

DEMONIACAL TIMELINE
1982-1985 (SUCCAR KURI)

After meeting Gloria Pita when she is fourteen years old, the two marry. She is aware of "his defects, the fact that he likes little girls."

He leaves Acapulco following a failed attempt to abuse a minor and being threatened by the girl's parents. He keeps his apartment in the city.

He meets Miguel Ángel Yunes. He opens businesses in the Mexico City airport.

1986

Succar Kuri arrives in Cancun and purchases several retail stores in the Nautilus shopping center. Assisted by Alejandro Góngora Vera, he makes deals with FONATUR.

He purchases units at the Solymar Villas and, thanks to his friendships and influence, begins doing business with his associate and friend Kamel Nacif.

2000

August. Emma is a student at the La Salle school and tells her Morality teacher, Margarita, about the abuses she suffered at the hands of Succar Kuri. Emma's mother contacts her brother (Emma's uncle), Ricardo Cetina, and the latter forbids her from reporting Succar.

2003

March. Kamel Nacif asks Succar Kuri to bring him a girl from Florida and another from El Salvador so that they can "fornicate" in a ménage à trois. Kamel asks how much each girl will cost him, and Succar tells him it's US$2,000 each and that he'll have them brought to the Solymar Villas in Cancun. (Telephone recording revealed by the journalist Carmen Aristegui. Nacif admits to the daily newspaper *Reforma* in 2007 that the recorded calls are authentic.)

October. Emma seeks out her former teacher Margarita and asks her to assist her in reporting Succar Kuri. Emma is introduced to the lawyer Verónica Acacio of the nonprofit organization Protégeme, who agrees to represent her and other underage girls in their accusation free of charge.

October 27. Quintana Roo state attorney general Celia Pérez Gordillo authorizes the state assistant attorney general to make a video recording of a conversation between Emma and Succar Kuri in order to obtain evidence against the latter. Succar admits to having raped girls as young as five.

The Quintana Roo newspaper *Por esto!* offers full, real-time coverage of the case. All the state media outlets follow suit.

October 29. Succar's lawyers orchestrate the pedophile's escape, after having been warned that he was going to be arrested the following day.

October 30. Gloria Pita, alias "La Ochi," telephones Emma and her mother and threatens to kill them if they do not retract the accusation against Pita's husband, Jean Succar. Two telephone calls are recorded in which Gloria can be heard admitting clearly and expressly to having explicit knowledge of her husband's pedophiliac activities.

November 2. Emma reports Jean Succar Kuri to the PGR for child pornography and for raping her when she was thirteen years old, and her younger sister and cousin when they were eight and nine years old, respectively, as well as other six-year-old girls. She testifies that Succar established contact with girls from the United States for the purpose of bringing them to Kamel Nacif Borge, Miguel Ángel Yunes Linares, and Alejandro Góngora Vera.

November. Emma gets in touch with Óscar Cadena and asks him to interview her on his television program *Encadénate*, because she fears for her life after having reported the man who raped her. Cadena broadcasts the interview on Televisión de Quintana Roo and on SKY.

November 4. The underage girl Carmen reports to the PGR that Succar has been raping her and filming videos with her since she was six years old. Another girl, Laura, reports that she met Succar Kuri when she was in kindergarten, at the home of a neighbor woman, and that he began abusing her when she was five years old. Three more underage girls who have never met Emma also file reports.

November 4. Emma locates Lydia Cacho and asks that she help her, as a journalist, to tell her story, explaining that her life has been threatened. Emma later accepts the assistance offered by CIAM Cancun to herself and other victims.

November 7. Alejandro Góngora (head of FONATUR) claims that he does not know the girl Emma.

Emma testifies to the PGR that she met Alejandro Góngora and his wife, Rocía, at the Solymar Villas—she was in the room and Succar introduced her to them as his daughter "La Pecas" ["Freckles"]. Emma explains that she accompanied Succar to FONATUR several times to do "business" with Góngora. The details she provides are later corroborated by the authorities.

November 12. INTERPOL reports that it has initiated an investigation into Jean Thouma Hanna Succar Kuri for "money laundering" in at least eight tourist resort cities around the country, where he also owns homes, clothing and jewelry shops, restaurants, and other properties.

November 13. The PGR has Emma and the other victims submit to psychological evaluations.

November 21. Governor Joaquín Hendricks promises to take action in the Succar case and declares, "I will see to it that the law is rigorously enforced," in the event that public servants at the State Attorney General's Office are proven to have been complicit in the escape of the pedophile Succar Kuri.

November 22. Kamel Nacif telephones Governor Hendricks to assure him that his friend Succar Kuri is innocent.

Succar Kuri telephones Lydia Cacho and threatens to kill her for having "meddled in his life" by publishing an analysis of the case in her newspaper column and going on television to discuss his acts of abuse.

Novmber 24. Attorney General of Mexico Rafael Macedo announces that the U.S. Marshals Service has reported having located Succar Kuri at his residence in Downey, California. They announce that they will seek a warrant for his arrest. (The PGR waits two months before sending the U.S. Marshals Service the documentation required for the arrest.)

November 26. The PGR hears testimony from American witnesses residing at the Solymar Villas. The latter declare that they inquired whether pedophilia of the sort Succar practiced with young girls was not illegal in Mexico. EJ and RC testify to having witnessed some of Succar's people removing boxes and documents from Solymar's Villa #1. They contacted the police but were ignored.

The PGR interrogates Kamel Nacif Borge, who declares under oath that he has seen Succar Kuri on only one occasion, at the inauguration of the Marriott hotel in Cancun, and that the two are not friends.

November 29. Víctor Manuel Echeverría Tun, third criminal court judge for Cancun, issues an arrest warrant against Succar Kuri for child pornography, corruption of minors, and statutory rape.

Yunes Linares categorically denies knowing Succar Kuri.

Sandra Moreno, Yunes Linares's secretary, admits to the PGR that she has been to the Solymar Villas in the company of Yunes, but she denies that her daughter or niece was ever molested.

The PGR's General Division of Extradition and Mutual Legal Assistance requests that the accused pedophile be handed over for trial in Mexico.

December. The magazine *Proceso* publishes investigations conducted by the American DEA and the Mexican AFI (the Federal Investigations Agency, a body under the direction of the PGR) into Miguel Ángel Yunes Linares, as well as the testimonies of captured narcotraffickers revealing that Yunes received US$15 million while serving as Veracruz Secretary General of Government. SEIDO assistant attorney general Eduardo Berdón reports that Patricio Chirinos and Miguel Ángel Yunes "supported narcotrafficking activities and, specifically, received approximately US$15 million" from drug boss Albino Quintero.

2004

January. Kamel Nacif succeeds in acquiring a 100 percent ownership stake in the American company Tarrant Apparel Group, with offices and factories in China, Thailand, Korea, New York, and Los Angeles.

February. Kamel Nacif hires San Diego–headquartered law firm Seltzer, Caplan, McMahon & Vitek and requests that Charles L. Goldberg be assigned to his case. Goldberg was named "Best Criminal Lawyer" in San Diego in 2000; he resigned from Kamel Nacif's case in 2005.

February 4. Jean Succar Kuri is arrested in Chandler, Arizona, at the request of INTERPOL.

March 10. Succar Kuri is ordered to undergo criminal proceedings for child pornography, in case number 447/2003-IV.

April **6.** The Secretariat of Finance and Public Credit sends the Federal Public Ministry twenty-two files containing information pursuant to the analysis of reports into 144 "unusual" banking transactions made by the company Kanan Banana that may be related to money-laundering activities.

June. Judge Armando Chiñas orders the "freezing" of US$20 million from accounts held in the name of Jean Succar Kuri, owner of Kanan Banana.

July. Succar Kuri's cellmate reports to prison authorities at the Arizona jail that Kuri has hired Felipe de Jesús Argüelles Mandujano, alias "El Rayo" ["Lightning"], to kill Emma, Lydia Cacho, Verónica Acacio, and their former lawyers, Edmart and Gabino Andrade.

2005

January **10.** President Vicente Fox appoints Miguel Ángel Yunes Lunares to the post of assistant secretary of public security. Yunes is a former federal deputy, a former member of the PRI, and is currently a PAN activist and right-hand-man to Elba Esther Gordillo.

January **18.** Assistant attorney general Miguel Ángel Pech Cen signs his name to a note given by him to the attorney general in which he states, "In prior enquiry 7431/2003, it must be added that there are in fact indications that Miguel Yunes [sic] was engaging in sexual relations with one of the underage girls. As per instructions, this finding has been 52-ed [legal code used to refer to cases that have been frozen]."

March. SEIDO detains the Municipal Public Security Office's assistant operative director, Felipe de Jesús Argüelles Mandujano, alias "El Rayo," for having run security for vehicles used in hit operations by the Gulf Cartel in Cancun. He is held in custody for his connections to criminal and narcotrafficking activities.

May **19.** The journalist Lydia Cacho Ribeiro publishes the book *The Demons of Eden: The Powers Protecting Child Pornography*, an investigation based on the testimonies of the victims of a pedophilia ring headed by businessman and American legal resident Jean Succar Kuri. The book is presented by Carlos Loret de Mola and Jorge Zepeda at the Jaime Sabines Cultural Center.

June 22. Businessman Kamel Nacif Borge reports Lydia Cacho to the Puebla authorities for defamation and libel; he requests that the state's governor, Mario Marín, use his influence to have the journalist arrested for the publication of *The Demons of Eden*, which linked him to textile magnate Succar Kuri.

July 11. Federal prosecutor Reid Charles Pixler, acting in representation of the government of Mexico, presents a file of new evidence to a federal court in the United States of America in support of the former country's request to have Succar extradited. Among this new evidence, there are videos showing Succar raping girls, setting up cameras in order to film pornographic scenes on his bed, and preparing a massage table on which to film still more girls.

December 16. Lydia Cacho is arrested by the Cancun Judicial Police in Cancun, Quintana Roo, and transported overland in conditions of torture to the city of Puebla. After spending almost thirty hours under arrest, she is released on the historically large bail sum of 70,000 pesos.

December 23. Judge Pérez Gonzáles, after allowing three working days for the submission of evidence, orders that Cacho Ribeiro be remanded to prison for the crimes of defamation and libel.

December 23. Cacho's lawyers resign for fear of reprisals from Marín's government, which was threatening and firing individuals supportive of Cacho even as she was being released from prison.

2006

January. In an interview on TV Azteca, Kamel Nacif admits to being friends with Succar and having taken care of his immigration papers upon the latter's arrival in Mexico twenty years earlier. (Nacif had denied this information previously when questioned by the authorities.)

January 17. Lydia Cacho is absolved of the crime of libel for lack of evidence, in an appeal made by her lawyers before the Superior Court of Justice (TSJ) of Puebla, but the charges of defamation are allowed to stand.

January 20. The Puebla TSJ rules in favor of the journalist, acknowledges Judge Pérez González's lack of jurisdiction, and transfers the case from Puebla to Cancun.

February 14. La Jornada publishes recorded telephone conversations between textile magnate Kamel Nacif Borge and the governor of Puebla, Mario Marín Torres, which lay bare the conspiracy between Puebla and Quintana Roo public servants to have Lydia Cacho arrested.

February 27. Close to forty thousand people take to the streets of Puebla to demand Governor Marín's removal.

March 13. The journalist files a report with the PGR against Puebla governor Mario Marín, businessman Kamel Nacif, Puebla state attorney general Blanca Laura Villeda Martínez, and judge Rosa Celia Pérez González for the crimes of bribery, influence peddling, abuse of authority, attempted rape, and false testimony.

April 4. American judge David K. Duncan authorizes the extradition of the alleged pedophile Jean Succar Kuri—denounced by the journalist Lydia Cacho in her book *The Demons of Eden*—to Mexico for his role as the head of an international pedophilia network.

April 18. The Congress of the Union requests that the Supreme Court of Justice of the Nation (SCJN) assert jurisdiction and investigate the alleged violation of Lydia Cacho's human rights; the nation's highest court accepts the request and rules to create an initial investigative commission whose aim will be to determine whether there is sufficient evidence to bring impeachment charges against Governor Mario Marín.

July 5. Jean Succar Kuri is extradited to Mexico and incarcerated at the Cancun jail.

August. Quintana Roo criminal court judge Sergio López Camejo requests that the Federal Preventive Police (PFP) transfer Succar Kuri—at this point considered a high-risk inmate—to the La Palma detention center, as an investigation carried out by the state's Secretariat of Public Security (SSP) had learned that he was involved in a dangerous extortion ring operating from within the Chetumal and Cancun prisons.

August. Three more underage girls file reports against Succar Kuri with the PGR's SEIDO division.

August 1. Quintana Roo state attorney general Bello Melchor Rodríguez Carrillo declares that "during Governor Hendricks's term of office, his public servants were known to have aided Succar in his escape, and appropriate response measures were never taken."

Jean Succar Kuri, alias "El Johnny," confirms that Miguel Ángel Yunes Linares, assistant secretary of public security at the federal level, is a friend of his and that he has known him for fifteen years. In a Televisa interview conducted by Carlos Loret de Mola from the Cancun municipal jail, Succar Kuri also admits that Kamel Nacif contributed US$300,000 to his defense.

August 3. Lydia Cacho's case file, which was opened just months previously at the request of the journalist herself, is stolen from the headquarters of the National Human Rights Commission. The Commission files a criminal report with the Mexico City Attorney General's Office (PGJDF) to have the robbery investigated.

August 17. The authorities transfer Succar Kuri to the Chetumal correctional facility. Information is leaked to the effect that Succar Kuri and other inmates are organizing a jailbreak from the Cancun prison.

September. Succar Kuri admits on Loret de Mola's news broadcast that he met Yunes Linares when the latter was employed as the commercial director of the Mexico City airport and that Yunes came to dine at his Solymar Villas in Cancun "with his wife."

September 9. By a vote of seven to three, the Supreme Court rules to widen its investigation into the possible violation of Lydia Cacho's rights in order to include an analysis of the so-called "Precious Guv'." A second special commission is created.

September 28. The PGR asserts jurisdiction in the case involving the theft of Lydia Cacho's case file from the CNDH. Four people are arrested as a result of the ensuing probe.

September 29. A second face-to-face session between the journalist and Kamel Nacif is held before a judge headquartered in Cancun.

October 25. Inmates Armando Bocanegra Priego and Juan Ramón González confess that they were hired by "El Johnny" Succar Kuri at the Chetumal prison to kill several witnesses, among them Lydia Cacho. Succar had given them a sketch of Cacho's residence.

November 16. Succar Kuri is transferred to the El Altiplano high-security prison in Toluca.

December 9. Nearly one hundred inmates escape from the Cancun municipal jail. Three are killed in the commotion. Authorities confirm that Succar was involved in the planning of this jailbreak, in which he himself had originally planned to escape, as well.

December 17. Emma files a civil suit in a Mexico City courthouse against Lydia Cacho for having published "her story" in *The Demons of Eden*. Emma also wrote to Lydia Cacho, stating that she had been forced to sign an agreement, written in English, with Kamel Nacif's lawyers in exchange for money.

2007

January 2. Kamel Nacif definitively loses the legal battle he began a year earlier against Cacho Ribeiro, whom he had accused of defamation. Fourth Criminal Court judge Lorenzo Medina Garzón of Mexico City ruled to throw out the proceedings initiated in December 2005 by the Puebla judge Rosa Celia Pérez González and decrees that the journalist be absolved.

March. The Supreme Court's second special investigative commission initiates investigations in Quintana Roo and Puebla. Public servants involved in the case, Jean Succar Kuri's victims, Lydia Cacho, and various members of the media are all formally questioned.

March 23. Lydia Cacho receives the Amnesty International Ginetta Sagan Award for her work in defense of human rights.

May 3. In a session lasting nearly thirteen hours, Lydia Cacho gives further testimony against alleged pedophile Jean Succar Kuri, who, in the presence of the journalist, admits to having had sexual relations with a minor. At the end of the face-to-face session, Succar Kuri threatens the journalist's life.

May 8. Lydia Cacho reports an attempt on her life. After the PGR assigns her an SUV and chauffeur as part of the precautionary measures being taken to protect her, Cacho gets into the vehicle at the Mexico City airport. After five minutes of traveling, the vehicle is stopped by the driver, because he notices a problem with one of the wheels. The security team discovers that the vehicle has been intentionally tampered with in order to provoke an accident. Three months later, the PGR has still not made an analysis of the vehicle or taken any witness testimonies. It does, however, arrange an appointment for Cacho to submit to a psychological examination, as a precondition to investigating the attack.

May 24. Governor Mario Marín appears before Justice Juan N. Silva Meza and submits to the latter a document with his version of the events. The text is filled with errors and political arguments in defense of the governor.

June 6. Justice Silva Meza circulates among his fellow justices at the nation's highest court a copy of the special investigative commission's findings report for the Lydia Cacho case, in order for them to analyze its contents prior to the public session that will be held to discuss the topic.

June 17. The secretary of the congressional Committee for Radio, Television, and Cinematography, José Antonio Díaz García, petitions the State Information and Communications System (SICOM) to broadcast the Supreme Court session in which the findings for the Lydia Cacho case will be announced.

June 21. A group of intellectuals, artists, film directors, and civil society bodies publishes a full-page spread in a variety of newspapers under the title "Once Upon a Time There Was a Pedophile . . ." It is signed by Alfonso Cuarón, Luis Mandoki, González Iñárritu, Guillermo del Toro, Salma Hayek, Noam Chomsky, and more than three thousand others.

June 26. Results of the Supreme Court's investigative committee: Silva Meza's conclusions establish that Marín, Guillermo Pachecho Pulido, Blanca Laura Villeda, and judge Rosa Celia Pérez González conspired to act to the advantage of businessman Kamel Nacif, through the apprehension and torture of Lydia Cacho, whose journalistic work uncovered a network of political and financial forces supporting and protecting child pornography and pedophilia rings as well as self-proclaimed pedophile Jean Succar Kuri himself.

Report by the Supreme Court of Justice of the Nation: "The Special Prosecutor for the Detection of Sexual Crimes, under the direction of the Office of the Attorney General for the State of Quintana Roo, reported 1,595 prior inquiries having been initiated for sexual crimes committed against minors (2006). The actions highlighted herein show the individual guarantee contained in Article IV of the Constitution, pursuant to the right of children to secure the fulfillment of all necessary elements for their complete and proper development in the states of Puebla and Quintana Roo, to be in a state of absolute neglect."

August. Proceedings are concluded in the Succar case at the federal court, which hopes to deliver a sentence of at least sixteen years' incarceration on federal charges of child pornography and twenty years on state charges of rape and corruption of minors. (Federal and state sentences may not be combined.)

Succar Kuri's lawyer, Wenceslao Cisnero, steps down publicly from the defense after viewing one of the pornographic videos in which his former client is seen raping small girls. He admits that Succar Kuri is a pedophile and that a Salvadoran girl whom the latter had been exploiting for use in the sex tourism industry is, according to Succar Kuri, dead.

The special federal prosecutor for crimes against women, Alicia Elena Pérez Duarte, acknowledges that Succar Kuri is part of an international network involved in the trafficking of girls and teenagers. Despite this, none of his accomplices are investigated.

August. Kamel Nacif is starting up new businesses in Costa Rica and Cuba. The factory where he manufactures Disney-brand children's products—Skytex de México, a variable capital company—is a huge commercial success.

The Congress of the Union has received the Supreme Court's resolution allowing impeachment charges to be brought against Mario Marín. Top PRI leaders have declared that they will protect Marín at all costs.

LAWYERS WHO HAVE ATTEMPTED TO DEFEND SUCCAR KURI AND LATER STEPPED DOWN

2003: Sidharta Bermúdez, Edmart and Gabino Andrade.

2004: Joaquín Espinosa (who, on Succar Kuri's orders, coordinated an attack against the Andrades that ended in a gunfight on March 23).

2004: Charles L. Goldberg (USA) is hired by Kamel Nacif and steps down after he is pressured to try to buy off judges and witnesses.

2005: Patrick Hall and an unnamed Cuban lawyer (whose voice is heard in recorded telephone conversations with Kamel Nacif).

2005: Elías Abdalá Delgado and Ena Rosa Valencia Rosado (who, as part of their defense of Succar, put Emma in touch with Carlos Loret de Mola for the purpose of having the latter interview her).

2006: Efraín Trujeque Arcila and Armando René Ancona Araujo (who worked as a Federal Public Ministry agent and as such had access to the underage girls' reports against Succar before becoming the latter's defender).

2006: José Wenceslao Cisneros Amaya and Hernán Cisneros Montes (who stepped down in 2007 after coaching some girls for the witness stand subsequent to the latter having been threatened and given money by Succar Kuri in exchange for a partial retraction of the accusation they had made against him).

2007: Dr. Alfredo Delgadillo Aguirre (president of the Academic Board at the National Institute for Higher Studies in Criminal Law [INDEPAC]—as of the date of this book's publication, he continues to defend Succar Kuri).

TELEPHONE CONVERSATIONS

My case took a turn, as I have previously explained, on February 14, 2006, when recordings surfaced of telephone conversations between Kamel Nacif and Governor Mario Marín, as well as conversations the former held with other public figures, including three governors and the PRI's congressional leader, Emilio Gamboa. Marín denied that the voice on the tapes is his, only to feel remorse and recant this statement later, claiming now that it was his voice, but that his words had been manipulated. For his part, Nacif declared in a statement to the daily newspaper *Reforma* that he had asked the governor to arrest me, and that the governor had obliged. Now desperate, the governor used public money to hire a number of American specialists who would analyze the calls and provide him with an "expert witness" in an attempt to prove that they had been faked. But on November 19, 2006, Kamel Nacif involuntarily dealt the final blow to his friend the Governor—whom he affectionately called "Daddy,"

"Precious," and "my hero"—when he put out an editorial explaining that his then wife (they have since divorced) recorded the calls because the two were experiencing marital troubles:

> Until today, I had chosen to proceed with the accusation I filed against Ms. Cacho under conditions of the strictest adherence to the law, limiting my dispute with her to appropriate forums, such as the courts, and not the media, but the events of a few days ago in which recordings obtained illicitly from my telephone lines were made public make it necessary for me to write this open letter to the public.

> I never imagined that sentiments I had expressed privately would be made public, fundamentally due to the nature of the setting in which my words were originally spoken. Morally speaking, I am the sole bearer of responsibility, it is I who can be heard speaking in those conversations, and the offensive words used were my own, in these conversations that—and I stress this once more—were of a private nature.

In these conversations, Nacif can be heard planning a hostile buyout of residential property with Succar Kuri and asking him to bring over some girls from Florida and El Salvador "to fornicate" with them in Cancun. Later dates have Nacif planning and celebrating my arrest, as well as discussing having me raped and beaten in the Puebla jail. All of the conversations you will read below are extracted and transcribed directly from the audio files provided to us by *La Jornada* and journalist Carmen Aristegui. The language used in them is uncouth, at times vulgar and offensive. In the interest of preserving authenticity, mispronounced words and disjointed ideas have been left untouched.[27]

---

27. To hear the original recordings of these and all the other telephone conversations, see the *La Jornada* and *El Universal* websites.

THE "PRECIOUS GUV'"

Christmas 2005 is approaching, it is December 23. Puebla judge Rosa Celia Pérez had remanded me to prison just a few hours earlier. There is the voice of a secretary, who mentions both men by name before connecting them, then the following conversation transpires:

Governor Mario Marín (GMM): Talk to me, Kamel.

Kamel Nacif (KN): My precious guv'.

GMM: Hey, my hero.

KN: No, you're the hero of this movie, Daddy.

GMM: So yesterday I finally gave that old bitch a goddamn good smacking. I told her that here in Puebla we respect the law, and there's no impunity, and if a person commits a crime, we call them a delinquent. And she better not go around playing the victim and trying to use this to get publicity for herself, either. I sent her a message, and now we'll see how she reacts. But she just keeps screwing around with us, so she can take her smacking and everyone else can goddamn well learn from it.

KN: I know, these bastards keep coming out with one bullshit thing after another. But I made a statement. I went on TV.

GMM: Hey, great. There in Mexico or here in Puebla?

KN: Here, but they said they were gonna send it there. It was shown here. And I told them at *Milenio*—if you want, you can read it—I told them, yeah, well the governor doesn't pussyfoot around.

GMM: No we do not, and we're not gonna start.

KN: Fucking bunch a rats. What have they done? What is this shit, huh?

GMM: No! They think they're God on high.

KN: Exactly. I called to thank you. I know I got you into a mess with this, but . . .

GMM: No, don't worry about it, I like this stuff. I agree with you that, sons a bitches, this stuff . . . I mean . . . we're no saints, clearly, but if anyone has any proof, then let them show it. And if not, they can shut the hell up.

KN: I know, but it's all just so shameful, my distinguished friend. It really is shameful.

GMM: It is.

KN: And to thank you, I've got a beautiful bottle of Cognac here for you, but I don't know where to send it.

GMM: Send it over to Casa Puebla.[28]

KN: I wanted to give it to you personally, but you're so busy.

GMM: Send it to me at Casa Aguayo,[29] that way I can drink it.

KN: You're gonna drink it? Then I'll send you two, not one.

TELEPHONE CONVERSATION BETWEEN KAMEL NACIF AND "JUANITO" NAKAD ON THE DAY OF LYDIA CACHO'S LAWFUL KIDNAPPING

"Juanito" Nakad (JN): Hey, *patrón*.[30]

Kamel Nacif (KN): Hey, Juanito.

JN: Listen, I'm down here at the Attorney General's. I couldn't see Alfonso Karam [the chief of police] because he's at a press conference. (. . .) I spoke to the judge. The judge is here now at the courthouse.

KN: And what did she say?

JN: She says "Juanito, I can't have you coming down here today." So I say, "Why not?" And she says, "Later, I'll tell you in a little while." It seems they've been talking to her since yesterday. "I don't wanna see you around here, don't worry, you're in good hands."

KN: So . . . what, then? Is she gonna let her out on bail?

---

28. Translator's Note: Official residence of the governor of the state of Puebla.
29. Translator's Note: The building that houses the official offices of the governor of the state of Puebla.
30. Q.v. footnote #6.

JN: I don't think so. I don't think so. But—she did say we'd talk soon. I don't know what orders she's got from above. It was the same last time . . . s'all right, listen, we'll talk in a sec, I'm gonna catch Alfonso Karam here, I'll call you in two minutes, five minutes. (Hangs up.)

FOLLOW-UP CALL I

Juanito calls Kamel from his cell phone twenty minutes later while monitoring the police's actions at the state attorney general's office.

JN: Listen, that woman's here now. Jesus Christ.

KN: And? Was it a whole big fucking thing or just nothing?

JN: Not a big thing, but . . . no. No sign of her husband. And Televisa showed up and the whole deal, and they brought her down from where she was being held. Because I told her—on orders of the governor, even if it's just for five minutes, you lock her up in a cell. And they were gonna stick her in there, and they brought her down, took her picture, I don't know what the fuck else. Then she left. He [Nakad is referring to the head of the State Judicial Police] was standing right in front of me talking to López Zavala, telling him to tell the governor that this woman [Lydia Cacho] was on her way over to the correctional facility, that she'd be at the correctional facility in five minutes. [It's clear that Juanito is giving orders in the name of the governor, as I was indeed locked in a cell after my photograph and fingerprints were taken.]

KN: Mm-hmm.

JN: And I was gonna go, but the judge told me not to, said she'd talk to me later. (. . .) Anyhow, they brought her [Lydia Cacho] in, blackmailed her. They say she's a mess. 'Cause she says they brought her over in a piece of shit car. I told her that was on purpose, that they sent an old car on purpose. In the twenty-four hours she was with them, they only let her eat once. We'll see what happens.

FOLLOW-UP CALL 2

In this conversation, "Juanito" Nakad and Kamel Nacif chat about the advisability of corrupting the authorities so that a person getting arrested never finds out about their impending detention ahead of time. They revel in influence peddling.

> **JN:** Don't you remember when we were filing the report? He said he had to notify her about it. And the Public Ministry guy said no, if we notify her, she'll get herself an injunction, and then she'll never go to jail. Do you remember that?
>
> **KN:** Of course.
>
> **JN:** He said it then: Juan knows what he's doing. Your lawyer wanted us to notify her about it. I said no. We have to hit her hard. When you start notifying people, they never go to jail. (. . .) She never found out, she never found out that there's an accusation and an arrest warrant out against her. Otherwise we'd have never gotten this far. That's how you succeed, that's how you gotta do things.
>
> **KN:** Goddamn right. What did the guy say?
>
> **JN:** He's saying she's being escorted by the AFI because she'd gotten a death threat. They're gonna be with her the whole way. She's being escorted like a star. [Laughs.] She's coming here with your people and also some other people who're gonna make sure your people don't *do anything* to her on the way over. That's normal here. If you're awake, you can see your friend López Dóriga at 10:30, he's sure to broadcast something about it. [Although Nakad is insisting here that my AFI escort is traveling in another car behind me, in reality the leader of my own security detail, Óscar Cienfuegos, called his boss on the phone while I was

being held and he was given the order to let me go with Judicial
Police agents. The AFI agents gave testimony to the PGR stating
that they never attempted to stop the arrest, nor did they follow
behind us. The other vehicle of armed men belonged, in fact, to
Kamel Nacif.]

KN: I doubt it.

JN: I bet you anything this is gonna end up on TV. And especially
if you're saying a bunch of journalists from all over Mexico called
the governor to ask him if the news is true or not. The news went
national, Daddy.

KN: Let it go national.

JN: What the hell, we're into it now, anyways. [Laughs.]

KN: [Laughs.] We're into it now.

CALL FROM WEDNESDAY THE 21ST

On the eve of the hearing to determine whether I would be
remanded to prison, Nacif lets his nervousness show in this conversation with Nakad:

KN: So is the judge gonna fuck around and change her mind?

JN: No, look, I was with the judge today. (. . .) Adolfo Meneses told
me he doesn't think the judge is gonna get cold feet, because
that's going against her own decision. The only thing I said to
Valentín was: Don't get all up in the judge's life, the judge doesn't
give a shit, the judge is gonna be all about the law. But if she
gets orders from the court, because they screw her over, then she
can't say no, you see what I'm saying? [Valentín Meneses was
Governor Marín's spokesman.]

KN: You know why she can't go back on her decision? Because
they'd come off looking like fucking idiots.

JN: Exactly. Another thing she told me, they were talking on
Saturday, they called her thirty times, *get her out of there, do*

whatever you have to, to get her out. She told her 104 thousand pesos. No, wait, 140 thousand. So they negotiate it: five,
ten, fourteen. She said, "I can't lower it." In the end she only
dropped it by 30. So she got 30 of it dropped and paid 70 in
cash. When I went to see her on Monday, she said, "Juan,
I've got the money that bunch of assholes put together when
they came down here to defend her. They drained their bank
accounts and emptied their wallets and put up 70 thousand
in cash." And she said, "Juan, as far as I'm concerned, she's
getting remanded to prison." [According to the Supreme Court
of Justice's investigation, the highest amount ever to have been
set as bail for similar crimes, in the entire history of the Fifth
Criminal Court, was 12 thousand pesos.]

KN: That's right!

JN: But I know how she is in her personal life. She takes a lot of
shit. Poor woman, she should really be on vacation. (. . .)

KN: Tell her I'll set her up with a vacation.

JN: That's what I'm saying. She's gonna have to stay there working
all week, 'cause she goes to work on Saturday, too. She's a true
brother to us, a thousand times over.

KN: Where does she want to go on vacation? Tell her I'll set her
up. Tell her I'll send her wherever she likes, anywhere at all.

JN: I'll tell her.

KN: Tell the judge I'll send her to Las Vegas, all expenses paid.

Later, Nacif exclaims:

KN: Man, I look really ugly on TV, don't I? I look really ugly.

JN: [Laughs.] Saw yourself, did you?

KN: Fucking old, bald son of a bitch.

JN: 'Ats all right. It comes off good here . . . it's fitting because you
can see the old bitch hurt you, fucking cunt. [Laughs again.]

EMMA, ONE OF THE VICTIMS, INTERVIEWS "EL JOHNNY"

Quintana Roo state attorney general Rosa Celia Pérez Gordillo ordered in October 2003 that Jean Succar Kuri be recorded in order to obtain further proof of his involvement in the rape of minors. She never guessed that Succar would be so exhaustive and detailed in his explanations. This is the transcription of the video footage taken when one of the victims, whom we will call Emma, interviewed him with a hidden camera, aided by agents of the Attorney General's Office. The transcription is literal.

> **Jean Succar Kuri (JSK):** I don't do it with fifteen-year-old girls anymore. Do you know why I don't? Because I only do that when I'm somewhere isolated. Like with Marína, when she was at my house and she disappeared and I told her, "Talk to me . . ."
>
> **Emma (E):** Who's Marína?
>
> **JSK:** I met her at your school, before I met you.
>
> **E:** Ahh . . . Marína.
>
> **JSK:** What was her name?
>
> **E:** Leticia Marína.
>
> **JSK:** But she has another name, she told me another name. I asked her, "Where are you?" and after two days she's standing in front of me, just there in the bedroom, shouting at the top of her voice.
>
> **E:** But when I came by, I came with Sandra. Well, at the beginning . . .
>
> **JSK:** Yeah, but the two of you came. Sandra was coming by alone back then. When I met you, I had just slept with Sandra for the first time, and that was when she bled, a shitload of blood came out of her, and she said, "My mom's gonna fucking kill me."
>
> **E:** Why? Was she a virgin?
>
> **JSK:** Hey, you know, I really couldn't tell you.
>
> **E:** How old was she?
>
> **JSK:** Sixteen or seventeen. They all bleed with me, my wife bled, a bunch of different housemaids I've fucked bled. Plus, they don't

bleed because they're virgins, they bleed because they're really small. I didn't know anything about this one girl.

E: You started seeing her when she was fifteen?

JSK: No, I told you, I approached your friend once, because she was looking for me, so I approached the girl's dad and there was no problem.

E: But when you took her with you, you touched her.

JSK: That's a whole different matter, as long as you don't have relations, as long as you don't consummate the act, everything's fine. But you've got a past I don't like . . . [Said mockingly.]

E: Why don't you like my past?

JSK: Forget it, it doesn't matter. [He fiddles with the straw in his glass of juice.]

E: It does matter, because those three years I was with you, who did I ever mess around with when I was a girl. No one, I'm telling you, no one.

JSK: You just want to block it out.

E: I want to block it out . . .

JSK: And everything you did when you were there with the girls, I kept bringing out the bottles . . .

E: I didn't know anything, you asked me to and you turned on your little camera for me to sleep with them . . .

JSK: It's done. If you enjoyed it or if you still enjoy it, that's your problem, I'm not telling you to do it or not to do it, after all, it's your own private life.

E: But you have to understand something, you take a thirteen-year-old girl who doesn't have any idea about anything and you start to teach her that that's what the world is like, that that's how people live, that all of this is normal, then pretty much what she's gonna learn is that all of this is normal.

J: You don't remember a lot of things, but I remember when we were at the pool, I told you, "M'*ija*, they tell me you're a lesbian," and I told you, "Lesly told me, even Nadia told me . . ."

E: It's not true.

JSK: Don't try to justify it, because there are things you don't remember, but the most consistent thing about you, the most screwed up of all, is that you don't remember everything I did for you.

E: I do, I do remember . . .

JSK: Yeah, but then whenever it suits you, you forget.

E: I remember a lot of things. What is it that might not suit me, according to you? Let's hear it . . .

JSK: Look, it's like I told you, I didn't know you were a lesbian until I saw you screwing Nadia.

E: I did no such thing . . .

JSK: And now you're coming out with all this oh, you taught me, oh, you forced me.

E: You taught me to do that, you taught me that if you need some medicine, I had to give you your medicine [sex]. Why? Because you were suffering . . .

JSK: Yes, I told you that I was a womanizer and I liked girls, and that if you love me, you have to bring me girls, but I didn't tell you, "Lick them . . ."

E: You told me—

JSK: Motherfucker! I didn't tell you . . . Look, let's make a deal.

E: Okay.

JSK: Look, it'll be really easy, we get some witnesses, some people, I swear on my children. I'm gonna bring you a girl and we'll see if you'll lick her, and if not, you can stay with me awhile.

E: But why?

JSK: To see if you're a lesbian or not.

E: But why would we do that?

JSK: Because if you're not a lesbian, you'll never lick her, you'll never do it, you'll never do it, not for all the money in the world. You won't be able to bring yourself to do it . . . there are some things that just . . . listen, one person might do it out of obligation, or necessity, but the other person—what are they guilty of? What need, what obligation do they have?

E: All the girls that were there . . . they were the same way. [According to testimony, he forced them to perform cunnilingus on one another while he filmed them.]

JSK: Who?

E: Pilar, Pocahontas, what's her name . . . Citlalli.

JSK: No, with you it's not a question of principles, it's a question of what makes sense for you.

E: You told me it was the only way to make sure the little girls weren't going to talk, because that way they'd be ashamed and their own reputations would be compromised, remember what you said!

JSK: All right [he tries to calm her down, he is visibly nervous, he looks from side to side], I love you very much and you've made me realize I still love you. . . . So, let's change the subject. Let's talk about something else.

E: About what?

JSK: I'm worried about this other girl at the house, she's saying she's gonna talk.

E: Why are you worried?

JSK: Because she's a little girl and the day her goddamn mother figures out she's already been fucked, the first thing her mind's gonna go to is me.

E: But if she goes home . . .

JSK: That's what I'm saying, but if the girl says it wasn't me, I can stop worrying.

E: But so she wants to go home?

JSK: I'm not gonna be held responsible for something that's not my fault.

E: Yeah, I know, what I'm saying is—

JSK: Lesly was coming to my place from when she was eight until she was twelve. Lesly took baths with me, she spent a long time with me, she slept whole weeks at my place, and I never did a thing to her.

E: But you would kiss her, and touch her.

JSK: But I'm telling you, that's all allowed! Because that's the risk you take when you go to some lonely old fuck's house, it's all part of the risk. Her parents just said, "Oh, he takes care of my daughter, he takes care of my daughter." All that's allowed. For instance, I say to Lesly, "Bring me a girl who's four," and if she says, "She's already been fucked," and I see if she's been fucked already, then I see if I'm gonna stick my dick in her or not. You know this is my weakness, it's my kink, and I know it's a crime and it's not allowed, but it's so much easier this way, because a tiny little girl like that doesn't stand a chance, because you can convince her really easily, and then you fuck her. I've been doing it my whole life, and sometimes they try to trick me, because they want to stay with me, because I've got a reputation for being a good father . . .

KAMEL NACIF AND JEAN SUCCAR,
TELEPHONE CALL FROM THE YEAR 2000

Just when it seemed that nothing could surprise us anymore, Carmen Aristegui used her news program to reveal new recordings that provided a clear picture of sex tourism and the trafficking and sexual exploitation of women in Cancun. The federal police believe this telephone call to took place at some point in the year 2000, basing their calculations on the timing of the hostile negotiations being undertaken by Succar Kuri to muscle American citizens out of their residential properties in Cancun. This is the literal transcription of the call, which Kamel Nacif would later admit was recorded in secret by his wife—who fled their home five years ago after he tried to kill her during a domestic dispute, as reported in the divorce filing. Part of the conversation was conducted in Spanish and the rest in Arabic. The Arabic portions were translated for W Radio by Dr. Alfredo Jalife Rahme, a specialist in international relations and a native-born Lebanese man who is fluent in several languages, including Lebanese Arabic.[31]

KN: Hello?

JSK: Yes?

KN: Who is this?

JSK: Hello, there, my dear Kamel!

KN: Jean Succar, how are you?

JSK: Where are you, are you over in Acapulco yet?

KN: I'm back in Puebla.

JSK: Ahh, just a quick visit, then, there and straight back again.

KN: Just had to talk to him . . . your friend wasn't there . . . eh.

JSK: I'll call you. Are you at home or at the factory?

KN: No, I'm at my house.

JSK: I'll call you.

KN: Or I can call you. Where are you at?

JSK: 9-2-3-0-3-3-3.

KN: Hold on, you son of a bitch!

JSK: [Laughs.]

KN: I'm not some genius like you, you know . . .

JSK: Same area code.

KN: 5-6-2-9-2-3 . . . Nine what?

JSK: 9-2-3-0-3. Bye.

[Operator speaking in English.]

JSK: Hellooo.

KN: Hey.

JSK: Hellooo, how's it going?

KN: What's up, what are you up to?

---

31. Translator's Note: For the present edition of this book, the English translation of this portion of the conversation is based on Dr. Alfredo Jalife Rahme's Spanish version rather than on the original Arabic.

JSK: Not much . . . so just a quick visit, then, you got there and since your friend wasn't there, you didn't want to stick around.

KN: You got me figs, you got me cheese, you got me a whole fucking spread.

JSK: I'm just trying to make you happy, I move heaven and earth to make you happy.

KN: No, unfortunately I couldn't eat any of it.

JSK: [Laughs.] But you're going back next week, right?

KN: I told Mari to set it aside for me, and to be careful nobody fucks with it.

JSK: You know what? I've got a special bottle here for you, you can take it back with you when you go, remind me when you come. I brought it back on my last trip, I've got it here in the refrigerator, but it slipped my mind.

KN: So what else are you up to?

JSK: Not much, just packing to get ready to leave again.

KN: What time are you leaving?

JSK: It leaves, it leaves here at like 12. I get in at like 7 in the evening.

KN: Hmm.

JSK: I'll be there till the 7th, 8th of May. The 4th of May I have the fucking condo board meeting.

KN: What's that all about, Daddy?

JSK: Oh, they're all pissed 'cause I got the hotel, they're gonna wanna scheme up something against me . . . they can suck my cock.

KN: 'Ats all right, bro, let 'em scheme.

JSK: [Laughs.]

KN: What do they want?

JSK: They're just dying of jealousy, I've already got 30 percent of the building . . .

KN: How's that?

JSK: They're a bunch of old folks, you know . . . retired, jealous,

they're afraid I'm gonna kick 'em out, that maintainance costs
are gonna go up, I'm taking over the whole building, they're jealous. I gotta keep 'em at bay, I'm trying to be really nice to them.
Once I get 51 percent, they can suck it.

KN: So . . . the condo board, huh . . . And what's gonna happen on
the 4th?

JSK: Nothing, they wanna kick the manager out and I'm supporting him. The manager means shit all to me, but if they kick him
out, it's a victory for them. [Inaudible.]

KN: Don't get in a fight. And when can we get the 51 percent?

JSK: We're still short like $2 million.

KN: 2 million?

JSK: [Laughs.]

KN: To buy them all out?

JSK: No, not to buy them out . . . to get to 51 percent.

KN: Okay. And is it worth it?

JSK: Yes, that land is worth $20 million, easy.

KN: What?

JSK: The land is worth $20 million, easy.

KN: What land? It's not yours, man.

JSK: No, but it's gonna be. Once I get to 51 percent, we control the
whole thing.

KN: No, no, no, Daddy.

JSK: Sure, then you can do whatever you like, then you control the
majority of votes.

KN: But what are you gonna do? I mean, I mean, I mean. How
much to buy them out?

JSK: Three more.

KN: Is $5 million enough to buy?

JSK: At most.

KN: Then fuck it, I'll just give it to you, buy them all out and tell
them to go fuck themselves already, right?

JSK: We'll talk when you come. If you're serious, we'll talk.

KN: Serious, serious? No, no, course I'm serious, man.

JSK: You love me, whatever I want, you give me, but I want you to feel positively about this.

KN: Yeah, positively. How many rooms are there?

JSK: Total it's like 250 rooms.

KN: Ok, so we put up $5 million. And how much is it gonna cost us to remodel the whole thing? Nicely, I mean, not that bullshit stuff you do, all that fucking ugly ass shit you do.

JSK: One, another million.

KN: You sure? That's all?

JSK: You need a million to set up, you know, the conference room and a gym and all that, I've already got the specs.

KN: Right, and to remodel the whole thing?

JSK: Another million.

KN: 'Kay, so it's 7 million. How much do you have? How many rooms are there?

JSK: 250, I've got 50.

KN: Right, so 200 rooms for 7 million, remodeling and everything, $35,000 a room—Do it! Right now!

JSK: There's a problem, not everyone wants to sell . . .

KN: Ohhh!

JSK: It's gotta be done all gangster, you have to study the thing, that's what I'm telling you . . . once you have 51 percent . . .

KN: How much did those people pay?

JSK: Here? On average, thirty-five or forty.

KN: It's what they paid, you're giving them their money, so now they can just run along and fuck themselves!

JSK: [Laughs.] That's what's gonna have to happen, I'm telling you . . . right now half of Solymar is up for sale, because they're scared, and if they find out I bought, that I have 51 percent the next day everyone [inaudible] it's logical, the few that don't sell because they wanna mess with me are gonna have to [inaudible]. It's a nice place, Kamel, it's cozy, it's private, it's not some building, some cold tower, it's got charm, it'll be a real jewel when it's all fixed up, a nice one, all pretty and fixed up.

KN: All right. Set it up.

JSK: When are you coming to Cancun? Are you coming next week?

KN: No, this coming week I can't, Daddy, the week after that.

JSK: Don't just come one night so you have to go back the next day, bro, come for two, three days and walk around on the beach with me. Disconnect for two days.

KN: What?

JSK: Disconnect for two nights.

KN: 'Kay, but [begins speaking in Arabic].

Literal translation from Lebanese Arabic:

KN: Don't you have any whores? [In Arabic] So why didn't you sent me one? [In Spanish]

JSK: I'm no good at that stuff [laughs]. [In Spanish]

KN: You're an asshole. [In Spanish]

JSK: I'm good at . . . I know what I'm good at. [In Spanish]

KN: You're an asshole, man . . . I'm gonna tell your wife what you're doing. [In Arabic]

JSK: [Laughs.] If she drops dead, it's because she doesn't love you.

KN: You want me to tell your wife? [In Arabic]

JSK: It's not worth your while, you're going to Cancun, I'll be waiting for you with one. [In Spanish]

KN: You want me to?

JSK: Forget her, poor thing, those five sons of hers all doing sports, soccer . . . she's very busy with them. It's a blessing she's so busy with those five sons.

KN: Where's the girl from Miami?

JSK: She's in Tampa, I get in on Sunday, and she gets in Sunday, too.

KN: That little whore is just like you.

JSK: You'll see when you see her.

KN: How much do you pay her?

JSK: $2,000.

KN: You're such an asshole.

JSK: You'll see for yourself when I bring her to you.

KN: When? Next week. Motherfucker . . . but you're bringing her to fornicate.

JSK: First one to chicken out is a rotten egg . . .

KN: But you understand me? She's coming, but to fornicate.

JSK: She's just as big a whore as you are.

KN: Just see how we fuck her! Maybe she'll bring her little friend along. You feeling bad about it or something?

JSK: What do I know, it's your business, not mine.

KN: No, no, no, bring her. Tell me when, and we'll bring her over.

JSK: I'm telling you, my friend is really pretty, this short little blond girl.

KN: Why are you speaking in Spanish?

JSK: My wife's not here, she went to the supermarket.

KN: All right, in Arabic then . . . but you understand, right, we're bringing this one over to fornicate. [In Arabic]

JSK: Tell me when you're coming. [In Arabic]

KN: When's the other girl coming? [In Spanish]

JSK: She gets in from Tampa on Sunday, she's staying with me until the 6th of May, whenever I tell her. Talk to your friend, we'll send her her ticket, cause she's in El Salvador, the friend's in El Salvador.

KN: Does she have a visa for *le Mexique?*

JSK: I'm not sure . . .

KN: So?

JSK: That's why we have to find out.

KN: So find out, man! Have the bitch get one in Tampa.

JSK: [Laughs.] All right.

KN: One who's just as big a whore as she is, who won't get all bitchy, and don't you be a little bitch, either, we're gonna make them have a ménage à trois.

JSK: Mine's a virgin, man [laughing].

KN: Yeah, right, a virgin. She can suck a cock like a lollipop, she's such a virgin! Ahhh, fucking Succar.

JSK: I told you what happened with the Viagra, right? She sucks my cock and she tells me . . . this time it was different [inaudible] different like . . . well, I don't know what was different. [Laughs].

KN: Hey, you got that fucking fat one working now, right?

JSK: Which? Oh yeah. And now what do I do with her? I finally got her out of my hair.

KN: Exactly, put her to work, it's Emma, you need her around here, so get over here and get to work already, you fucking cunt. No, you don't need her at the house.

JSK: No, I don't bring her to the house anymore.

KN: Do it and don't, don't do it and bring her to the house. Hey, you got rid of the DIRECTV in the fucking suite.

JSK: No, I dropped the ball on that one, I didn't get rid of it, it's not gotten rid of, I dropped the ball, the box gets taken to the lobby and when I need the suite, I ask for the box. I completely dropped the ball on that one, excuse me.

KN: Ohhh . . . might as well save money anyways man, you're right. So what else is going on, man?

JSK: Not much, like I said, I'm hoping everything works out at Solymar, I'm a little nervous. I'll tell you about it later . . .

KN: Nervous? Why? You want me to tell you something, Jean Succar? Take the whole thing easy . . . Whatever happens happens.

This telephone call corroborates the information provided by different witnesses who had given statements to the PGR to the effect that Succar Kuri was bringing girls and boys to the United States without their parents. One of the witnesses under federal protection, who worked with Succar at his shops in the Cancun airport, even told the authorities that the latter would take the children and their airplane tickets and "store" them at his shop until it was time to catch the plane to Los Angeles. "He told us on several occasions, 'Take care of them until I come for them,'" the witness explained. "I saw the children leaving, but we never saw them come back. He would bring little girls over from the United States, as well, and they were never accompanied by any adults."

EMILIO GAMBOA AND KAMEL NACIF, THE PROOF OF THEIR "FRIENDSHIP"

A few days after he became chair of the Senate's Political Coordination Board, PRI-affiliated politician Emilio Gamboa acknowledged that the conversation he held with Kamel Nacif in which the two discussed a gambling law that would affect betting at the Hipódromo [horseracing track] was not the only such talk they had had, stating that there were at least six or seven others. To inoculate himself against any new leaks, Gamboa, who heads the PRI in the senate, revealed further conversations with the Lebanese-born businessman but stressed that he regrets the calls and their contents.

A recording in the possession of *El Universal* shows that businessman Kamel Nacif demanded that Emilio Gamboa, then a senator, block proposed legal reforms that would have allowed the opening of a casino at the Hipódromo de las Américas racetrack in Mexico City. In February 2004, PRI deputies realized it was in their interest to push through a bill for a proposed Law on Gambling and Lotteries. They drafted a document containing 175 articles and 3 stipulation clauses to regulate the operation of gambling and betting venues. The changes debated in Congress in April 2004 were not passed in the end, and the bill died in September of that same year.

Emilio Gamboa (EG): Hey, Daddy, where you been, man?

Kamel Nacif (KN): Oh, you know, still here in this fucking demon town, Daddy.

EG: But where've you been, my king? 'Cause a person can go around all day saying good things about you, but then you up and disappear, you son of a bitch.

KN: I've just been working my ass off, you know how it is.

EG: But you're doing all right?

KN: Hey, you know, as long as I'm alive, I'm doing all right.

EG: No, no, seriously, you all right?

KN: Yes, my king.

EG: All right, take care of yourself, and I'll see you soon.

KN: And how are you, Senator?

EG: Pfff . . . busy as hell, just having some lunch right now with a couple of senators, if I told you, you'd . . . Jesus Christ.

KN: Where . . . ?

EG: We're gonna do the Hipódromo reform, not the gambling one anymore . . . just the Hipódromo one.

KN: What for . . . ?

EG: To put some gambling in there, man . . .

KN: What . . .? Oh . . .

EG: What do you think?

KN: No, don't fuck around with that stuff.

EG: Whatever you say, then, man, whatever you say, that's the direction we're going, man.

KN: No, block it, Daddy.

EG: All right then, it's blocked, that shit's not getting through the Senate, right?

KN: Hell, no!

EG: Okay.

KN: Hell, no!

EG: All my best.

KN: When are we gonna get together?

EG: Whenever you like, my Kamelito.

KN: Just say the word . . .

EG: I'm going to Washington to see a couple of assholes up there, but I'll see you when I get back.

KN: When are you going to Washington?

EG: I'm leaving Sunday . . . Friday, no, Saturday . . . and I'm back at 11 o'clock Tuesday night.

KN: All right, let's try to get together on Wednesday.

EG: I'll call you when I get back . . . believe me when I say I'll call you . . . but don't you call me, now . . . I'll call you, friend.

KN: Sure thing, Senator . . .

EG: All my best.

KN: Take care. Bye.

EG: You too.

To listen to the recordings of these telephone calls, go to:
www.unafuente.com
www.jornada.unam.mx
www.eluniversal.com.mx

THE PRECIOUS FORTY

This story of conspiracy is jam-packed with names. All of these people participated, to greater or lesser degrees, in the plan to harass and intimidate me and violate my individual guarantees. The 1,205-page document containing the findings of Juan Silva Meza's investigation includes fingerprints and photographs of each one of these individuals.

Source: Alejandro Almazán and Viétnika Batres, "Cómo se armó la conspiración contra Lydia Cacho" ["How the Conspiracy against Lydia Cacho Was Hatched"], *emeequis*, number 87, October 1, 2007.

PUEBLA:
Mario Plutarco Marín Torres, the governor
José Kamel Nacif Borge, the businessman
Hanna Nakad Bayeh, the businessman's friend
Ana María Campeche Sánchez, the governor's secretary

Guillermo Pacheco Pulido, the chief justice of the Superior Court of Justice of the State

Rosa Celia Pérez González, the judge

Blanca Laura Villena Martínez, the state attorney general

Enrique Ruiz Delgadillo, the adjunct secretary of the Superior Court of Justice of the State

Javier López Zavala, the state secretary of the interior

Carlos Escobar, the governor's personal secretary

Mario Edgar Tepox, the coordinator of the governor's agenda

Ricardo Velásquez Cruz, the governor's legal advisor

Hugo Adolfo Karam Beltrán, the former head of the State Judicial Police

Leonardo Fabio Briceño Moreno, the secretary to the chief justice of the Superior Court of Justice of the State

Heriberto Galindo Martínez, the head of the Social

Readaptation Center (Cereso) of Puebla (also known as the San Miguel prison)

Aldo Enrique Cruz Pérez, the director general of the Social Readaptation System for the state of Puebla

Arsenio Farell Campa, Luis Jorge Castro Trejo, Agustín Ruiz

Parra, Manuel Farrera Villalobos, and **Jorge Miguel Echeverría,** the businessman's lawyers

Igor Archundia Sierra, the assistant attorney general in charge of prior inquiries

Gerardo Villar Borja, Juan José Barriento Granda, and **Fernando García Rosas,** the justices serving on the

Superior Court of Justice of the State

Martín Macías Pérez, the general agreements secretary of the Superior Court of Justice of the State

José Hernández Corona, the assistant secretary for political

affairs and civil protection of the Secretariat of the Interior.

Juan Sánchez Moreno, the commander of the arrest party from the now defunct warrant-issuing station.

Rómulo Arredondo Gutiérrez, the secretary of transportation

Luis Guillermo Arsención Serna, the director in charge of prior inquiries

Rosaura Espejel Prado and **Ignacio Sarabia Martínez,** the Public Ministry workers

José Montaño Quiroz and **Jesús Pérez Vargas,** the Judicial Police agents

QUINTANA ROO:

Bello Melchor Rodríguez y Carrillo, the state attorney general

Teodoro Manuel Sarmiento Silva, the state assistant attorney general for the Northern Zone

Javier Brito Rosellón, the former director of legal affairs at the Office of the Assistant Attorney General for the Northern Zone

Jaime Alberto Ongay Ortiz, the former head of the Judicial Police for the Northern Zone

Jorge Félix Humberto Adolfo Molina Osuna, the former commander of the Apprehension Group at the Office of the Assistant Attorney General for the Northern Zone

Miguel Mora Olvera, the Judicial Police agent

PRESS RELEASE, JUNE 21, 2007:
ONCE UPON A TIME THERE WAS A PEDOPHILE WHO WAS PROTECTED BY HIS VERY POWERFUL FRIENDS . . .

FOR THE PUBLIC'S CONSIDERATION

The report filed in 2003 by a group of girls and boys who had been sexually abused by Jean Succar Kuri in Cancun unleased a long series of scandals that has not yet run its course. It is a case that reveals the hurdles the Mexican people are met with whenever an attempt is made to bring authorities and other powerful men with ties to organized crimes before the courts.

THE FACTS

It could have been no easy task for the victims in this case to work up the courage required to report their tormentor, a man of great riches and connections. The authorities responded to this brave, civic act first with an attempt to extort the criminal, and later with negligence by allowing him to escape. Thanks to pressure put on INTERPOL by the victims themselves, Succar Kuri was detained in the United States, but his extradition process was stalled as a result of footdragging at the PGR when it came time to provide the American authorities with documentation of the crime. Evidence and testimony documenting the pedophile's crimes, some of it irreplaceable, have disappeared from files. Influence peddling has caused the legal process to become completely bogged down.

Thanks to the publication of journalist Lydia Cacho's book *The Demons of Eden* and the coverage her case has received, the PGR eventually sped up extradition proceedings. But the network of powerful individuals protecting Succar dealt a harsh punishment to the journalist for having had the audacity to expose them. Businessman Kamel Nacif and Puebla governor Mario Marín undertook negotiations for a torturous version of justice to be meted out as a punishment to Lydia Cacho, as several different pieces of evidence, as well as the famous recordings that came to light on February 14, 2006, attest.

Like the girls Succar abused, Lydia Cacho turned to the law (the PGR), and she reported her tormentors for abuse of authority, torture, and attempted rape. Cacho made the decision to battle it out with her tormentors in the courts, the very arena they had chosen for her torture. The strategy was a risky one, but it was born of a conviction that the country's democratization might make it possible for a case brought by a citizen against a governor and a state attorney general to succeed.

The backlash has been unrelenting. The judicial system has set resources and subterfuges in motion to punish her daring: the disappearance of evidence, including the CNDH computer on which the testimonies of key witnesses were stored; the intimidation of witnesses; the repetition ad nauseum of interrogation sessions designed to exhaust the journalist; the attack on a PGR-issued SUV in which she was traveling; the Puebla governor's campaign to discredit Cacho, which was aided by his illegal access to materials in the power of the State Attorney General's Office; the intentional foot-dragging of Public Ministry workers and judges. The two cases—the case involving the pedophile Succar Kuri and the case of Cacho vs. Marín—are inextricably intertwined. Throughout the entire process, the Puebla authorities have used the courts as though the latter were an extension of the apparatus of the state, rather than a public space in which to hear citizens' complaints.

To every violation and abuse, Lydia Cacho's defense has provided a timely response in the courts, never failing to report irregularities and abuses. Every legal maneuver has been met invariably with further harassment and harsher retributions against the journalist.

FOR YOUR CONSIDERATION

The case involving Lydia Cacho and the governor of Puebla has reached the Supreme Court for the second time, thanks to a request made by the Chamber of Deputies and the Senate of the Republic. The matter at hand is of vital importance for the country. There is much more under examination than a single violation of the human rights of a journalist who is known to protect and give voice to abused boys and girls. What is at stake here is the chance to know, for once and for all, if we average Mexican men and women have any chance at all of getting the state to protect us from criminals who ally themselves with public servants, those in the executive and the judiciary who use the criminal justice system to protect all manner of criminal rings, including networks promoting child pornography and the corruption of minors. For the Puebla authorities involved in this case did not need to participate directly in the act of pedophilia to become accomplices; it was enough that they form an illegal pact to send the public a message—the rights of attackers are protected, and victims and journalists who dare to reveal the true facts of matters are punished.

We urge the justices of the Supreme Court to return to the citizens of Mexico our right to trust the courts. So far, the reprisals dealt to Succar's victims and the campaign of persecution against Lydia Cacho would appear to confirm the views of eight out of every ten Mexicans, who believe the reporting of crimes to be useless because the institutions of the state will not afford them the proper protection. If the Puebla authorities are cleared of all responsibility, if the obvious existence of networks propagating child pornography, child abuse, and the trafficking of minors in Mexico is not recognized, it is highly unlikely that any other citizen will dare to step forward and challenge in court those men who use the power of the state to corrupt society and strengthen criminal activities in Mexico.

WE, THE UNDERSIGNED, DEMAND RESPECT FOR THE CHILDREN AND STAND AGAINST ABUSE AND IMPUNITY:

Adolfo Castañón, Agustín Coppel, Alan Ibarra, Alfonso Cuarón, Alberto Begné, Alberto Ruy Sánchez, Alejandra Islas, Alejandro González Iñarritu, Alejandro Páez Varela, Alicia Leal, Alison Thompson, Álvaro Enrigue, Ana Claudia Talancón, Ana Colchero, Ana de la Reguera, Angeles Mastretta, Ángeles Ochoa, Ashley Judd, Astrid Haddad, Avi Lewis, Bart Freundlich, Beatriz Novaro, Benicio del Toro, Berta Hiriart, Berta Navarro, Blanca Guerra, Bridget

Fonda, Blanca Rico, Blue Demon Jr. Carla Faesler, Carlos Carrera, Carlos Fazio, Carlos García Agraz, Carlos Martínez Assad, Carlos Monsiváis, Carlos Reygadas, Carmen Boullosa, Carmen Giménez Cacho, Carmina Narro, Caroline Coskren, Cecilia Suárez Charlize Theron, Chema Yazpik Clara Jusidman, Clara Montes, Clara Scherer, Clive Owen, Committee of Protection of Journalists, Cristina del Valle, Damien Rice, Dana Rotberg, Debra Winger, Demi Moore, Daniel Giménez Cacho, Darren Aranovsky, David Bialostozky, David Heyman, Daya Fernandez, Debora Holtz, Denise Dresser, Diana Washington Valdéz, Diego Luna, Eduardo Gamboa, Edward Norton, Elena Poniatowska, Elsa Cross, Emi Norris, Emilienne de León, Emmanuel Lubezki, Enrique Berruga, Epigmenio Ibarra, Eric Newman, Ernesto Gómez Cruz, Eugenia León, Eugenio Caballero, Eugenio Derbez, Eve Ensler, Fabrizio Eva, Federico Campbell, Felipe Cazals, Felipe Garrido, Fernando Cámara, Fred Berger, Frederique Ulla Alonso, Gabriel Orozco, Gabriela García Luna, Gael García Bernal, Gerardo García, Gerardo Priego Tapia, Graciela Iturbide, Grupo Elefante, Guadalupe Loaeza, Guillaume Canet, Guillermo del Toro, Gus Van Sant, Harrison Lobdell, Heather Graham, Héctor de Mauleón, Henry Holmes, Huberto Bátiz, Humberto Musacchio, Ignacio Ortiz, Ignacio Rodríguez Reyna, Jackie Joiner, Jacquelyn Langberg, James Schamus, Jenaro Villamil, Jeniffer Hoffmeister, Jesusa Rodríguez, John Hecht, Jonás Cuarón, Jordi Soler, Jorge Fons, Jorge Volpi, Jorge Zepeda Patterson, José Gordon, Jose Luis Garcia Agraz José Pérez-Espino, Josefina Zoraida Vázquez, Josh Lucas, Juan Antonio de la Riva, Juan Carlos Casasola, Julianne Moore, Julie Delpy, Julio Pomar, Julio Scherer Ibarra, Karla Moles, Kristel Laiblin, Kyzza Terrazas, Kate del Castillo, Katia D' Artigues, Laura de Ita, Leonardo de Leozzane, Liliana Felipe, Lorena Maza, Lucía Álvarez, Lucía Melgar, Lucina Jiménez, Luis Farnox, Luis Javier Solana, Luis Mandoki, Luis Mario Moncada, Manuel Carrillo, Manuel Pereira, Marc Abraham, Marc Weiss, Marcela Lagarde, Marco Lara Kahr, Margarita De Orellana, María Consuelo Mejía,

María Elena Chapa, María Rojo, María Teresa Priego, Mariana Castaneda, Mariana Rodríguez, Mariana Winocour, Marie Claire Acosta, Mariestela Fernández, Marina Arvizu, Marina Castañeda, Marta Lamas, Mary Browning, Mateo Gil, Mauricio Carrera, Maximiliano Vega Tato, Mia Maestro, Michael Mann, Mike Davis, Milos Forman, Mira Nair, Moderatto, Molotov, Monica Hoge, Mónica Lavín, Naomi Klein, Naomi Watts, Natalie Imbruglia, Nerio Barberis, Nicole Teeny, Olallo Rubio, Oscar Figueroa, Pablo Cruz, Paloma Torres, Noam Chomsky, Patricia Mercado, Patricia Reyes, Espíndola, Paul Lalberty, Pedro Armendáriz, Pilar Ordoñez, Polly Cohen, Priscila Amescua, Priya Shelly, Rafael Pérez Gay, Random House Mondadori, Randy Ebright, Rebeca Miller, Regina Orozco, Reporteros Sin Fronteras, Ricardo Rocha, Richard Fox, Rita Varela, Rosa Nissan, Rosario Dawson, Rosaura Barahona, Rose McGowan, Ross Katz, Rossana Fuentes, Robert Rodríguez, Robin Wright Penn, Ryan Gosling, Sabina Berman, Salma Hayek, Salvador Camarena, Salvador Frausto, Sara Sefchovich, Sasha Sokol, Saul Hernández, Sean Penn, Sergio Aguayo, Sergio González, Sigfrido Barjau, Slavo Zízek, Stasia de la Garza, Steve Rabineau, Steven Czitrom, Susan Sarandon, Taylor McNulty, Thomas Vinterberg, Timothy J.Sexton, Toni Kuhn, Vicente Leñero, Warren Olney, Woody Harrelson

... AND OVER 2,000 MORE SIGNATURES—
ALL SIGNING AS ONE—AVAILABLE FOR VIEWING AT:
www.unafuente.com

Full-page spread published June 21, 2007, signed by artists, intellectuals, journalists, and millions of other individuals from a variety of countries, urging the justices at the Supreme Court of Justice of the Nation to halt impunity.

MORE INFORMATION ON HOW TO STOP CHILD PORNOGRAPHY

AUSTRALIA
Australian Broadcasting Authority   www.aba.gov.au
Australian Federal Police   www.afp.gov.au
New South Wales Police/Crime Stoppers   www.police.nsw.gov.au
Phone toll-free: (800) 333-000

AUSTRIA
Stopline   www.stopline.at

BELGIUM
Child Focus   www.childfocus-net-alert.be
Judicial Police of Belgium   www.ecops.be

CANADA
Cybertip   www.cybertip.ca
Cyber Tipline – National Center for Missing & Exploited Children
www.missingkids.org/cybertipline
  Phone: (703) 274-3900, toll-free: (800) 843-567
  The NCMEC Hotline can be used in the United States, Canada, and Mexico.

Ontario Provincial Police Child Pornography Unit
www.opp.ca/ecms/index.php?id=185
  Contact person: Bob Matthews, Child Pornography Unit,
  phone: (416) 235-4552

DENMARK
Red Barnet   www.redbarnet.dk

EUROPA
INHOPE Association   www.inhope.org
P.O. BOX 737, Woking GU22 8SY   United Kingdom

INTERPOL www.interpol.int

FINLAND
Pelastakaa Lapset   www.pelastakaalapset.fi/nettivihje/report.htm

FRANCE
AFA Point de Contact   www.pointdecontact.net

GERMANY
Anti-Kinderporno   www.anti-kinderporno.de/start_adressen.htm

GREECE
SafeLine   www.safeline.gr

HOLLAND
Meldpunt Kinderporno NL   www.meldpunt.org

HONG KONG
Hong Kong Child Protection Unit   http://www.swd.gov.hk/en/index/
site_pubsvc/page_family/sub_listofserv/id_familyandc/
Phone: 2804 1437

ICELAND
Barnaheill   www.barnaheill.is

IRELAND
ISPA of Ireland Child Pornography Reporting   www.hotline.ie
Phone: 1890 610 710

ITALY
Stop-iT   www.stop-it.it/

JAPAN
Japan National Police Agency   www.npa.go.jp

SPAIN
Protegeles.Com   www.protegeles.com

SOUTH KOREA
ICEC   http://www.cecinfo.org/country-by-country-information/
status-availability-database/countries/south-korea/

SWEDEN
Rüdda Barnen   www.rb.se/hotline/

TAIWAN
ECPAT Taiwan   www.ecpat.org.tw/

NEW ZEALAND
DIA New Zealand
www.dia.govt.nz/web/submitforms.nsf/cencomp?OpenForm

UNITED KINGDOM
CrimeStoppers   Freephone: 0800 555 111
Internet Watch Fundation   www.iwf.org.uk
New Scotland Yard Child Pornography Division
http://content.met.police.uk/Site/tellsomebody
Freephone: 0808 100 0040

INDEX OF NAMES

ABOUT THE AUTHOR

LYDIA CACHO is a Mexican journalist, author, and a feminist activist. She has published seven books, including the award-winning *Manual to Prevent, Detect and Heal Child Sexual Abuse (Con Mi Hijo No)* and *Slavery, Inc.* Currently Ms. Cacho is a columnist with *El Universal*, the main daily newspaper in Mexico, and a workshop teacher on successful approaches to help trafficking victims, and on Community Schools for Peace, a holistic method to negotiate conflicts.